BHARATIYA NYAY SANHITA 2023

Written By:

BHUPENDER SINGH

Advocate

(B.Sc.LLB)

(Supreme court of India)

Bhupender Singh
1st Edition

Publication Date: July 2024
Price: ₹655 | $15
ISBN: *978-93-5847-336-0*
Published by:
Adhyyan Books
Office No. 125,
Opposite Vivanta by Taj,
DDA SFS. Pocket-1, Dwarka,
Sec-22, New Delhi-110077
Website: http://adhyyanbooks.com
E-mail: contact@adhyyanbooks.com

Printed at: Repro Printers, Delhi

Contents

AS INTRODUCED IN LOK SABHA

Bill No. 173 of 2023

LS passes Bharatiya Nyaya Sanhita Bill;

"From the Red Fort, PM Modi had said that we need to free ourselves from the colonial laws. The new laws have been framed keeping in mind three basic principles — civil liberty of citizens, human rights and equality. Some are unable to visualise this. The current laws have no scope for justice — punishment is seen as justice," he added.

The Bharatiya Nyaya (Second) Sanhita will replace the Indian Penal Code, the Bharatiya Nagrik Suraksha (Second) Sanhita the Code of Criminal Procedure, and Bharatiya Saksha (Second) Bill the Evidence Act, 1872.

IPC, which deals with a majority of criminal offences, was brought by the British in 1860. It was adopted by the Indian government after Independence and has been amended around 77 times, but there were calls from some quarters for revamping the entire criminal justice system as it was considered obsolete and a colonial legacy.

The bills were first tabled in Parliament on August 11, and then sent to a parliamentary standing committee. Some of the suggestions of the panel were incorporated, and a set of new bills (labelled as "second") were tabled on December 12.LS passes Bharatiya Nyaya Sanhita Bill;

Before the members voted on the bills, Shah said the key feature was that these were "citizen-centric", explained how criminal laws would be in sync with the advancement in technology over the last 100 years, and gave a point-by-point rejoinder to some Opposition members who said that the new law gives unbridled powers to the police and make the country a police state.

"There will not be any police state in this country until this government is here... On many fronts, the power of the police has been curtailed. On others, police are also being watched," Shah said in his address.

"After this bill is passed, there will be a uniform justice system throughout the country. From Kashmir to Kanyakumari and from Dwarka to Assam, there will be one criminal legal procedure across the country," he said.

hon'ble home minister Amit Shah says it focuses on justice rather than punishment

Home Minister Amit Shah said that by bringing the new Bills, the government is erasing the '150-year-old' law that was created by colonisers

Union Home Minister Amit Shah in the Lok Sabha during the Winter session of Parliament, in New Delhi on Wednesday, December 20, 2023. (Photo | PTI)By PTI

The Lok Sabha on Wednesday passed the Bharatiya Nyaya (Second) Sanhita Bill by a voice vote.

The Central government on Tuesday took up the three bills to replace the existing British-era criminal laws for consideration, in the absence of a majority of Opposition MPs in Lok Sabha.

The new Bills, Bharatiya Nyaya Sanhita, Bharatiya Nagarik Suraksha Sanhita, and the Bharatiya Sakshya Adhiniyam, were introduced in Lok Sabha in August to replace the Code of Criminal Procedure Act, 1898; the Indian Penal Code, 1860, and the Indian Evidence Act, 1872, respectively.

Addressing the remaining members of the Lok Sabha, Home Minister Amit Shah said that Bharatiya Nyaya Sanhita, which will replace the Indian Penal Code, focuses on justice rather than punishment.

He said that the three proposed criminal laws will free people from the colonial mindset and its symbols.

Replying to a protest on the criminal law bills, he said, "If someone opposes govt, he shouldn't be punished as it's his freedom of speech."

However, he said, "If anyone works against the country, he or she must not be spared and must be given the strictest punishment," emphasizing that criminal law bills will ensure victim-centric justice.

"Act of terrorism is the worst human rights violation, anyone involved in terror must be given harsh punishment," he added.

"I have not only read every line of proposed criminal laws but have gone through every comma, full stop; held 158 meetings," he said.

Changes

India's Historical Legal Reform: The Introduction of Bharatiya Nyaya Sanhita- Major Changes By Law Trend December 31, 2023

In a historic move, three bills passed by the Indian Parliament have now become law, marking a significant transformation in the country's legal system.

In the BNS, 20 new offences have been added to and 19 provisions in the repealed IPC have been dropped. The punishment of imprisonment has been increased for 33 offences, and fines have been increased for 83 offences. A mandatory minimum punishment has been introduced for 23 offences. A sentence of community service has been introduced for six offences.

Offences against the body: The BNS retains the provisions of the IPC on murder, abetment of suicide, assault and causing grievous hurt. It adds new offences such as organised crime, terrorism, and murder or grievous hurt by a group on certain grounds.

Sexual offences against women: The BNS retains the provisions of the IPC on rape, voyeurism, stalking and insulting the modesty of a woman. It increases the threshold for the victim to be classified as a major, in the case of gang rape, from 16 to 18 years of age.

Offences against property: The BNS retains the provisions of the IPC on theft, robbery, burglary and cheating. It adds new offences such as cybercrime and financial fraud.

Offences against the state: The BNS removes sedition as an offence. Instead, there is a new offence for acts endangering India's sovereignty, unity and integrity.

Offences against the public: The BNS adds new offences such as environmental pollution and human trafficking.

Structure

The Bharatiya Nyaya Sanhita comprises 20 chapters and 358 sections. Its structure is similar to that of the IPC. The outline of the Sanhita is as follows:

The Bharatiya Nyaya Sanhita, 2023

Chapters Clauses Classification of Offences

Chapter 1 Clauses 1 to 3 Preliminary

Chapter 2 Clauses 4 to 13 Of Punishments

Chapter 3 Clauses 14 to 44 General Exceptions of the Right to Private Defence (sections 34 to 44)

Chapter 4 Clauses 45 to 62 Of Abetment, Criminal Conspiracy and Attempt

Chapter 5 Clauses 63 to 97 Of Offences against Women and Children Of Sexual Offences (63 to 72) Of Criminal Force and Assault against Women (73 to 78) Of Offences relating to Marriage (79 to 85) Of the Causing of Miscarriage, etc. (86 to 97)

Chapter 6 Clauses 98 to 144 Of Offences Affecting the Human Body Of Offences Affecting Life (98 to 111) Of Hurt (112 to 125) Of

1. Definitions [Section 2 of BNS/Sections 8 to 52A of IPC]

General

In IPC, there was no definition clause. All the interpretation clauses were spread over sections 8 to 52A of IPC.

The definition of 'section' in section 50 of IPC stands omitted by BNS as it is now a word of extensive usage in various legislations and it needs no definition or elucidation.

Most of these interpretation clauses in sections 8 to 52A of IPC,1860 have been retained in BNS without any change and have been compactly grouped in section 2 of BNS in alphabetical dictionary sequence for ease of reading and reference.

Unless context otherwise requires

Though most of the interpretation rules in sections 8 to 52A of IPC have been included in section 2 of BNS without any change, it must be noted that the applicability of these interpretation rules in BNS is subject to requirements of the context of a provision as all definitions in BNS in section 2 are subject to the qualificatory phrase "unless the context otherwise requires". The applicability of interpretation clauses in sections 8 to 52A of IPC, except definitions in sections 9, 32 and 46, were not made subject to contextual requirements.

Child

New definition of 'child' in section 2(3) of BNS

Transgender

The definition of "gender" in section 8 of IPC recognizes only male and female genders. The new definition of "gender" in section 2(10) of BNS recognizes "transgender" in addition to genders of "male" and "female".

Taxmann's New Criminal Major Acts

2. Child [Section 2(3) of BNS]

Child

Section 2(3) of BNS is a new provision [NEW]

Section 2(3) of BNS defines 'child' to means any person below the age of 18 years.

3. Court [Section 2(5) of BNS/Section 20 of IPC]

Omission of illustration

Illustration below section 20 of IPC referring to "Regulation VII, 1816, of the Madras Code" has been omitted from the definition in section 2(5) of BNS, as the illustration had become redundant long back with the repeal of Regulation VII by the Madras Civil Courts Act, 1873.

4. Document [Section 2(8) of BNS/Section 29 of IPC]

Electronic and digital record

Section 2(8) of BNS provides that documents includes 'electronics and digital record'.

5. Gender [Section 2(10) of BNS/Section 8 of IPC]

Transgender recognised as gender and defined

Definition in section 2(10) expressly refers to transgender and defines the term which was not the case in section 8 of IPC.

6. Judge [Section 2(16) of BNS/Section 19 of IPC]

Old Law – Section 19 (IPC, 1860) – "Judge"

The old law's definition of "Judge" is quite detailed.

It states that the term "Judge" includes not only individuals officially designated as Judges but also those who have the authority to render definitive judgments in any legal proceeding, whether civil or criminal.

This definition encompasses individuals who can make judgments that, if not appealed against, would be considered definitive.

It also includes members of a body of persons authorized by law to render such judgments.

The illustrations provided clarify this definition further, including examples of Collectors, Magistrates, and members of a panchayat.

New Law – Section 2(16) – “Judge”

The new law’s definition of “Judge” is more concise and follows a similar pattern.

The new law aligns with the old law’s definition but presents the information in a more streamlined manner.

7. Month and Year [Section 2(20) of BNS/Section 49 of IPC]

Reference to British calendar replaced with reference to Gregorian calendar

Section 49 of IPC required year or month to be reckoned as per British calendar while section 2(20) of BNS requires year or month to be reckoned as per the Gregorian calendar.

8. Movable Property [Section 2(21) of BNS/Section 22 of IPC]

Scope of “Movable property” in section 2(21) not limited to property in corporeal form, unlike the definition in section 22

Section 2(21) of BNS omits the word “are intended to include corporeal” before the word “property” which was there in the definition of movable property in section 22 of IPC.

Therefore, movable property includes property of every description other than immovable property whether such property is in corporeal (tangible physical) form or not.

Definition of movable property under BNS will include intangible assets like patents, copyrights, etc., also as well as actionable claims.

Taxmann's New Criminal Laws Combo – BNS | BNSS | BSA

9. Public Servant [Section 2(28) of BNS/Section 21 of IPC]

Juryman

References to juryman omitted from definition in section 2(28) of BNS

Local authority

"Local authority" is defined by referring to clause (31) of section 3 of the General Clauses Act, 1897 and section 2(45) of the Companies Act, 2013.

10. Punishments [Section 4 of BNS/Section 53 of IPC]

Community service

Section 53 of IPC provided for 5 types of punishments viz. (1) Death; (2) Imprisonment for life; (3) Imprisonment which is of two descriptions–rigorous and simple; (4) Forfeiture of property and (5) Fine. Section 4(f) of BNS has introduced a new 6th type of punishment – Community service.

To reduce the burden on jails, community service has been included in BNS as a punishment for the first time and it is being given legal status. [PIB Press Release, dated 20-12-2023]

BNS prescribes Community Service as punishment for petty offences like non-appearance in response to a proclamation, attempt to commit suicide, to compel or restraint exercise of lawful power of public servant, petty theft on return of theft money, misconduct in public by a drunken person, defamation, etc.

The term "community service" is not defined in BNS. However, it is defined by Explanation to section 23 of BNSS to mean the work which the Court may order a convict to perform as a form of punishment that benefits the community, for which he shall not be entitled to any remuneration.

Life imprisonment

The punishment of imprisonment for life has been clearly defined as imprisonment for remainder of a person's natural life.

11. Sentence, Commutation of [Section 5 of BNS/Sections 54 and 55 of IPC]

Changes in commutation provisions: Section 433 of Cr.PC vis-a-vis section 474 of Bharatiya Nagarik Suraksha Sanhita, 2023 (BNSS)

The comparison between section 433 of Cr.PC and section 474 of BNSS is tabulated below:

Sentence

What the sentence in Col. (1) may be commuted for by appropriate govt. under section 433 of Cr.PC

What the sentence in Col.(1) may be commuted for by appropriate govt. under section 474 of BNSS

Sentence of death Appropriate Government may commute a death sentence for any other punishment provided by the Indian Penal Code Death sentence may be commuted for imprisonment for life

Sentence of imprisonment for life Sentence may be commuted for imprisonment for a term not exceeding fourteen years or for fine; Sentence may be commuted for imprisonment for a term not less than 7 years

A sentence for imprisonment for seven years or more

Sentence may be commuted for imprisonment for a term not less than 3 years

Sentence of rigorous imprisonment Sentence may be commuted for simple imprisonment for any term to which that person might have been sentenced, or for fine; Sentence may be commuted for simple imprisonment for any term to which that person might have been sentenced

Sentence of simple

imprisonment

Sentence may be commuted for fine

Sentence for imprisonment for less than seven years

Sentence may be commuted for fine

12. Punishment, Fractions of Terms of [Section 6 of BNS/Section 57 of IPC]

Unless otherwise provided

Unlike section 57 of IPC, section 6 applies “unless otherwise provided”.

The words “unless otherwise provided” which were not there in section 57 have been added in section 6 at the end of the provision.

13. Fine, Liability in Default of Payment of Fine, etc. [Section 8 of BNS/Sections 63 to 70 of IPC]

Community service

IPC only provided for imprisonment in default of fine only. As there was no punishment of community service in IPC, there was also no imprisonment in default of community service in IPC.

Consequent upon introduction of new punishment of community service [See section 4 of BNS] by the BNS, sub-sections (4) and (5) of section 8 of BNS provide for imposing imprisonment in default of community service.

Fine of community service, default in payment of

Under old law for default in payment of fine following punishment followed:

Fine not exceeding ` 50 – Imprisonment not exceeding 2 months

Fine not exceeding ` 100 – Imprisonment not exceeding 4 months

In any other case – Imprisonment not exceeding 6 months

Under BNS for default in payment of fine or default of community service following punishment follows:

Fine not exceeding ` 5000 or community service – Imprisonment not exceeding 2 months

Fine not exceeding ` 10,000 or community service – Imprisonment not exceeding 4 months

In any other case – Imprisonment not exceeding 1 year

14. Private Defence of Property, When Right of, Extends to Causing Death [Section 41 of BNS/Section 103 of IPC]

House breaking

Old law provided for 'House breaking by night'. Section 41 of BNS provides for 'house breaking after sunset and before sunrise'.

Section 103 of Cr.PC provided for 'mischief by fire'. Section 41 of BNS provides for 'mischief by fire or any explosive substance'.

15. Private Defence of Property, Commencement and Continuance of Right of [Section 43 of BNS/Section 105 of IPC]

House breaking 'after sunset and before sunrise'

Section 105 of IPC provided for 'house breaking by night'. Section 43 of BNS provides for 'house breaking after sunset and before sunrise'.

16. Abetment Outside India for Offence in India (New) [Section 48 of BNS]

Abetment outside India

Section 48 of BNS is a new provision [NEW]

Section 48 of BNS provides that a person abets an offence within the meaning of this Sanhita who, without and beyond India, abets the commission of any act in India which would constitute an offence if committed in India.

Abetment by a person outside India has been made an offence under section 48 to allow prosecution of person located in foreign country.

17. Abetting Commission of Offence By Public or By More Than Ten Persons [Section 57 of BNS/Section 117 of IPC]

Prescribed punishment

Section 117 of IPC provided for imprisonment upto 3 years or fine or both. Section 57 of BNS provides for imprisonment of either description for a term which may extend to 7 years and fine.

18. Rape [Section 63 of BNS/Section 375 of IPC]

Age of Consent

Exception 2 to section 63 of BNS provides that sexual intercourse or sexual acts by a man with his own wife, the wife not being under 18 years of age, is not rape. Under section 375 of IPC the age limit was 15 years.

19. Rape, Punishment for [Section 64 of BNS/Section 376 of IPC]

Consent

Clause (i) of section 64(2) of BNS provides for 'commits rape, on a woman incapable of giving consent'. Section 376(2)(i) of IPC provided for 'commits rape on woman when she is under 16 years of age'.

20 Rape, Punishment for, in Certain Cases [Section 65 of BNS/Section 376AB of IPC]

Age categories

Section 65 of BNS combines both age categories (under 12 and under 16) into a single section, simplifying the legal framework.

21. Sexual Intercourse by Employing Deceitful Means, etc. [Section 69 of BNS]

Sexual intercourse by employing deceitful means

Section 69 of BNS is a new provision [NEW]

Section 69 of BNS provides that whoever, by deceitful means or making by promise to marry a woman without any intention of fulfilling the same, and has sexual intercourse with her, such sexual intercourse not amounting to the offence of rape, shall be punished with imprisonment of either description for a term which may extend to ten years and shall also be liable to fine.

"Deceitful means" shall include the false promise of employment or promotion, inducement or marring after suppressing identity.

22. Rape, Gang [Section 70 of BNS/Sections 376D to 376DB of IPC]

Death penalty for gang rape of woman under 18 years of age

Death sentence was provided under section 376DB of IPC for gang rape of woman under 12 years of age. No death penalty was provided for gang rape of woman aged below 16 but above 12 in section 376DA. Now, section 70(2) of BNS provides death penalty for gangrape of woman under 18 years of age.

23. Woman, Assault or Use of Criminal Force With Intent to Disrobe [Section 76 of BNS/Section 354B of IPC]

Neutral Gender

Word "whoever" is used in sections 76 and 77 of BNS. Earlier word 'man' was used in section 354B/354C of IPC

24. Voyeurism [Section 77 of BNS/Section 354C of IPC]

Neutral Gender

Word "whoever" is used in sections 75 and 76 of BNS. Earlier word 'man' was used in section 354B/354C of IPC

25. Woman, Enticing or Taking Away or Detaining With Criminal Intent a Married Woman [Section 84 of BNS/Section 498 of IPC]

Woman under husband care or any other person

Words 'from that man, or from any person having the care of her on behalf of that man' are omitted from section 498 of IPC

Thus, unlike section 498 of IPC, offence under section 84 of BNS is committed whether or not a married woman is taken or enticed away from her husband or from any person having care of her on behalf of her husband.

Section 84 protects a married woman whether or not she is living in the care of her husband or any other person who is taking care of her on behalf of her husband.

26. Child, Hiring, Employing or Engaging to Commit an Offence [Section 95 of BNS] [NEW]

Hiring child to commit an offence

Section 95 of BNS is a new provision

Section 95 of BNS provides that whoever hires, employs or engages any person below the age of eighteen years to commit an offence shall be punished for with imprisonment of either description or fine provided for that offence as if the offence has been committed by such person himself.

Hiring, employing, engaging or using a child for sexual exploitation or pornography is covered within the meaning of this section.

27. Child, Procuration of [Section 96 of BNS/Section 366A of IPC]

Neutral Gender

Section 366A of IPC provided for offence of procuration of minor girl (under the age of eighteen years). Section 96 of BNS deals with offence of procuration of any child below the age of eighteen years (irrespective of gender).

The protection accorded by section 96 of BNS to children is wider than that accorded by section 366A of IPC since protection under section 96 is available to all children irrespective of gender while section 366A protected only minor girls.

28. Child, Selling for Purposes of Prostitution, etc. [Section 98 of BNS/Section 372 of IPC]

Child

Word "child" is substituted for "any person" in section 372 of IPC

29. Child, Buying for Purposes of Prostitution, etc. [Section 99 of BNS/Section 373 of IPC]

Child

Word 'child' is substituted for 'person' in section 99 of BNS

Prescribed imprisonment

Imprisonment prescribed is 'not less than 7 years but which may extend to 14 years'. Earlier prescribed imprisonment was 'ten years'.

30. Mob Lynching [Section 103(1) of BNS/Section 302 of IPC]

Section 103(2) of BNS is a new provision [NEW]

Section 103(2) of BNS provides that when a group of five or more persons acting in concert commits murder on the ground of race, caste or community, sex, place of birth, language, personal belief or any other ground each member of such group shall be punished with death or with imprisonment for life, and shall also be liable to fine.

31. Murder, Punishment for by Life-convict [Section 104 of BNS/Section 303 of IPC]

Prescribed imprisonment

Unlike IPC, it is not mandatory to award death sentence for murder by a life-convict. BNS given an option to the Judge to sentence the life-convict murderer to death or with imprisonment for life, which shall mean the remainder of that person's natural life.

32. Culpable Homicide not Amounting to Murder, Punishment for [Section 105 of BNS/Section 304 of IPC]

Prescribed punishment

Section 105 of BNS prescribes imprisonment of 'not less than 5 years which may extend to 10 years' with fine. It was upto 10 years with fine or both under section 304 of IPC

Lesser punishment if accused reports the case to Police and takes the victim to hospital for medical treatment

As per the Home Minister's statement in Lok Sabha on 20.12.2023-See PIB's Press Release, dated 20.12.2023 in case of culpable homicide, there is a provision for lesser punishment if the accused goes to police to report the case and takes the victim to the hospital for medical treatment. [However, there is no such provision in the text of BNS]

33. Death, Causing by Negligence [Section 106 of BNS/Section 304A of IPC]

Increased punishment

Section 106(1) of BNS provides that whoever causes death of any person by doing any rash or negligent act not amounting to culpable homicide, shall be punished with imprisonment of either description for a term which may extend to five years.

The new law increases the punishment for causing death by negligence from a maximum of two years to a maximum of five years. This change reflects a stricter approach to cases of negligence resulting in death.

Offender escaping or failing to report [NEW]

Section 106(2) introduces an additional provision in sub-section (2) to section 106 of BNS, which addresses situations where the offender escapes from the scene of the incident without reporting it to a police officer or Magistrate after the incident. In such cases, the punishment is very severe, with a maximum term of imprisonment of ten years with fine. [Section 106(2)]

As the instances of hit and run cases are on the rise, a new provision under section 106(2) of BNS has been made. Currently hit and run cases resulting in death due to reckless and negligent driving are registered u/s 304A of IPC, with maximum penalty of two years of imprisonment. As per Delhi Road Crash Report of 2021, there were 555 cases (46.01% of total cases) where the registration number of vehicles involved in crime were unknown, signifying hit and run cases. The Supreme Court had in several cases observed on the inadequacy of law in view of increased vehicular accident. To address this issue, the new provision has been introduced under clause 106(2), which was long overdue.

Section 106(2) has been introduced to cover the hit and run accidents and to ensure reporting of accident immediately. This has been introduced with an aim to save the victim within the critical 'Golden

Hour' a term introduced in the Motor Vehicles Act, 1988 in the year 2019.

Punishment under section 106(2) is not attracted merely by virtue of driver escaping from the scene after the incident to escape the wrath of bystanders who might mob-lynch him. Offence is committed only if escape from scene is coupled with non-reporting by him to Police or Magistrate soon after the incident.

Medical practitioner [NEW]

In case of registered medical practitioner if negligent act is done by a registered medical practitioner while performing medical procedure, he shall be punished with imprisonment of either description for a term which may extend to two years, and shall also be liable to fine.

For the purposes of this sub-section, "registered medical practitioner" means a medical practitioner who possesses any medical qualification recognised under the National Medical Commission Act, 2019 (30 of 2019) and whose name has been entered in the National Medical Register or a State Medical Register under that Act.

34. Suicide of Child or Person of Unsound Mind, Abetment of [Section 107 of BNS/Section 305 of IPC]

Unsound mind

Reference to "insane person"/"any idiot" in section 305 of IPC is replaced with reference to "person of unsound mind" in BNS

35. Murder, Attempt to [Section 109 of BNS/Section 307 of IPC]

Prescribed punishment

Under IPC, section 307 prescribed only death penalty for attempt to murder by a life-convict. For attempt to murder by life-convict, section 109 of BNS provides for death or with imprisonment for life, which shall mean the remainder of that person's natural life

36. Organised Crime [Section 111 of BNS] [New]

Section 111 of BNS is a new provision

Section 111 provides as under:

Any continuing unlawful activity including kidnapping, robbery, vehicle theft, extortion, land grabbing, contract killing, economic offence, cyber-crimes, trafficking of persons, drugs, weapons or illicit goods or services, human trafficking for prostitution or ransom, by any person or a group of persons acting in concert, singly or jointly, either as a member of an organised crime syndicate or on behalf of such syndicate, by use of violence, threat of violence, intimidation, coercion, or by any other unlawful means to obtain direct or indirect material benefit including a financial benefit, shall constitute an organised crime.

For the purposes of this sub-section,--

(i) "organised crime syndicate" means a group of two or more persons who, acting either singly or jointly, as a syndicate or gang indulge in any continuing unlawful activity;

(ii) "continuing unlawful activity" means an activity prohibited by law which is a cognizable offence punishable with imprisonment of three years or more, undertaken by any person, either singly or jointly, as a member of an organised crime syndicate or on behalf of such syndicate in respect of which more than one charge-sheets have been filed before a competent Court within the preceding period of ten years and that Court has taken cognizance of such offence, and includes economic offence;

(iii) "economic offence" includes criminal breach of trust, forgery, counterfeiting of currency-notes, bank-notes and Government stamps, hawala transaction, mass-marketing fraud or running any scheme to defraud several persons or doing any act in any manner with a view to defraud any bank or financial institution or any other institution or organisation for obtaining monetary benefits in any form.

Whoever commits organised crime shall,—

if such offence has resulted in the death of any person, be punished with death or imprisonment for life, and shall also be liable to fine which shall not be less than ten lakh rupees; in any other case, be punished with imprisonment for a term which shall not be less than five years but which may extend to imprisonment for life, and shall also be liable to fine which shall not be less than five lakh rupees.

Whoever abets, attempts, conspires or knowingly facilitates the commission of an organised crime, or otherwise engages in any act preparatory to an organised crime, shall be punished with imprisonment for a term which shall not be less than five years but which may extend to imprisonment for life, and shall also be liable to fine which shall not be less than five lakh rupees.

Any person who is a member of an organised crime syndicate shall be punished with imprisonment for a term which shall not be less than five years but which may extend to imprisonment for life, and shall also be liable to fine which shall not be less than five lakh rupees.

Whoever, intentionally, harbours or conceals any person who has committed the offence of an organised crime shall be punished with imprisonment for a term which shall not be less than three years but which may extend to imprisonment for life, and shall also be liable to fine which shall not be less than five lakh rupees. This provision shall not apply to any case in which the harbour or concealment is by the spouse of the offender.

Whoever possesses any property derived or obtained from the commission of an organised crime or proceeds of any organised crime or which has been acquired through the organised crime, shall be punishable with imprisonment for a term which shall not be less than three years but which may extend to imprisonment for life and shall also be liable to fine which shall not be less than two lakh rupees.

If any person on behalf of a member of an organised crime syndicate is, or at any time has been in possession of movable or immovable property which he cannot satisfactorily account for, shall be punishable with imprisonment for a term which shall not be less than three years but which may extend to imprisonment for ten years and shall also be liable to fine which shall not be less than one lakh rupees.

37. Organised Crime, Petty [Section 112 of BNS] [New]

Section 112 of BNS is a new provision

Section 112 provides as under :

Whoever, being a member of a group or gang, either singly or jointly, commits any act of theft, snatching, cheating, unauthorised selling of tickets, unauthorised betting or gambling, selling of public examination question papers or any other similar criminal act, is said to commit petty organised crime. For the purposes of this sub-section "theft" includes trick theft, theft from vehicle, dwelling house or business premises, cargo theft, pick pocketing, theft through card skimming, shoplifting and theft of Automated Teller Machine.

Whoever commits any petty organised crime shall be punished with imprisonment for a term which shall not be less than one year but which may extend to seven years, and shall also be liable to fine.

38. Terrorist Act [Section 113 of BNS] [New]

Section 113 of BNS is a new provision

New definition – definition of 'terrorist act'

Section 113 provides as under:

Whoever does any act with the intent to threaten or likely to threaten the unity, integrity, sovereignty, security, or economic security of India or with the intent to strike terror or likely to strike terror in the people or any section of the people in India or in any foreign country,--

(a) by using bombs, dynamite or other explosive substance or inflammable substance or firearms or other lethal weapons or poisonous or noxious gases or other chemicals or by any other substance (whether biological, radioactive, nuclear or otherwise) of a hazardous nature or by any other means of whatever nature to cause or likely to cause,—

(i) death of, or injury to, any person or persons; or

(ii) loss of, or damage to, or destruction of, property; or

(iii) disruption of any supplies or services essential to the life of the community in India or in any foreign country; or

(iv) damage to, the monetary stability of India by way of production or smuggling or circulation of counterfeit Indian paper currency, coin or of any other material; or

(v) damage or destruction of any property in India or in a foreign country used or intended to be used for the defence of India or in connection with any other purposes of the Government of India, any State Government or any of their agencies; or

(b) overawes by means of criminal force or the show of criminal force or attempts to do so or causes death of any public functionary or attempts to cause death of any public functionary; or

(c) detains, kidnaps or abducts any person and threatening to kill or injure such person or does any other act in order to compel the Government of India, any State Government or the Government of a foreign country or an international or inter-governmental organisation or any other person to do or abstain from doing any act, commit a terrorist act.

For the purpose of this sub-section,—

(a) "public functionary" means the constitutional authorities or any other functionary notified in the Official Gazette by the Central Government as public functionary;

(b) "counterfeit Indian currency" means the counterfeit currency as may be declared after examination by an authorised or notified forensic authority that such currency imitates or compromises with the key security features of Indian currency.

Punishment for commission of 'terrorist act'

Whoever commits a terrorist act shall,—

if such offence has resulted in the death of any person, be punished with death or imprisonment for life, and shall also be liable to fine; in any other case, be punished with imprisonment for a term which shall not be less than five years but which may extend to imprisonment for life, and shall also be liable to fine.

ORGANISED CRIME

Bharatiya Nyaya Sanhita has specific provisions on organised crime, in a first for national laws

Though the IPC has no provisions on organised crime, there are several State laws on the offence, starting with MCOCA; BNS introduces higher punishment for attempted offences that result in death

Organised crime is being addressed in a comprehensive way at the national level for the first time, with its introduction in a specific section of the recently enacted Bharatiya Nyaya (Second) Sanhita (BNS), 2023. The new statute will replace the Indian Penal Code, 1860, which does not have any clauses pertaining to organised crimes, though the offence has inter-State and even international ramifications.

"To allow for an effective prosecution of such an offence, the Maharashtra State Legislative Assembly had passed the Maharashtra Control of Organised Crime Act (MCOCA), 1999. Thereafter, similar laws were adopted in various States. However, there was a need for a legal framework at the national level to combat the menace efficiently," a senior police officer said.

A comparison of the BNS' provisions on organised crime with the MCOCA shows that several sections are substantially the same.

Section 109 of the BNS defines organised crime as "any continuing unlawful activity" committed by "groups of individuals acting in concert, singly or jointly, either as a member of an organised crime syndicate or on behalf of such syndicate, by use of violence, threat of violence, intimidation, coercion, corruption or related activities or other unlawful means to obtain direct or indirect, material benefit including a financial benefit".

The types of organised crime explicitly included in the provision are kidnapping, robbery, vehicle theft, extortion, land grabbing, contract killing, economic offences, cyber-crimes having severe consequences, trafficking in people, drugs, illicit goods or services and weapons, human trafficking racket for prostitution or ransom.

The definition differ from the MCOCA only insofar as the specific types of organised crimes which have been included in the BNS.

Section 109 provides detailed explanations to terms such as "organised crime syndicate" and "continuing unlawful activity", which have also been explained in the MCOCA. However, it further adds explanations for the terms "benefit" and "economic offences".

In both the laws, the punishments for various degrees of offences linked to organised crime are also almost the same. However, a major difference is that in the BNS, whoever "attempts" to commit, or commits an offence of organised crime, which has resulted in the death of any person, will be punishable with death or imprisonment for life and are liable for a fine of not less than ₹10 lakh.

In the MCOCA, only the commission of organised crime which results in the death of any person attracts the punishment of death or life imprisonment, apart from a minimum fine of ₹1 lakh.

"There are several issues involved... First, that MCOCA-like State laws are properly enacted by the State legislature and many of them have also been approved by the Central Home Ministry and President. The validity of those laws have been endorsed by High Courts and the Supreme Court.

"There is no conflict between the two laws [MCOCA and BNS]. Then the questions are of quantum of punishment, and whether the case will be taken up before a regular or special court. Under MCOCA, there are powers of preventive detention and the law has wider details and deeper implications to address the organised crimes. Therefore, the respective States may very well continue to invoke it,"

In Section 110, the BNS also defines "petty organised crime or organised crime in general" as "any crime that causes general feelings of insecurity among citizens". The provision highlights various types of such offences, which include the theft of or from a vehicle, domestic and business theft, trick theft, cargo crime, theft (attempt to theft, theft of personal property), organised pick-pocketing, and snatching.

In view of the new criminal law, that appropriate amendments would have to be made in some other related laws, including the Prevention of Money Laundering Act, for a coordinated approach towards combating organised crime.

THE BHARATIYA NYAYA (SECOND) SANHITA, 2023

———— ARRANGEMENT OF CLAUSES ————

CHAPTER IX

OF OFFENCES RELATING TO ELECTIONS

CLAUSES

CHAPTER X

OF OFFENCES RELATING TO COIN, CURRENCY-NOTES, BANK-NOTES, AND GOVERNMENT STAMPS

CLAUSES

CHAPTER XII

OF OFFENCES BY OR RELATING TO PUBLIC SERVANTS

CHAPTER XIII

OF CONTEMPTS OF THE LAWFUL AUTHORITY OF PUBLIC SERVANTS

CLAUSES

CHAPTER XIV

OF FALSE EVIDENCE AND OFFENCES AGAINST PUBLIC JUSTICE

CLAUSES

CLAUSES

AS INTRODUCED IN LOK SABHA

Bill No. 173 of 2023

THE BHARATIYA NYAYA (SECOND) SANHITA, 2023

A

BILL

to consolidate and amend the provisions relating to offences and for matters connected therewith or incidental thereto.

BE it enacted by Parliament in the Seventy-fourth Year of the Republic of India as follows:––

CHAPTERI PRELIMINARY

1. (*1*) This Act may be called the Bharatiya Nyaya (Second) Sanhita, 2023.

(*2*) It shall come into force on such date as the Central Government may, by notification in the Official Gazette, appoint, and different dates may be appointed for different provisions of this Sanhita.

Short title, commencement and application.

(*3*) Every person shall be liable to punishment under this Sanhita and not otherwise for every act or omission contrary to the provisions thereof, of which he shall be guilty within India.

Definitions.

(*4*) Any person liable, by any law for the time being in force in India, to be tried for an offence committed beyond India shall be dealt with according to the provisions of this 5 Sanhita for any act committed beyond India in the same manner as if such act had been committed within India.

(*5*) The provisions of this Sanhita shall also apply to any offence committed by—

(*a*) any citizen of India in any place without and beyond India;

(*b*) any person on any ship or aircraft registered in India wherever it may be;

(*c*) any person in any place without and beyond India committing offence targeting a computer resource located in India.

Explanation.—In this section, the word "offence" includes every act committed outside

India which, if committed in India, would be punishable under this Sanhita.

Illustration.

A, who is a citizen of India, commits a murder in any place without and beyond India. He can be tried and convicted of murder in any place in India in which he may be found.

(*6*) Nothing in this Sanhita shall affect the provisions of any Act for punishing mutiny and desertion of officers, soldiers, sailors or airmen in the service of the Government of India or the provisions of any special or local law.

2. In this Sanhita, unless the context otherwise requires,––

(*1*) "act" denotes as well a series of acts as a single act;

(*2*) "animal" means any living creature, other than a human being;

(*3*) "child" means any person below the age of eighteen years;

(*4*) "counterfeit".––A person is said to "counterfeit" who causes one thing to resemble another thing, intending by means of that resemblance to pratise deception, or knowing it to be likely that deception will thereby be practised.

Explanation 1.—It is not essential to counterfeiting that the imitation should be exact.

Explanation 2.—When a person causes one thing to resemble another thing, and the resemblance is such that a person might be deceived thereby, it shall be presumed, until the contrary is proved, that the person so causing the one thing to resemble the other thing intended by means of that resemblance to practise deception or knew it to be likely that deception would thereby be practised;

(*5*) "Court" means a Judge who is empowered by law to act judicially alone, or a body of Judges which is empowered by law to act judicially as a body, when such Judge or body of Judges is acting judicially;

(*6*) "death" means the death of a human being unless the contrary appears from the context;

(*7*) "dishonestly" means doing anything with the intention of causing wrongful gain to one person or wrongful loss to another person;

(*8*) "document" means any matter expressed or described upon any substance by means of letters, figures or marks, or by more than one of those means, and includes electronic and digital record, intended to be used, or which may be used, as evidence of that matter.

Explanation 1.—It is immaterial by what means or upon what substance the letters, figures or marks are formed, or whether the evidence is intended for, or may be used in a Court or not.

Illustrations.

(*a*) A writing expressing the terms of a contract, which may be used as evidence of the contract, is a document.

(*b*) A cheque upon a banker is a document.

(*c*) A power-of-attorney is a document.

(*d*)A map or plan which is intended to be used or which may be used as evidence, is a document.

(*e*) A writing containing directions or instructions is a document.

Explanation 2.—Whatever is expressed by means of letters, figures or marks as explained by mercantile or other usage, shall be deemed to be expressed by such letters, figures or marks within the meaning of this section, although the same may not be actually expressed.

Illustration.

A writes his name on the back of a bill of exchange payable to his order. The meaning of the endorsement, as explained by mercantile usage, is that the bill is to be paid to the holder. The endorsement is a document, and shall be construed in the same manner as if the words "pay to the holder" or words to that effect had been written over the signature;

(*9*) "fraudulently" means doing anything with the intention to defraud but not otherwise;

(*10*) "gender".—The pronoun "he" and its derivatives are used of any person, whether male, female or transgender.

Explanation.–– "transgender" shall have the meaning assigned to it in clause (*k*)

of section 2 of the Transgender Persons (Protection of Rights) Act, 2019;

(*11*) "good faith".—Nothing is said to be done or believed in "good faith" which is done or believed without due care and attention;

(*12*) "Government" means the Central Government or a State Government;

(*13*) "harbour" includes supplying a person with shelter, food, drink, money, clothes, arms, ammunition or means of conveyance, or the assisting a person by any means, whether of the same kind as those enumerated in this clause or not, to evade apprehension;

(*14*) "injury" means any harm whatever illegally caused to any person, in body, mind, reputation or property;

(*15*) "illegal" and "legally bound to do".—The word "illegal" is applicable to everything which is an offence or which is prohibited by law, or which furnishes ground for a civil action; and a person is said to be "legally bound to do" whatever it is illegal in him to omit;

(*16*) "Judge" means a person who is officially designated as a Judge and includes a person,--

(*i*) who is empowered by law to give, in any legal proceeding, civil or criminal, a definitive judgment, or a judgment which, if not appealed against, would be definitive, or a judgment which, if confirmed by some other authority, would be definitive; or

(*ii*) who is one of a body or persons, which body of persons is empowered by law to give such a judgment.

Illustration.

A Magistrate exercising jurisdiction in respect of a charge on which he has power to sentence to fine or imprisonment, with or without appeal, is a Judge;

(*17*) "life" means the life of a human being, unless the contrary appears from the context;

(*18*) "local law" means a law applicable only to a particular part of India; (*19*) "man" means male human being of any age;

(*20*) "month" and "year".––Wherever the word "month" or the word "year" is used, it is to be understood that the month or the year is to be reckoned according to the Gregorian calendar;

(*21*) "movable property" includes property of every description, except land and things attached to the earth or permanently fastened to anything which is attached to the earth;

(*22*) "number".—Unless the contrary appears from the context, words importing the singular number include the plural number, and words importing the plural number include the singular number;

(*23*) "oath" includes a solemn affirmation substituted by law for an oath, and any declaration required or authorised by law to be made before a public servant or to be used for the purpose of proof, whether in a Court or not;

(*24*) "offence".—Except in the Chapters and sections mentioned in sub-clauses (*a*) and (*b*), the word "offence" means a thing made punishable by this Sanhita, but––

(a) in Chapter III and in the following sections, namely, sub-sections (*2*), (*3*), (*4*) and (*5*) of section 8, sections 9, 49, 50, 52, 54, 55, 56, 57, 58, 59, 60, 61, 119, 120, 123, sub-sections (*7*) and (*8*) of section 127, 222, 230, 231, 240, 248, 250, 251, 259, 260, 261, 262, 263, sub-sections (*6*) and (*7*) of section 308 and sub-section (*2*) of section 330, the word "offence" means a thing punishable under this Sanhita, or under any special law or local law; and

(*b*) in sub-section (*1*) of section 189, sections 211, 212, 238, 239, 249, 253 and sub-section (*1*) of section 329, the word "offence" shall have the same meaning when the act punishable under the special law or local law is punishable under such law with imprisonment for a term of six months or more, whether with or without fine;

(*25*) "omission" denotes as well as a series of omissions as a single omission;

(*26*) "person" includes any company or association or body of persons, whether incorporated or not;

(*27*) "public" includes any class of the public or any community;

(*28*) "public servant" means a person falling under any of the descriptions, namely:—

(*a*) every commissioned officer in the Army, Navy or Air Force;

(*b*) every Judge including any person empowered by law to discharge, whether by himself or as a member of any body of persons, any adjudicatory functions;

(*c*) every officer of a Court including a liquidator, receiver or commissioner whose duty it is, as such officer, to investigate or report on any matter of law or 45 fact, or to make, authenticate, or keep any document, or to take charge or dispose of any property, or to execute any judicial process, or to administer any oath, or to interpret, or to preserve order in the Court, and every person specially authorised by a Court to perform any of such duties;

(*d*) every assessor or member of a panchayat assisting a Court or public servant;

(*e*) every arbitrator or other person to whom any cause or matter has been referred for decision or report by any Court, or by any other competent public authority;

(*f*) every person who holds any office by virtue of which he is empowered to place or keep any person in confinement;

(*g*) every officer of the Government whose duty it is, as such officer, to prevent offences, to give information of offences, to bring offenders to justice, or to protect the public health, safety or convenience;

(*h*) every officer whose duty it is, as such officer, to take, receive, keep or expend any property on behalf of the Government, or to make any survey, assessment or contract on behalf of the Government, or to execute any revenue-process, or to investigate, or to report, on any matter affecting the pecuniary interests of the Government, or to make, authenticate or keep any document relating to the pecuniary interests of the Government, or to prevent the infraction of any law for the protection of the pecuniary interests of the Government;

(*i*) every officer whose duty it is, as such officer, to take, receive, keep or expend any property, to make any survey or assessment or to levy any rate or tax for any secular common purpose of any village, town or district, or to make, authenticate or keep any document for the ascertaining of the rights of the people of any village, town or district;

(*j*) every person who holds any office by virtue of which he is empowered to prepare, publish, maintain or revise an electoral roll or to conduct an election or part of an election;

(*k*) every person—

(*i*) in the service or pay of the Government or remunerated by fees or commission for the performance of any public duty by the Government;

(*ii*) in the service or pay of a local authority as defined in clause (*31*) of section 3 of the General ClausesAct, 1897, a corporation established by or under a Central or State Act or a Government company as defined in clause (*45*) of section 2 of the Companies Act, 2013.

Explanation.—

(*a*) persons falling under any of the descriptions made in this clause are public servants, whether appointed by the Government or not;

(*b*) every person who is in actual possession of the situation of a public servant, whatever legal defect there may be in his right to hold that situation is a public servant;

(*c*) "election" means an election for the purpose of selecting members of any legislative, municipal or other public authority, of whatever character, the method of selection to which is by, or under any law for the time being in force.

Illustration.

A Municipal Commissioner is a public servant; General explanations.

(*29*) "reason to believe".—A person is said to have "reason to believe" a thing, if he has sufficient cause to believe that thing but not otherwise;

(*30*) "special law" means a law applicable to a particular subject;

(*31*) "valuable security" means a document which is, or purports to be, a document whereby any legal right is created, extended, transferred, restricted, extinguished or released, or whereby any person acknowledges that he lies under legal liability, or has not a certain legal right.

Illustration.

A writes his name on the back of a bill of exchange. As the effect of this endorsement is to transfer the right to the bill to any person who may become the lawful holder of it, the endorsement is a "valuable security";

(*32*) "vessel" means anything made for the conveyance by water of human beings or of property;

(*33*) "voluntarily".—A person is said to cause an effect "voluntarily" when he causes it by means whereby he intended to cause it, or by means which, at the time of employing those means, he knew or had reason to believe to be likely to cause it.

Illustration.

A sets fire, by night, to an inhabited house in a large town, for the purpose of facilitating a robbery and thus causes the death of a person. Here, A may not have intended to cause death; and may even be sorry that death has been caused by his act; yet, if he knew that he was likely to cause death, he has caused death voluntarily;

(*34*) "will" means any testamentary document;

(*35*) "woman" means a female human being of any age;

(*36*) "wrongful gain" means gain by unlawful means of property to which the person gaining is not legally entitled;

(*37*) "wrongful loss" means the loss by unlawful means of property to which the person losing it is legally entitled;

(*38*) "gaining wrongfully" and "losing wrongfully".—A person is said to gain wrongfully when such person retains wrongfully, as well as when such person acquires wrongfully. Aperson is said to lose wrongfully when such person is wrongfully kept out of any property, as well as when such person is wrongfully deprived of property; and

(*39*) words and expressions used but not defined in this Sanhita but defined in the InformationTechnologyAct, 2000 and the Bharatiya Nagarik Suraksha Sanhita, 2023 shall have the meanings respectively assigned to them in that Act and Sanhita:

Provided that any reference in this Sanhita to the Bharatiya Nagarik Suraksha Sanhita, 2023, shall be construed as a reference to the Bharatiya Nagarik Suraksha (Second) Sanhita, 2023.

3. (*1*) Throughout this Sanhita every definition of an offence, every penal provision, and every *Illustration* of every such definition or penal provision, shall be understood subject to the exceptions contained in the Chapter entitled "General Exceptions", though those exceptions are not repeated in such definition, penal provision, or *Illustration*.

Illustrations.

(*a*) The sections in this Sanhita, which contain definitions of offences, do not express that a child under seven years of age cannot commit such offences; but the definitions are to be understood subject to the general exception which provides that nothing shall be an offence which is done by a child under seven years of age.

(*b*) A, a police officer, without warrant, apprehends Z, who has committed murder. Here A is not guilty of the offence of wrongful confinement; for he was bound by law to apprehend Z, and therefore the case falls within the general exception which provides that "nothing is an offence which is done by a person who is bound by law to do it".

(*2*) Every expression which is explained in any Part of this Sanhita, is used in every Part of this Sanhita in conformity with the explanation.

(*3*) When property is in the possession of a person's spouse, clerk or servant, on account of that person, it is in that person's possession within the meaning of this Sanhita.

Explanation.—A person employed temporarily or on a particular occasion in the capacity of a clerk or servant, is a clerk or servant within the meaning of this sub-section.

(*4*) In every Part of this Sanhita, except where a contrary intention appears from the context, words which refer to acts done extend also to illegal omissions.

(*5*) When a criminal act is done by several persons in furtherance of the common intention of all, each of such persons is liable for that act in the same manner as if it were done by him alone.

(*6*) Whenever an act, which is criminal only by reason of its being done with a criminal knowledge or intention, is done by several persons, each of such persons who joins in the act with such knowledge or intention is liable for the act in the same manner as if the act were done by him alone with that knowledge or intention.

(*7*) Wherever the causing of a certain effect, or an attempt to cause that effect, by an act or by an omission, is an offence, it is to be understood that the causing of that effect partly by an act and partly by an omission is the same offence.

Illustration.

A intentionally causes Z's death, partly by illegally omitting to give Z food, and partly by beating Z. A has committed murder.

(*8*) When an offence is committed by means of several acts, whoever intentionally cooperates in the commission of that offence by doing any one of those acts, either singly or jointly with any other person, commits that offence.

Illustrations.

(*a*)Aand B agree to murder Z by severally and at different times giving him small doses of poison.A and B administer the poison according to the agreement with intent to murder Z. Z dies from the effects the several doses of poison so administered to him. Here A and B intentionally cooperate in the commission of murder and as each of them does an act by which the death is caused, they are both guilty of the offence though their acts are separate.

(*b*) A and B are joint jailors, and as such have the charge of Z, a prisoner, alternatively for six hours at a time. Aand B, intending to cause Z's death, knowingly cooperate in causing that effect by illegally omitting, each during the time of his attendance, to furnish Z with food supplied to them for that purpose. Z dies of hunger. Both A and B are guilty of the murder of Z. (*c*) A, a jailor, has the charge of Z, a prisoner. A, intending to cause Z's death, illegally omits to supply Z with food; in consequence of which Z is much reduced in strength, but the starvation is not sufficient to cause his death. A is dismissed from his office, and B succeeds him. B, without collusion or cooperation with A, illegally omits to supply Z with food, knowing that he is likely thereby to cause Z's death. Z dies of hunger. B is guilty of murder, but, as A did not cooperate with B. A is guilty only of an attempt to commit murder.

(*9*) Where several persons are engaged or concerned in the commission of a criminal act, they may be guilty of different offences by means of that act.

Illustration.

A attacks Z under such circumstances of grave provocation that his killing of Z would be only culpable homicide not amounting to murder. B, having ill-will towards Z and intending to kill him, and not having been subject to the provocation, assists A in killing Z. Here, though A and B are both engaged in causing Z's death, B is guilty of murder, and A is guilty only of culpable homicide.

Punishments.

Commutation are—

Bill No. 173 of 2023

THE BHARATIYA NYAYA (SECOND) SANHITA, 2023

A

BILL

to consolidate and amend the provisions relating to offences and for matters connected therewith or incidental thereto.

BE it enacted by Parliament in the Seventy-fourth Year of the Republic of India as follows:––

Chapter One

PRELIMINARY

1. (*1*) This Act may be called the Bharatiya Nyaya (Second) Sanhita, 2023.

(*2*) It shall come into force on such date as the Central Government may, by notification in the Official Gazette, appoint, and different dates may be appointed for different provisions of this Sanhita.

Short title, commencement and application.

(*3*) Every person shall be liable to punishment under this Sanhita and not otherwise for every act or omission contrary to the provisions thereof, of which he shall be guilty within India.

Definitions.

(*4*) Any person liable, by any law for the time being in force in India, to be tried for an offence committed beyond India shall be dealt with according to the provisions of this 5 Sanhita for any act committed beyond India in the same manner as if such act had been committed within India.

(*5*) The provisions of this Sanhita shall also apply to any offence committed by—

(*a*) any citizen of India in any place without and beyond India;

(*b*) any person on any ship or aircraft registered in India wherever it may be;

(*c*) any person in any place without and beyond India committing offence targeting a computer resource located in India.

Explanation.—In this section, the word "offence" includes every act committed outside

India which, if committed in India, would be punishable under this Sanhita.

Illustration.

A, who is a citizen of India, commits a murder in any place without and beyond India. He can be tried and convicted of murder in any place in India in which he may be found.

(*6*) Nothing in this Sanhita shall affect the provisions of any Act for punishing mutiny and desertion of officers, soldiers, sailors or airmen in the service of the Government of India or the provisions of any special or local law.

2. In this Sanhita, unless the context otherwise requires,––

(*1*) "act" denotes as well a series of acts as a single act;

(*2*) "animal" means any living creature, other than a human being;

(*3*) "child" means any person below the age of eighteen years;

(*4*) "counterfeit".--A person is said to "counterfeit" who causes one thing to resemble another thing, intending by means of that resemblance to pratise deception, or knowing it to be likely that deception will thereby be practised.

Explanation 1.—It is not essential to counterfeiting that the imitation should be exact.

Explanation 2.—When a person causes one thing to resemble another thing, and the resemblance is such that a person might be deceived thereby, it shall be presumed, until the contrary is proved, that the person so causing the one thing to resemble the other thing intended by means of that resemblance to practise deception or knew it to be likely that deception would thereby be practised;

(*5*) "Court" means a Judge who is empowered by law to act judicially alone, or a body of Judges which is empowered by law to act judicially as a body, when such Judge or body of Judges is acting judicially;

(*6*) "death" means the death of a human being unless the contrary appears from the context;

(*7*) "dishonestly" means doing anything with the intention of causing wrongful gain to one person or wrongful loss to another person;

(*8*) "document" means any matter expressed or described upon any substance by means of letters, figures or marks, or by more than one of those means, and includes electronic and digital record, intended to be used, or which may be used, as evidence of that matter.

Explanation 1.—It is immaterial by what means or upon what substance the letters, figures or marks are formed, or whether the evidence is intended for, or may be used in a Court or not.

Illustrations.

(*a*) A writing expressing the terms of a contract, which may be used as evidence of the contract, is a document.

(*b*) A cheque upon a banker is a document.

(*c*) A power-of-attorney is a document.

(*d*)A map or plan which is intended to be used or which may be used as evidence, is a document.

(*e*) A writing containing directions or instructions is a document.

Explanation 2.—Whatever is expressed by means of letters, figures or marks as explained by mercantile or other usage, shall be deemed to be expressed by such letters, figures or marks within the meaning of this section, although the same may not be actually expressed.

Illustration.

A writes his name on the back of a bill of exchange payable to his order. The meaning of the endorsement, as explained by mercantile usage, is that the bill is to be paid to the holder. The endorsement is a document, and shall be construed in the same manner as if the words "pay to the holder" or words to that effect had been written over the signature;

(*9*) "fraudulently" means doing anything with the intention to defraud but not otherwise;

(*10*) "gender".—The pronoun "he" and its derivatives are used of any person, whether male, female or transgender.

Explanation.–– "transgender" shall have the meaning assigned to it in clause (*k*)

of section 2 of the Transgender Persons (Protection of Rights) Act, 2019;

(*11*) "good faith".—Nothing is said to be done or believed in "good faith" which is done or believed without due care and attention;

(*12*) "Government" means the Central Government or a State Government;

(*13*) "harbour" includes supplying a person with shelter, food, drink, money, clothes, arms, ammunition or means of conveyance, or the assisting a person by any means, whether of the same kind as those enumerated in this clause or not, to evade apprehension;

(*14*) "injury" means any harm whatever illegally caused to any person, in body, mind, reputation or property;

(*15*) "illegal" and "legally bound to do".—The word "illegal" is applicable to everything which is an offence or which is prohibited by law, or which furnishes ground for a civil action; and a person is said to be "legally bound to do" whatever it is illegal in him to omit;

(*16*) "Judge" means a person who is officially designated as a Judge and includes a person,––

(*i*) who is empowered by law to give, in any legal proceeding, civil or criminal, a definitive judgment, or a judgment which, if not appealed against, would be definitive, or a judgment which, if confirmed by some other authority, would be definitive; or

(*ii*) who is one of a body or persons, which body of persons is empowered by law to give such a judgment.

Illustration.

A Magistrate exercising jurisdiction in respect of a charge on which he has power to sentence to fine or imprisonment, with or without appeal, is a Judge;

(*17*) "life" means the life of a human being, unless the contrary appears from the context;

(*18*) "local law" means a law applicable only to a particular part of India; (*19*) "man" means male human being of any age;

(*20*) "month" and "year".––Wherever the word "month" or the word "year" is used, it is to be understood that the month or the year is to be reckoned according to the Gregorian calendar;

(*21*) "movable property" includes property of every description, except land and things attached to the earth or permanently fastened to anything which is attached to the earth;

(*22*) "number".—Unless the contrary appears from the context, words importing the singular number include the plural number, and words importing the plural number 15 include the singular number;

(*23*) "oath" includes a solemn affirmation substituted by law for an oath, and any declaration required or authorised by law to be made before a public servant or to be used for the purpose of proof, whether in a Court or not;

(*24*) "offence".—Except in the Chapters and sections mentioned in sub-clauses (*a*) and (*b*), the word "offence" means a thing made punishable by this Sanhita, but––

(a) in Chapter III and in the following sections, namely, sub-sections (*2*), (*3*), (*4*) and (*5*) of section 8, sections 9, 49, 50, 52, 54, 55, 56, 57, 58, 59, 60, 61, 119, 120, 123, sub-sections (*7*) and (*8*) of section 127, 222, 230, 231, 240, 248, 250, 251, 259, 260, 261, 262, 263, sub-sections (*6*) and (*7*) of section 308 and sub-section (*2*) of section 330, the word "offence" means a thing punishable under this Sanhita, or under any special law or local law; and

(*b*) in sub-section (*1*) of section 189, sections 211, 212, 238, 239, 249, 253 and sub-section (*1*) of section 329, the word "offence" shall have the same meaning when the act punishable under the special law or local law is punishable under such law with imprisonment for a term of six months or more, whether with or without fine;

(*25*) "omission" denotes as well as a series of omissions as a single omission;

(*26*) "person" includes any company or association or body of persons, whether incorporated or not;

(*27*) "public" includes any class of the public or any community;

(*28*) "public servant" means a person falling under any of the descriptions, namely:—

(*a*) every commissioned officer in the Army, Navy or Air Force;

(*b*) every Judge including any person empowered by law to discharge, whether by himself or as a member of any body of persons, any adjudicatory functions;

(*c*) every officer of a Court including a liquidator, receiver or commissioner whose duty it is, as such officer, to investigate or report on any matter of law or 45 fact, or to make, authenticate, or keep any document, or to take charge or dispose of any property, or to execute any judicial process, or to administer any oath, or to interpret, or to preserve order in the Court, and every person specially authorised by a Court to perform any of such duties;

(*d*) every assessor or member of a panchayat assisting a Court or public servant;

(*e*) every arbitrator or other person to whom any cause or matter has been referred for decision or report by any Court, or by any other competent public authority;

(*f*) every person who holds any office by virtue of which he is empowered to place or keep any person in confinement;

(*g*) every officer of the Government whose duty it is, as such officer, to prevent offences, to give information of offences, to bring offenders to justice, or to protect the public health, safety or convenience;

(*h*) every officer whose duty it is, as such officer, to take, receive, keep or expend any property on behalf of the Government, or to make any survey, assessment or contract on behalf of the Government, or to execute any revenue-process, or to investigate, or to report, on any matter affecting the pecuniary interests of the Government, or to make, authenticate or keep any document relating to the pecuniary interests of the Government, or to prevent the infraction of any law for the protection of the pecuniary interests of the Government;

(*i*) every officer whose duty it is, as such officer, to take, receive, keep or expend any property, to make any survey or assessment or to levy any rate or tax for any secular common purpose of any village, town or district, or to make, authenticate or keep any document for the ascertaining of the rights of the people of any village, town or district;

(*j*) every person who holds any office by virtue of which he is empowered to prepare, publish, maintain or revise an electoral roll or to conduct an election or part of an election;

(*k*) every person—

(*i*) in the service or pay of the Government or remunerated by fees or commission for the performance of any public duty by the Government;

(*ii*) in the service or pay of a local authority as defined in clause (*31*) of section 3 of the General ClausesAct, 1897, a corporation established by or under a Central or State Act or a Government company as defined in clause (*45*) of section 2 of the Companies Act, 2013.

Explanation.—

(*a*) persons falling under any of the descriptions made in this clause are public servants, whether appointed by the Government or not;

(*b*) every person who is in actual possession of the situation of a public servant, whatever legal defect there may be in his right to hold that situation is a public servant;

(*c*) "election" means an election for the purpose of selecting members of any legislative, municipal or other public authority, of whatever character, the method of selection to which is by, or under any law for the time being in force.

Illustration.

A Municipal Commissioner is a public servant; General explanations.

(*29*) "reason to believe".—A person is said to have "reason to believe" a thing, if he has sufficient cause to believe that thing but not otherwise;

(*30*) "special law" means a law applicable to a particular subject;

(*31*) "valuable security" means a document which is, or purports to be, a document whereby any legal right is created, extended, transferred, restricted, extinguished or released, or whereby any person acknowledges that he lies under legal liability, or has not a certain legal right.

Illustration.

A writes his name on the back of a bill of exchange. As the effect of this endorsement is to transfer the right to the bill to any person who may become the lawful holder of it, the endorsement is a "valuable security";

(*32*) "vessel" means anything made for the conveyance by water of human beings or of property;

(*33*) "voluntarily".—A person is said to cause an effect "voluntarily" when he causes it by means whereby he intended to cause it, or by means which, at the time of employing those means, he knew or had reason to believe to be likely to cause it.

Illustration.

A sets fire, by night, to an inhabited house in a large town, for the purpose of facilitating a robbery and thus causes the death of a person. Here, A may not have intended to cause death; and may even be sorry that death has been caused by his act; yet, if he knew that he was likely to cause death, he has caused death voluntarily;

(*34*) "will" means any testamentary document;

(*35*) "woman" means a female human being of any age;

(*36*) "wrongful gain" means gain by unlawful means of property to which the person gaining is not legally entitled;

(*37*) "wrongful loss" means the loss by unlawful means of property to which the person losing it is legally entitled;

(*38*) "gaining wrongfully" and "losing wrongfully".—A person is said to gain wrongfully when such person retains wrongfully, as well as when such person acquires wrongfully. Aperson is said to lose wrongfully when such person is wrongfully kept out of any property, as well as when such person is wrongfully deprived of property; and

(*39*) words and expressions used but not defined in this Sanhita but defined in the InformationTechnologyAct, 2000 and the Bharatiya Nagarik Suraksha Sanhita, 2023 shall have the meanings respectively assigned to them in that Act and Sanhita:

Provided that any reference in this Sanhita to the Bharatiya Nagarik Suraksha Sanhita, 2023, shall be construed as a reference to the Bharatiya Nagarik Suraksha (Second) Sanhita, 2023.

3. (*1*) Throughout this Sanhita every definition of an offence, every penal provision, and every *Illustration* of every such definition or penal provision, shall be understood subject to the exceptions contained in the Chapter entitled "General Exceptions", though those exceptions are not repeated in such definition, penal provision, or *Illustration*.

Illustrations.

(*a*) The sections in this Sanhita, which contain definitions of offences, do not express that a child under seven years of age cannot commit such offences; but the definitions are to be understood subject to the general exception which provides that nothing shall be an offence which is done by a child under seven years of age.

(*b*) A, a police officer, without warrant, apprehends Z, who has committed murder. Here A is not guilty of the offence of wrongful confinement; for he was bound by law to apprehend Z, and therefore the case falls within the general exception which provides that "nothing is an offence which is done by a person who is bound by law to do it".

(*2*) Every expression which is explained in any Part of this Sanhita, is used in every Part of this Sanhita in conformity with the explanation.

(*3*) When property is in the possession of a person's spouse, clerk or servant, on account of that person, it is in that person's possession within the meaning of this Sanhita.

Explanation.—A person employed temporarily or on a particular occasion in the capacity of a clerk or servant, is a clerk or servant within the meaning of this sub-section.

(*4*) In every Part of this Sanhita, except where a contrary intention appears from the context, words which refer to acts done extend also to illegal omissions.

(*5*) When a criminal act is done by several persons in furtherance of the common intention of all, each of such persons is liable for that act in the same manner as if it were done by him alone.

(*6*) Whenever an act, which is criminal only by reason of its being done with a criminal knowledge or intention, is done by several persons, each of such persons who joins in the act with such knowledge or intention is liable for the act in the same manner as if the act were done by him alone with that knowledge or intention.

(*7*) Wherever the causing of a certain effect, or an attempt to cause that effect, by an act or by an omission, is an offence, it is to be understood that the causing of that effect partly by an act and partly by an omission is the same offence.

Illustration.

A intentionally causes Z's death, partly by illegally omitting to give Z food, and partly by beating Z. A has committed murder.

(*8*) When an offence is committed by means of several acts, whoever intentionally cooperates in the commission of that offence by doing any one of those acts, either singly or jointly with any other person, commits that offence.

Illustrations.

(*a*)Aand B agree to murder Z by severally and at different times giving him small doses of poison.A and B administer the poison according to the agreement with intent to murder Z. Z dies from the effects the several doses of poison so administered to him. Here A and B intentionally cooperate in the commission of murder and as each of them does an act by which the death is caused, they are both guilty of the offence though their acts are separate.

(*b*) A and B are joint jailors, and as such have the charge of Z, a prisoner, alternatively for six hours at a time. Aand B, intending to cause Z's death, knowingly cooperate in causing that effect by illegally omitting, each during the time of his attendance, to furnish Z with food supplied to them for that purpose. Z dies of hunger. Both A and B are guilty of the murder of Z. (*c*) A, a jailor, has the charge of Z, a prisoner. A, intending to cause Z's death, illegally omits to supply Z with food; in consequence of which Z is much reduced in strength, but the starvation is not sufficient to cause his death. A is dismissed from his office, and B succeeds him. B, without collusion or cooperation with A, illegally omits to supply Z with food, knowing that he is likely thereby to cause Z's death. Z dies of hunger. B is guilty of murder, but, as A did not cooperate with B. A is guilty only of an attempt to commit murder.

(*9*) Where several persons are engaged or concerned in the commission of a criminal act, they may be guilty of different offences by means of that act.

Illustration.

45 A attacks Z under such circumstances of grave provocation that his killing of Z would be only culpable homicide not amounting to murder. B, having ill-will towards Z and intending to kill him, and not having been subject to the provocation, assists A in killing Z. Here, though A and B are both engaged in causing Z's death, B is guilty of murder, and A is guilty only of culpable homicide.

Punishments.

Commutation are—

Chapter Two

OF PUNISHMENTS

4. The punishments to which offenders are liable under the provisions of this Sanhita

(*a*) Death;

(*b*) Imprisonment for life;

(*c*) Imprisonment, which is of two descriptions, namely:—

(*1*) Rigorous, that is, with hard labour; (*2*) Simple;

(*d*) Forfeiture of property; (*e*) Fine;

(*f*) Community Service.

5. The appropriate Government may, without the consent of the offender, commute

of sentence.

Fractions of terms of

punishment.

Sentence may be (in certain cases of

imprisonment) wholly or partly rigorous or simple.

Amount of fine, liability in default of payment of fine, etc.

any punishment under this Sanhita to any other punishment in accordance with section 474 of the Bharatiya Nagarik Suraksha Sanhita, 2023.

Explanation.--For the purposes of this section the expression "appropriate

Government" means,--

(*a*) in cases where the sentence is a sentence of death or is for an offence against any law relating to a matter to which the executive power of the Union extends, the Central Government; and

(*b*) in cases where the sentence (whether of death or not) is for an offence against any law relating to a matter to which the executive power of the State extends, the Government of the State within which the offender is sentenced.

6. In calculating fractions of terms of punishment, imprisonment for life shall be reckoned as equivalent to imprisonment for twenty years unless otherwise provided.

7. In every case in which an offender is punishable with imprisonment which may be

of either description, it shall be competent to the Court which sentences such offender to direct in the sentence that such imprisonment shall be wholly rigorous, or that such imprisonment shall be wholly simple, or that any part of such imprisonment shall be rigorous and the rest simple.

8. (*1*) Where no sum is expressed to which a fine may extend, the amount of fine to which the offender is liable is unlimited, but shall not be excessive.

(*2*) In every case of an offence––

(*a*) punishable with imprisonment as well as fine, in which the offender is sentenced to a fine, whether with or without imprisonment;

(*b*) punishable with imprisonment or fine, or with fine only, in which the offender

is sentenced to a fine,

it shall be competent to the Court which sentences such offender to direct by the sentence that, in default of payment of the fine, the offender shall suffer imprisonment for a certain term, in which imprisonment shall be in excess of any other imprisonment to which he may have been sentenced or to which he may be liable under a commutation of a sentence.

(*3*) The term for which the Court directs the offender to be imprisoned in default of payment of a fine shall not exceed one-fourth of the term of imprisonment which is the maximum fixed for the offence, if the offence be punishable with imprisonment as well as fine.

(*4*) The imprisonment which the Court imposes in default of payment of a fine or in default of community service may be of any description to which the offender might have been sentenced for the offence.

(*5*) If the offence is punishable with fine or community service, the imprisonment which the Court imposes in default of payment of the fine or in default of community service shall be simple, and the term for which the Court directs the offender to be imprisoned, in default of payment of fine or in default of community service, shall not exceed,—

(*a*) two months when the amount of the fine does not exceed five thousand rupees;

(*b*) four months when the amount of the fine does not exceed ten thousand rupees; and

(*c*) one year in any other case.

(*6*) (*a*) The imprisonment which is imposed in default of payment of a fine shall terminate whenever that fine is either paid or levied by process of law;

(*b*) If, before the expiration of the term of imprisonment fixed in default of payment, such a proportion of the fine be paid or levied that the term of imprisonment suffered in default of payment is not less than proportional to the part of the fine still unpaid, the imprisonment shall terminate.

Illustration.

A is sentenced to a fine of one thousand rupees and to four months' imprisonment in default of payment. Here, if seven hundred and fifty rupees of the fine be paid or levied before the expiration of one month of the imprisonment, A will be discharged as soon as the first month has expired. If seven hundred and fifty rupees be paid or levied at the time of the expiration of the first month, or at any later time while Acontinues in imprisonment, Awill be immediately discharged. If five hundred rupees of the fine be paid or levied before the expiration of two months of the imprisonment, A will be discharged as soon as the two months are completed. If five hundred rupees be paid or levied at the time of the expiration of those two months, or at any later time whileAcontinues in imprisonment,Awill be immediately discharged.

(*7*) The fine, or any part thereof which remains unpaid, may be levied at any time within six years after the passing of the sentence, and if, under the sentence, the offender be liable to imprisonment for a longer period than six years, then at any time previous to the expiration of that period; and the death of the offender does not discharge from the liability any property which would, after his death, be legally liable for his debts.

9. (*1*) Where anything which is an offence is made up of parts, any of which parts is itself an offence, the offender shall not be punished with the punishment of more than one of

40 such his offences, unless it be so expressly provided. (*2*) Where—

(*a*) anything is an offence falling within two or more separate definitions of any

law in force for the time being by which offences are defined or punished; or

Limit of punishment of offence made up of several offences.

Punishment of person guilty

of one of several

offences, judgment

stating that it is doubtful of which.

Solitary

confinement.

Limit of solitary

confinement.

Enhanced

punishment for certain

offences after previous

conviction.

Act done by a person bound, or by mistake of fact believing

himself bound, by law.

(*b*) several acts, of which one or more than one would by itself or themselves constitute an offence, constitute, when combined, a different offence,

the offender shall not be punished with a more severe punishment than the Court which tries him could award for any one of such offences.

Illustrations.

(*a*) A gives Z fifty strokes with a stick. Here A may have committed the offence of voluntarily causing hurt to Z by the whole beating, and also by each of the blows which make up the whole beating. If A were liable to punishment for every blow, he might be imprisoned for fifty years, one for each blow. But he is liable only to one punishment for the whole beating.

(*b*) But, if, while A is beating Z, Y interferes, and A intentionally strikes Y, here, as the blow given to Y is no part of the act wherebyA voluntarily causes hurt to Z, Ais liable to one punishment for voluntarily causing hurt to Z, and to another for the blow given to Y.

10. In all cases in which judgment is given that a person is guilty of one of several offences specified in the judgment, but that it is doubtful of which of these offences he is guilty, the offender shall be punished for the offence for which the lowest punishment is provided if the same punishment is not provided for all.

11. Whenever any person is convicted of an offence for which under this Sanhita the Court has power to sentence him to rigorous imprisonment, the Court may, by its sentence, order that the offender shall be kept in solitary confinement for any portion or portions of the imprisonment to which he is sentenced, not exceeding three months in the whole, according to the following scale, namely:—

(*a*) a time not exceeding one month if the term of imprisonment shall not exceed six months;

(*b*) a time not exceeding two months if the term of imprisonment shall exceed six months and shall not exceed one year;

(*c*) a time not exceeding three months if the term of imprisonment shall exceed one year.

12. In executing a sentence of solitary confinement, such confinement shall in no case exceed fourteen days at a time, with intervals between the periods of solitary confinement of not less duration than such periods; and when the imprisonment awarded shall exceed three months, the solitary confinement shall not exceed seven days in any one month of the whole imprisonment awarded, with intervals between the periods of solitary confinement of not less duration than such periods.

13. Whoever, having been convicted by a Court in India, of an offence punishable under Chapter X or Chapter XVII of this Sanhita with imprisonment of either description for a term of three years or upwards, shall be guilty of any offence punishable under either of those Chapters with like imprisonment for the like term, shall be subject for every such subsequent offence to imprisonment for life, or to imprisonment of either description for a term which may extend to ten years.

Chapter Three

GENERAL EXCEPTIONS

14. Nothing is an offence which is done by a person who is, or who by reason of a mistake of fact and not by reason of a mistake of law in good faith believes himself to be, bound by law to do it.
45

Illustrations.

(*a*) A, a soldier, fires on a mob by the order of his superior officer, in conformity with the commands of the law. A has committed no offence.

(*b*) A, an officer of a Court, being ordered by that Court to arrest Y, and, after due enquiry, believing Z to be Y, arrests Z. A has committed no offence.

15. Nothing is an offence which is done by a Judge when acting judicially in the exercise of any power which is, or which in good faith he believes to be, given to him by law.

16. Nothing which is done in pursuance of, or which is warranted by the judgment or order of, a Court; if done whilst such judgment or order remains in force, is an offence, notwithstanding the Court may have had no jurisdiction to pass such judgment or order, provided the person doing the act in good faith believes that the Court had such jurisdiction.

17. Nothing is an offence which is done by any person who is justified by law, or who by reason of a mistake of fact and not by reason of a mistake of law in good faith, believes himself to be justified by law, in doing it.

Illustration.

A sees Z commit what appears to A to be a murder. A, in the exercise, to the best of his judgment exerted in good faith, of the power which the law gives to all persons of apprehending murderers in the fact, seizes Z, in order to bring Z before the proper authorities. A has committed no offence, though it may turn out that Z was acting in self-defence.

18. Nothing is an offence which is done by accident or misfortune, and without any criminal intention or knowledge in the doing of a lawful act in a lawful manner by lawful means and with proper care and caution.

Illustration.

A is at work with a hatchet; the head flies off and kills a man who is standing by. Here, if there was no want of proper caution on the part of A, his act is excusable and not an offence.

19. Nothing is an offence merely by reason of its being done with the knowledge that it is likely to cause harm, if it be done without any criminal intention to cause harm, and in good faith for the purpose of preventing or avoiding other harm to person or property.

Explanation.—It is a question of fact in such a case whether the harm to be prevented or avoided was of such a nature and so imminent as to justify or excuse the risk of doing the act with the knowledge that it was likely to cause harm.

Illustrations.

(*a*) A, the captain of a vessel, suddenly and without any fault or negligence on his part, finds himself in such a position that, before he can stop his vessel, he must inevitably run down a boat B, with twenty or thirty passengers on board, unless he changes the course of his vessel, and that, by changing his course, he must incur risk of running down a boat C with only two passengers on board, which he may possibly clear. Here, if A alters his course without any intention to run down the boat C and in good faith for the purpose of avoiding the danger to the passengers in the boat B, he is not guilty of an offence, though he may run down the boat C by doing an act which he knew was likely to cause that effect, if it be found as a matter of fact that the danger which he intended to avoid was such as to excuse him in incurring the risk of running down the boat C.

(*b*) A, in a great fire, pulls down houses in order to prevent the conflagration from spreading. He does this with the intention in good faith of saving human life or property. Here, if it be found that the harm to be prevented was of such a nature and so imminent as to excuse A's act, A is not guilty of the offence.

Act of Judge when acting judicially.

Act done pursuant to judgment or order of

Court.

Act done by a person justified, or by mistake of fact believing himself justified, by law.

Accident in doing a lawful act.

Act likely to cause harm, but done

without

criminal

intent, and to prevent other harm.

Act of a child under seven years of age.

Act of a child above seven and under twelve years of age of

immature

understanding.

Act of a person of unsound mind.

Act of a person incapable of judgment by reason of

intoxication caused against his will.

Offence requiring a particular

intent or knowledge

committed by one who is

intoxicated.

Act not intended and

not known to be likely to cause death or grievous hurt, done by

consent.

Act not intended to cause death, done by

consent in good faith for person's

benefit.

Act done in good faith for benefit of child or

person of unsound mind, by, or by

consent of guardian.

20. Nothing is an offence which is done by a child under seven years of age.

21. Nothing is an offence which is done by a child above seven years of age and under twelve years of age, who has not attained sufficient maturity of understanding to judge of the nature and consequences of his conduct on that occasion.

22. Nothing is an offence which is done by a person who, at the time of doing it, by 5 reason of unsoundness of mind, is incapable of knowing the nature of the act, or that he is doing what is either wrong or contrary to law.

23. Nothing is an offence which is done by a person who, at the time of doing it, is, by reason of intoxication, incapable of knowing the nature of the act, or that he is doing what is either wrong, or contrary to law; provided that the thing which intoxicated him was administered to him without his knowledge or against his will.

24. In cases where an act done is not an offence unless done with a particular knowledge or intent, a person who does the act in a state of intoxication shall be liable to be dealt with as if he had the same knowledge as he would have had if he had not been intoxicated, unless the thing which intoxicated him was administered to him without his knowledge or against his will.

25. Nothing which is not intended to cause death, or grievous hurt, and which is not known by the doer to be likely to cause death or grievous hurt, is an offence by reason of any harm which it may cause, or be intended by the doer to cause, to any person, above eighteen years of age, who has given consent, whether express or implied, to suffer that harm; or by reason of any harm which it may be known by the doer to be likely to cause to any such person who has consented to take the risk of that harm.

Illustration.

A and Z agree to fence with each other for amusement. This agreement implies the consent of each to suffer any harm which, in the course of such fencing, may be caused without foul play; and if A, while playing fairly, hurts Z, A commits no offence.

26. Nothing, which is not intended to cause death, is an offence by reason of any harm which it may cause, or be intended by the doer to cause, or be known by the doer to be likely to cause, to any person for whose benefit it is done in good faith, and who has given a consent, whether express or implied, to suffer that harm, or to take the risk of that harm.

Illustration.

A, a surgeon, knowing that a particular operation is likely to cause the death of Z, who suffers under the painful complaint, but not intending to cause Z's death, and intending, in good faith, Z's benefit, performs that operation on Z, with Z's consent. A has committed no offence.

27. Nothing which is done in good faith for the benefit of a person under twelve years of age, or person of unsound mind, by or by consent, either express or implied, of the guardian or other person having lawful charge of that person, is an offence by reason of any harm which it may cause, or be intended by the doer to cause or be known by the doer to be likely to cause to that person:

Provided that this exception shall not extend to––

(*a*) the intentional causing of death, or to the attempting to cause death;

(*b*) the doing of anything which the person doing it knows to be likely to cause death, for any purpose other than the preventing of death or grievous hurt, or the curing of any grievous disease or infirmity;

(*c*) the voluntary causing of grievous hurt, or to the attempting to cause grievous hurt, unless it be for the purpose of preventing death or grievous hurt, or the curing of any grievous disease or infirmity;

(*d*) the abetment of any offence, to the committing of which offence it would not extend.

Illustration.

A, in good faith, for his child's benefit without his child's consent, has his child cut for the stone by a surgeon knowing it to be likely that the operation will cause the child's death, but not intending to cause the child's death. A is within the exception, in as much as his object was the cure of the child.

28. A consent is not such a consent as is intended by any section of this Sanhita,–– (*a*) if the consent is given by a person under fear of injury, or under a misconception of fact, and if the person doing the act knows, or has reason to believe, that the consent was given in consequence of such fear or misconception; or

(*b*) if the consent is given by a person who, from unsoundness of mind, or intoxication, is unable to understand the nature and consequence of that to which he gives his consent; or

(*c*) unless the contrary appears from the context, if the consent is given by a person who is under twelve years of age.

29. The exceptions in sections 25, 26 and 27 do not extend to acts which are offences independently of any harm which they may cause, or be intended to cause, or be known to be likely to cause, to the person giving the consent, or on whose behalf the consent is given.

Illustration.

Causing miscarriage (unless caused in good faith for the purpose of saving the life of the woman) is an offence independently of any harm which it may cause or be intended to cause to the woman. Therefore, it is not an offence "by reason of such harm"; and the consent of the woman or of her guardian to the causing of such miscarriage does not justify the act.

30. Nothing is an offence by reason of any harm which it may cause to a person for whose benefit it is done in good faith, even without that person's consent, if the circumstances are such that it is impossible for that person to signify consent, or if that person is incapable of giving consent, and has no guardian or other person in lawful charge of him from whom it is possible to obtain consent in time for the thing to be done with benefit:

Provided that this exception shall not extend to––

(*a*) the intentional causing of death, or the attempting to cause death;

(*b*) the doing of anything which the person doing it knows to be likely to cause death, for any purpose other than the preventing of death or grievous hurt, or the curing of any grievous disease or infirmity;

(*c*) the voluntary causing of hurt, or to the attempting to cause hurt, for any purpose other than the preventing of death or hurt;

(*d*) the abetment of any offence, to the committing of which offence it would not extend.

Consent known to be given under fear or misconception.

Exclusion of acts which are offences

independently of harm caused.

Act done in good faith for benefit of a

person without

consent.

Illustrations.

45 (*1*) Z is thrown from his horse, and is insensible. A, a surgeon, finds that Z requires to

Communication made in good

faith.

Act to which a person is compelled by

threats.

Act causing slight harm.

Things done in private defence.

Right of private defence of body and of property.

be trepanned. A, not intending Z's death, but in good faith, for Z's benefit, performs the trepan before Z recovers his power of judging for himself. A has committed no offence.

(*2*) Z is carried off by a tiger.Afires at the tiger knowing it to be likely that the shot may kill Z, but not intending to kill Z, and in good faith intending Z's benefit. A's bullet gives Z a mortal wound. A has committed no offence.

(*3*) A, a surgeon, sees a child suffer an accident which is likely to prove fatal unless an operation be immediately performed. There is no time to apply to the child's guardian. A performs the operation in spite of the entreaties of the child, intending, in good faith, the child's benefit. A has committed no offence.

(*4*) A is in a house which is on fire, with Z, a child. People below hold out a blanket. A drops the child from the house top, knowing it to be likely that the fall may kill the child, but not intending to kill the child, and intending, in good faith, the child's benefit. Here, even if the child is killed by the fall, A has committed no offence.

Explanation.—Mere pecuniary benefit is not benefit within the meaning of sections 26, 27 and this section.

31. No communication made in good faith is an offence by reason of any harm to the person to whom it is made, if it is made for the benefit of that person.

Illustration.

A, a surgeon, in good faith, communicates to a patient his opinion that he cannot live.

The patient dies in consequence of the shock. A has committed no offence, though he knew it to be likely that the communication might cause the patient's death.

32. Except murder, and offences against the State punishable with death, nothing is an offence which is done by a person who is compelled to do it by threats, which, at the time of doing it, reasonably cause the apprehension that instant death to that person will otherwise be the consequence:

Provided that the person doing the act did not of his own accord, or from a reasonable apprehension of harm to himself short of instant death, place himself in the situation by which he became subject to such constraint.

Explanation 1.—A person who, of his own accord, or by reason of a threat of being beaten, joins a gang of dacoits, knowing their character, is not entitled to the benefit of this exception, on the ground of his having been compelled by his associates to do anything that is an offence by law.

Explanation 2.—A person seized by a gang of dacoits, and forced, by threat of instant death, to do a thing which is an offence by law; for example, a smith compelled to take his tools and to force the door of a house for the dacoits to enter and plunder it, is entitled to the benefit of this exception.

33. Nothing is an offence by reason that it causes, or that it is intended to cause, or that it is known to be likely to cause, any harm, if that harm is so slight that no person of ordinary sense and temper would complain of such harm. *Of the right of private defence* 40

34. Nothing is an offence which is done in the exercise of the right of private defence.

35. Every person has a right, subject to the restrictions contained in section 37, to defend—

(*a*) his own body, and the body of any other person, against any offence affecting

the human body; 45

(*b*) the property, whether movable or immovable, of himself or of any other person, against any act which is an offence falling under the definition of theft, robbery, mischief or criminal trespass, or which is an attempt to commit theft, robbery, mischief or criminal trespass.

36. When an act, which would otherwise be a certain offence, is not that offence, by

5 reason of the youth, the want of maturity of understanding, the unsoundness of mind or the intoxication of the person doing that act, or by reason of any misconception on the part of that person, every person has the same right of private defence against that act which he would have if the act were that offence.

Illustrations.

(*a*) Z, a person of unsound mind, attempts to kill A; Z is guilty of no offence. ButA has the same right of private defence which he would have if Z were sane.

(*b*) A enters by night a house which he is legally entitled to enter. Z, in good faith, taking A for a house-breaker, attacks A. Here Z, by attacking A under this misconception, commits no offence. But A has the same right of private defence against Z, which he would have if Z were not acting under that misconception.

37. (*1*) There is no right of private defence,--

(*a*) against an act which does not reasonably cause the apprehension of death or of grievous hurt, if done, or attempted to be done, by a public servant acting in good faith under colour of his office, though that act, may not be strictly justifiable by law;

(*b*) against an act which does not reasonably cause the apprehension of death or of grievous hurt, if done, or attempted to be done, by the direction of a public servant acting in good faith under colour of his office, though that direction may not be strictly justifiable by law;

(*c*) in cases in which there is time to have recourse to the protection of the public authorities.

(*2*) The right of private defence in no case extends to the inflicting of more harm than it is necessary to inflict for the purpose of defence.

Explanation 1.—A person is not deprived of the right of private defence against an act done, or attempted to be done, by a public servant, as such, unless he knows or has reason to believe, that the person doing the act is such public servant.

Explanation 2.—A person is not deprived of the right of private defence against an act done, or attempted to be done, by the direction of a public servant, unless he knows, or has reason to believe, that the person doing the act is acting by such direction, or unless such person states the authority under which he acts, or if he has authority in writing, unless he

produces such authority, if demanded.

38. The right of private defence of the body extends, under the restrictions specified in section 37, to the voluntary causing of death or of any other harm to the assailant, if the offence which occasions the exercise of the right be of any of the descriptions hereinafter enumerated, namely:—

(*a*) such an assault as may reasonably cause the apprehension that death will otherwise be the consequence of such assault;

(*b*) such an assault as may reasonably cause the apprehension that grievous hurt will otherwise be the consequence of such assault;

(*c*) an assault with the intention of committing rape;

(*d*) an assault with the intention of gratifying unnatural lust; (*e*) an assault with the intention of kidnapping or abducting;

Right of private defence against act of a person of unsound mind, etc. Acts against which there is no right of private defence When right of private defence of body extends to causing death. When such right extends to causing any harm other than death. Commencement and continuance of right of private defence of body. When right of private defence of property extends to causing death.

When such right extends to causing any harm other than death. Commencement and continuance of right of private defence of property.

Right of private defence against deadly assault when there is risk of harm to innocent person.

(*f*) an assault with the intention of wrongfully confining a person, under circumstances which may reasonably cause him to apprehend that he will be unable to have recourse to the public authorities for his release;

(*g*) an act of throwing or administering acid or an attempt to throw or administer acid which may reasonably cause the apprehension that grievous hurt will otherwise be the consequence of such act.

39. If the offence be not of any of the descriptions specified in section 38, the right of private defence of the body does not extend to the voluntary causing of death to the assailant, but does extend, under the restrictions specified in section 37, to the voluntary causing to the assailant of any harm other than death.

40. The right of private defence of the body commences as soon as a reasonable apprehension of danger to the body arises from an attempt or threat to commit the offence though the offence may not have been committed; and it continues as long as such apprehension of danger to the body continues.

41. The right of private defence of property extends, under the restrictions specified in section 37, to the voluntary causing of death or of any other harm to the wrong-doer, if the offence, the committing of which, or the attempting to commit which, occasions the exercise of the right, be an offence of any of the descriptions hereinafter enumerated, namely:— (*a*) robbery;

(*b*) house-breaking after sunset and before sunrise;

(*c*) mischief by fire or any explosive substance committed on any building, tent or vessel, which building, tent or vessel is used as a human dwelling, or as a place for the custody of property;

(*d*) theft, mischief, or house-trespass, under such circumstances as may reasonably cause apprehension that death or grievous hurt will be the consequence, if such right of private defence is not exercised.

42. If the offence, the committing of which, or the attempting to commit which occasions the exercise of the right of private defence, be theft, mischief, or criminal trespass, not of any of the descriptions specified in section 41, that right does not extend to the voluntary causing of death, but does extend, subject to the restrictions specified in section 37, to the voluntary causing to the wrong-doer of any harm other than death.

43. The right of private defence of property,--

(*a*) commences when a reasonable apprehension of danger to the property commences;

(*b*) against theft continues till the offender has effected his retreat with the property or either the assistance of the public authorities is obtained, or the property has been recovered;

(*c*) against robbery continues as long as the offender causes or attempts to cause to any person death or hurt or wrongful restraint or as long as the fear of instant death or of instant hurt or of instant personal restraint continues;

(*d*) against criminal trespass or mischief continues as long as the offender continues in the commission of criminal trespass or mischief;

(*e*) against house-breaking after sunset and before sunrise continues as long as the house-trespass which has been begun by such house-breaking continues.

44. If in the exercise of the right of private defence against an assault which reasonably causes the apprehension of death, the defender be so situated that he cannot effectually exercise that right without risk of harm to an innocent person, his right of private defence extends to the running of that risk.

Illustration.

A is attacked by a mob who attempt to murder him. He cannot effectually exercise his right of private defence without firing on the mob, and he cannot fire without risk of harming young children who are mingled with the mob. Acommits no offence if by so firing he harms any of the children.

Chapter Four

OF ABETMENT, CRIMINAL CONSPIRACY AND ATTEMPT

of abetment

45. A person abets the doing of a thing, who—

(*a*) instigates any person to do that thing; or

(*b*) engages with one or more other person or persons in any conspiracy for the doing of that thing, if an act or illegal omission takes place in pursuance of that conspiracy, and in order to the doing of that thing; or

(*c*) intentionally aids, by any act or illegal omission, the doing of that thing.

Explanation 1.—A person who, by wilful misrepresentation, or by wilful concealment of a material fact which he is bound to disclose, voluntarily causes or procures, or attempts to cause or procure, a thing to be done, is said to instigate the doing of that thing.

Illustration.

A, a public officer, is authorised by a warrant from a Court to apprehend Z. B, knowing that fact and also that C is not Z, wilfully represents to Athat C is Z, and thereby intentionally causes A to apprehend C. Here B abets by instigation the apprehension of

Explanation 2.—Whoever, either prior to or at the time of the commission of an act,

does anything in order to facilitate the commission of that act, and thereby facilitates the commission thereof, is said to aid the doing of that act.

46. A person abets an offence, who abets either the commission of an offence, or the commission of an act which would be an offence, if committed by a person capable by law of committing an offence with the same intention or knowledge as that of the abettor.

Explanation 1.—The abetment of the illegal omission of an act may amount to an offence although the abettor may not himself be bound to do that act.

Explanation 2.—To constitute the offence of abetment it is not necessary that the act abetted should be committed, or that the effect requisite to constitute the offence should be caused.

Illustrations.

(*a*) A instigates B to murder C. B refuses to do so. A is guilty of abetting B to commit murder.

(*b*) A instigates B to murder D. B in pursuance of the instigation stabs D. D recovers from the wound. A is guilty of instigating B to commit murder.

Explanation 3.—It is not necessary that the person abetted should be capable by law of committing an offence, or that he should have the same guilty intention or knowledge as that of the abettor, or any guilty intention or knowledge.

Abetment of a thing.

Abettor.

Illustrations.

(*a*) A, with a guilty intention, abets a child or a person of unsound mind to commit an act which would be an offence, if committed by a person capable by law of committing an offence, and having the same intention as A. Here A, whether the act be committed or not, is guilty of abetting an offence.

(*b*) A, with the intention of murdering Z, instigates B, a child under seven years of age, to do an act which causes Z's death. B, in consequence of the abetment, does the act in the absence of A and thereby causes Z's death. Here, though B was not capable by law of committing an offence, Ais liable to be punished in the same manner as if B had been capable by law of committing an offence, and had committed murder, and he is therefore subject to the punishment of death.

(*c*) Ainstigates B to set fire to a dwelling-house. B, in consequence of his unsoundness of mind, being incapable of knowing the nature of the act, or that he is doing what is wrong or contrary to law, sets fire to the house in consequence of A's instigation. B has committed no offence, but A is guilty of abetting the offence of setting fire to a dwelling-house, and is liable to the punishment provided for that offence.

(*d*) A, intending to cause a theft to be committed, instigates B to take property belonging to Z out of Z's possession. A induces B to believe that the property belongs to A. B takes the property out of Z's possession, in good faith, believing it to be A's property. B, acting under

this misconception, does not take dishonestly, and therefore does not commit theft. But A is

guilty of abetting theft, and is liable to the same punishment as if B had committed theft.

Explanation 4.—The abetment of an offence being an offence, the abetment of such an abetment is also an offence.

Abetment in

India of offences outside India.

Abetment outside India for offence in India.

Illustration.

A instigates B to instigate C to murder Z. B accordingly instigates C to murder Z, and

C commits that offence in consequence of B's instigation. B is liable to be punished for his offence with the punishment for murder; and, as A instigated B to commit the offence, A is also liable to the same punishment.

Explanation 5.—It is not necessary to the commission of the offence of abetment by conspiracy that the abettor should concert the offence with the person who commits it. It is sufficient if he engages in the conspiracy in pursuance of which the offence is committed.

Illustration.

A concerts with B a plan for poisoning Z. It is agreed that Ashall administer the poison. B then explains the plan to C mentioning that a third person is to administer the poison, but without mentioning A's name. C agrees to procure the poison, and procures and delivers it to B for the purpose of its being used in the manner explained. A administers the poison; Z dies in consequence. Here, though A and C have not conspired together, yet C has been engaged in the conspiracy in pursuance of which Z has been murdered. C has therefore committed the offence defined in this section and is liable to the punishment for murder.

47. A person abets an offence within the meaning of this Sanhita who, in India, abets the commission of any act without and beyond India which would constitute an offence if committed in India.

Illustration.

A, in India, instigates B, a foreigner in country X, to commit a murder in that country,

A is guilty of abetting murder.

48. A person abets an offence within the meaning of this Sanhita who, without and beyond India, abets the commission of any act in India which would constitute an offence if committed in India.

Illustration.

A, in country X, instigates B, to commit a murder in India,Ais guilty of abetting murder.

49. Whoever abets any offence shall, if the act abetted is committed in consequence of the abetment, and no express provision is made by this Sanhita for the punishment of such abetment, be punished with the punishment provided for the offence.

Explanation.—An act or offence is said to be committed in consequence of abetment, when it is committed in consequence of the instigation, or in pursuance of the conspiracy, or with the aid which constitutes the abetment.

Illustrations.

(*a*) A instigates B to give false evidence. B, in consequence of the instigation, commits that offence. A is guilty of abetting that offence, and is liable to the same punishment as B.

(*b*) A and B conspire to poison Z. A, in pursuance of the conspiracy, procures the poison and delivers it to B in order that he may administer it to Z. B, in pursuance of the conspiracy, administers the poison to Z in A's absence and thereby causes Z's death. Here B is guilty of murder. A is guilty of abetting that offence by conspiracy, and is liable to the punishment for murder.

50. Whoever abets the commission of an offence shall, if the person abetted does the act with a different intention or knowledge from that of the abettor, be punished with the punishment provided for the offence which would have been committed if the act had been done with the intention or knowledge of the abettor and with no other.

51. When an act is abetted and a different act is done, the abettor is liable for the act done, in the same manner and to the same extent as if he had directly abetted it:

Provided that the act done was a probable consequence of the abetment, and was committed under the influence of the instigation, or with the aid or in pursuance of the conspiracy which constituted the abetment.

Illustrations.

(*a*) A instigates a child to put poison into the food of Z, and gives him poison for that purpose. The child, in consequence of the instigation, by mistake puts the poison into the food of Y, which is by the side of that of Z. Here, if the child was acting under the influence of A's instigation, and the act done was under the circumstances a probable consequence of the abetment,A is liable in the same manner and to the same extent as if he had instigated the child to put the poison into the food of Y.

(*b*) A instigates B to burn Z's house, B sets fire to the house and at the same time commits theft of property there. A, though guilty of abetting the burning of the house, is not guilty of abetting the theft; for the theft was a distinct act, and not a probable consequence of the burning.

(*c*) Ainstigates B and C to break into an inhabited house at midnight for the purpose of robbery, and provides them with arms for that purpose. B and C break into the house, and being resisted by Z, one of the inmates, murder Z. Here, if that murder was the probable consequence of the abetment, A is liable to the punishment provided for murder.

52. If the act for which the abettor is liable under section 51 is committed in addition to the act abetted, and constitute a distinct offence, the abettor is liable to punishment for each of the offences.

Punishment of abetment if act abetted is committed in consequence and where no express provision is made for its punishment.

Punishment of abetment if person abetted does act with different intention from that of abettor.

Liability of abettor when one act abetted and different act done.

Abettor when liable to cumulative

punishment

for act abetted and for act

done.

Liability of abettor for an effect caused by act abetted different from that intended by abettor.

Abettor present when offence is

committed.

Abetment of offence punishable with death or

imprisonment for life.

Abetment of offence punishable with

imprisonment.

Illustration.

A instigates B to resist by force a distress made by a public servant. B, in consequence, resists that distress. In offering the resistance, B voluntarily causes grievous hurt to the officer executing the distress. As B has committed both the offence of resisting the distress,

and the offence of voluntarily causing grievous hurt, B is liable to punishment for both these 5 offences; and, if A knew that B was likely voluntarily to cause grievous hurt in resisting the distress, A will also be liable to punishment for each of the offences.

53. When an act is abetted with the intention on the part of the abettor of causing a particular effect, and an act for which the abettor is liable in consequence of the abetment, causes a different effect from that intended by the abettor, the abettor is liable for the effect caused, in the same manner and to the same extent as if he had abetted the act with the intention of causing that effect, provided he knew that the act abetted was likely to cause that effect.

Illustration.

A instigates B to cause grievous hurt to Z. B, in consequence of the instigation, causes grievous hurt to Z. Z dies in consequence. Here, if A knew that the grievous hurt abetted was likely to cause death, A is liable to be punished with the punishment provided for murder.

54. Whenever any person, who is absent would be liable to be punished as an abettor,

is present when the act or offence for which he would be punishable in consequence of the

abetment is committed, he shall be deemed to have committed such act or offence.

55. Whoever abets the commission of an offence punishable with death or imprisonment for life, shall, if that offence be not committed in consequence of the abetment, and no express provision is made under this Sanhita for the punishment of such abetment, be punished with imprisonment of either description for a term which may extend to seven years, and shall also be liable to fine; and if any act for which the abettor is liable in consequence of the abetment, and which causes hurt to any person, is done, the abettor shall be liable to imprisonment of either description for a term which may extend to fourteen years, and shall also be liable to fine.

Illustration.

A instigates B to murder Z. The offence is not committed. If B had murdered Z, he would have been subject to the punishment of death or imprisonment for life. Therefore, Ais liable to imprisonment for a term which may extend to seven years and also to a fine; and if any hurt be done to Z in consequence of the abetment, he will be liable to imprisonment for a term which may extend to fourteen years, and to fine.

56. Whoever abets an offence punishable with imprisonment shall, if that offence be not committed in consequence of the abetment, and no express provision is made under this Sanhita for the punishment of such abetment, be punished with imprisonment of any description provided for that offence for a term which may extend to one-fourth part of the longest term provided for that offence; or with such fine as is provided for that offence, or with both; and if the abettor or the person abetted is a public servant, whose duty it is to prevent the commission of such offence, the abettor shall be punished with imprisonment of any description provided for that offence, for a term which may extend to one-half of the longest term provided for that offence, or with such fine as is provided for the offence, or with both.

Illustrations.

(*a*) A instigates B to give false evidence. Here, if B does not give false evidence, A has nevertheless committed the offence defined in this section, and is punishable accordingly.

(*b*) A, a police officer, whose duty it is to prevent robbery, abets the commission of robbery. Here, though the robbery be not committed, A is liable to one-half of the longest term of imprisonment provided for that offence, and also to fine.

(*c*) B abets the commission of a robbery by A, a police officer, whose duty it is to prevent that offence. Here, though the robbery be not committed, B is liable to one-half of the longest term of imprisonment provided for the offence of robbery, and also to fine.

57. Whoever abets the commission of an offence by the public generally or by any number or class of persons exceeding ten, shall be punished with imprisonment of either description for a term which may extend to seven years and with fine.

Illustration.

A affixes in a public place a placard instigating a sect consisting of more than ten members to meet at a certain time and place, for the purpose of attacking the members of an adverse sect, while engaged in a procession. A has committed the offence defined in this section.

58. Whoever intending to facilitate or knowing it to be likely that he will thereby facilitate the commission of an offence punishable with death or imprisonment for life, voluntarily conceals by any act or omission, or by the use of encryption or any other information hiding tool, the existence of a design to commit such offence or makes any representation which he knows to be false respecting such design shall,––

(*a*) if that offence be committed, be punished with imprisonment of either description for a term which may extend to seven years; or

(*b*) if the offence be not committed, with imprisonment of either description, for a term which may extend to three years, and shall also be liable to fine.

Illustration.

A, knowing that dacoity is about to be committed at B, falsely informs the Magistrate that a dacoity is about to be committed at C, a place in an opposite direction, and thereby misleads the Magistrate with intent to facilitate the commission of the offence. The dacoity is committed at B in pursuance of the design. A is punishable under this section.

59. Whoever, being a public servant, intending to facilitate or knowing it to be likely that he will thereby facilitate the commission of an offence which it is his duty as such public servant to prevent, voluntarily conceals, by any act or omission or by the use of encryption or any other information hiding tool, the existence of a design to commit such offence, or makes any representation which he knows to be false respecting such design shall,––

(*a*) if the offence be committed, be punished with imprisonment of any description provided for the offence, for a term which may extend to one-half of the longest term of such imprisonment, or with such fine as is provided for that offence, or with both; or

(*b*) if the offence be punishable with death or imprisonment for life, with imprisonment of either description for a term which may extend to ten years; or

(*c*) if the offence be not committed, shall be punished with imprisonment of any description provided for the offence for a term which may extend to one-fourth part of the longest term of such imprisonment or with such fine as is provided for the offence, or with both.

Abetting commission of offence by public or by more than ten persons.

Concealing design to commit offence punishable with death or imprisonment for life.

Public servant concealing design to commit offence which it is his duty to prevent.

Illustration.

45 A, an officer of police, being legally bound to give information of all designs to commit robbery which may come to his knowledge, and knowing that B designs to commit robbery, omits to give such information, with intent to so facilitate the commission of that offence.

Concealing design to

commit offence punishable with

imprisonment.

Criminal

conspiracy.

Punishment for attempting to

commit offences punishable with imprisonment for life or

other

imprisonment.

Here A has by an illegal omission concealed the existence of B's design, and is liable to punishment according to the provision of this section.

60. Whoever, intending to facilitate or knowing it to be likely that he will thereby facilitate the commission of an offence punishable with imprisonment, voluntarily conceals,

by any act or illegal omission, the existence of a design to commit such offence, or makes any 5 representation which he knows to be false respecting such design shall,––

(*a*) if the offence be committed, be punished with imprisonment of the description provided for the offence, for a term which may extend to one-fourth; and

(*b*) if the offence be not committed, to one-eighth,

of the longest term of such imprisonment, or with such fine as is provided for the offence, or with both.

Of criminal conspiracy

61. (*1*) When two or more persons agree with the common object to do, or cause to be done––

(*a*) an illegal act; or

(*b*) an act which is not illegal by illegal means, such an agreement is designated a criminal conspiracy:

Provided that no agreement except an agreement to commit an offence shall amount to a criminal conspiracy unless some act besides the agreement is done by one or more parties to such agreement in pursuance thereof.

Explanation.—It is immaterial whether the illegal act is the ultimate object of such agreement, or is merely incidental to that object.

(*2*) Whoever is a party to a criminal conspiracy,––

(*a*) to commit an offence punishable with death, imprisonment for life or rigorous imprisonment for a term of two years or upwards, shall, where no express provision is made in this Sanhita for the punishment of such a conspiracy, be punished in the same manner as if he had abetted such offence;

(*b*) other than a criminal conspiracy to commit an offence punishable as aforesaid shall be punished with imprisonment of either description for a term not exceeding six months, or with fine or with both.

Of attempt

62. Whoever attempts to commit an offence punishable by this Sanhita with imprisonment for life or imprisonment, or to cause such an offence to be committed, and in such attempt does any act towards the commission of the offence, shall, where no express

provision is made by this Sanhita for the punishment of such attempt, be punished with

imprisonment of any description provided for the offence, for a term which may extend to one-half of the imprisonment for life or, as the case may be, one-half of the longest term of imprisonment provided for that offence, or with such fine as is provided for the offence, or with both.

Illustrations.

(*a*)A makes an attempt to steal some jewels by breaking open a box, and finds after so opening the box, that there is no jewel in it. He has done an act towards the commission of theft, and therefore is guilty under this section.

(*b*) A makes an attempt to pick the pocket of Z by thrusting his hand into Z's pocket. A fails in the attempt in consequence of Z's having nothing in his pocket. A is guilty under this section.

Chapter Five

OF OFFENCES AGAINST WOMAN AND CHILD

Of sexual offences

63. A man is said to commit "rape" if he—

(*a*) penetrates his penis, to any extent, into the vagina, mouth, urethra or anus of a woman or makes her to do so with him or any other person; or

(*b*) inserts, to any extent, any object or a part of the body, not being the penis, into the vagina, the urethra or anus of a woman or makes her to do so with him or any other person; or

(*c*) manipulates any part of the body of a woman so as to cause penetration into the vagina, urethra, anus or any part of body of such woman or makes her to do so with him or any other person; or

(*d*) applies his mouth to the vagina, anus, urethra of a woman or makes her to do so with him or any other person,

under the circumstances falling under any of the following seven descriptions:— (*i*) against her will;

(*ii*) without her consent;

(*iii*) with her consent, when her consent has been obtained by putting her or any person in whom she is interested, in fear of death or of hurt;

(*iv*) with her consent, when the man knows that he is not her husband and that her consent is given because she believes that he is another man to whom she is or believes herself to be lawfully married;

(*v*) with her consent when, at the time of giving such consent, by reason of unsoundness of mind or intoxication or the administration by him personally or through another of any stupefying or unwholesome substance, she is unable to understand the nature and consequences of that to which she gives consent;

(*vi*) with or without her consent, when she is under eighteen years of age; (*vii*) when she is unable to communicate consent.

Explanation 1.—For the purposes of this section, "vagina" shall also include *labia majora.*

Explanation 2.—Consent means an unequivocal voluntary agreement when the woman by words, gestures or any form of verbal or non-verbal communication, communicates willingness to participate in the specific sexual act:

Provided that a woman who does not physically resist to the act of penetration shall not by the reason only of that fact, be regarded as consenting to the sexual activity.

Exception 1.––A medical procedure or intervention shall not constitute rape.

Exception 2.––Sexual intercourse or sexual acts by a man with his own wife, the wife not being under eighteen years of age, is not rape.

64. (*1*) Whoever, except in the cases provided for in sub-section (*2*), commits rape,

shall be punished with rigorous imprisonment of either description for a term which shall not be less than ten years, but which may extend to imprisonment for life, and shall also be liable to fine.

(*2*) Whoever,—

(*a*) being a police officer, commits rape,—

Rape.

Punishment for rape.

(*i*) within the limits of the police station to which such police officer is appointed; or

(*ii*) in the premises of any station house; or

(*iii*) on a woman in such police officer's custody or in the custody of a police officer subordinate to such police officer; or (*b*) being a public servant, commits rape on a woman in such public servant's custody or in the custody of a public servant subordinate to such public servant; or

(*c*) being a member of the armed forces deployed in an area by the Central Government or a State Government commits rape in such area; or

(*d*) being on the management or on the staff of a jail, remand home or other place of custody established by or under any law for the time being in force or of a women's or children's institution, commits rape on any inmate of such jail, remand home, place or institution; or

(*e*) being on the management or on the staff of a hospital, commits rape on a woman in that hospital; or

(*f*) being a relative, guardian or teacher of, or a person in a position of trust or authority towards the woman, commits rape on such woman; or

(*g*) commits rape during communal or sectarian violence; or

(*h*) commits rape on a woman knowing her to be pregnant; or

(*i*) commits rape, on a woman incapable of giving consent; or

(*j*) being in a position of control or dominance over a woman, commits rape on such woman; or

(*k*) commits rape on a woman suffering from mental or physical disability; or (*l*) while committing rape causes grievous bodily harm or maims or disfigures or endangers the life of a woman; or

(*m*) commits rape repeatedly on the same woman,

shall be punished with rigorous imprisonment for a term which shall not be less than ten years, but which may extend to imprisonment for life, which shall mean imprisonment for the remainder of that person's natural life, and shall also be liable to fine.

Explanation.—For the purposes of this sub-section,—

(*a*) "armed forces" means the naval, army and air forces and includes any member of the Armed Forces constituted under any law for the time being in force, including the paramilitary forces and any auxiliary forces that are under the control of the Central Government or the State Government;

(*b*) "hospital" means the precincts of the hospital and includes the precincts of any institution for the reception and treatment of persons during convalescence or of persons requiring medical attention or rehabilitation;

(*c*) "police officer" shall have the same meaning as assigned to the expression

"police" under the Police Act, 1861;

(*d*) "women's or children's institution" means an institution, whether called an orphanage or a home for neglected women or children or a widow's home or an institution called by any other name, which is established and maintained for the reception and care of women or children.

5 of 1861.

65. (*1*) Whoever, commits rape on a woman under sixteen years of age shall be punished with rigorous imprisonment for a term which shall not be less than twenty years, but which may extend to imprisonment for life, which shall mean imprisonment for the remainder of that person's natural life, and shall also be liable to fine:

Provided that such fine shall be just and reasonable to meet the medical expenses and rehabilitation of the victim:

Provided further that any fine imposed under this sub-section shall be paid to the victim.

(*2*) Whoever, commits rape on a woman under twelve years of age shall be punished with rigorous imprisonment for a term which shall not be less than twenty years, but which may extend to imprisonment for life, which shall mean imprisonment for the remainder of that person's natural life, and with fine or with death:

Provided that such fine shall be just and reasonable to meet the medical expenses and rehabilitation of the victim:

Provided further that any fine imposed under this sub-section shall be paid to the victim.

66. Whoever, commits an offence punishable under sub-section (*1*) or sub-section (*2*) of section 64 and in the course of such commission inflicts an injury which causes the death of the woman or causes the woman to be in a persistent vegetative state, shall be punished with rigorous imprisonment for a term which shall not be less than twenty years, but which may extend to imprisonment for life, which shall mean imprisonment for the remainder of that person's natural life, or with death.

67. Whoever has sexual intercourse with his own wife, who is living separately, whether under a decree of separation or otherwise, without her consent, shall be punished with

imprisonment of either description for a term which shall not be less than two years but which may extend to seven years, and shall also be liable to fine.

Explanation.—In this section, "sexual intercourse" shall mean any of the acts mentioned in clauses (*a*) to (*d*) of section 63.

68. Whoever, being—

(*a*) in a position of authority or in a fiduciary relationship; or

(*b*) a public servant; or

(*c*) superintendent or manager of a jail, remand home or other place of custody established by or under any law for the time being in force, or a women's or children's institution; or

(*d*) on the management of a hospital or being on the staff of a hospital,

abuses such position or fiduciary relationship to induce or seduce any woman either in his custody or under his charge or present in the premises to have sexual intercourse with him, such sexual intercourse not amounting to the offence of rape, shall be punished with rigorous imprisonment of either description for a term which shall not be less than five years, but which may extend to ten years, and shall also be liable to fine.

Explanation 1.—In this section, "sexual intercourse" shall mean any of the acts mentioned in clauses (*a*) to (*d*) of section 63.

Explanation 2.—For the purposes of this section, *Explanation* 1 to section 63 shall also be applicable.

Explanation 3.—"Superintendent", in relation to a jail, remand home or other place of custody or a women's or children's institution, includes a person holding any other office in such jail, remand home, place or institution by virtue of which such person can exercise any authority or control over its inmates.

Punishment for rape in certain cases.

Punishment for causing death or resulting in persistent vegetative state of

victim. Sexual intercourse by husband upon his wife during

separation.

Sexual intercourse by a person in

authority.

Sexual

intercourse

by employing deceitful means, etc.

Gang rape.

Punishment for repeat offenders.

Disclosure of identity of victim of certain offences, etc.

Explanation 4.—The expressions "hospital" and "women's or children's institution" shall respectively have the same meanings as in clauses (*b*) and (*d*) of the *Explanation* to sub-section (*2*) of section 64.

69. Whoever, by deceitful means or by making promise to marry to a woman without any intention of fulfilling the same, has sexual intercourse with her, such sexual intercourse not amounting to the offence of rape, shall be punished with imprisonment of either description for a term which may extend to ten years and shall also be liable to fine.

Explanation.—"deceitful means" shall include inducement for, or false promise of employment or promotion, or marrying by suppressing identity.

70. (*1*) Where a woman is raped by one or more persons constituting a group or acting in furtherance of a common intention, each of those persons shall be deemed to have committed the offence of rape and shall be punished with rigorous imprisonment for a term which shall not be less than twenty years, but which may extend to imprisonment for life which shall mean imprisonment for the remainder of that person's natural life, and with fine:

Provided that such fine shall be just and reasonable to meet the medical expenses and rehabilitation of the victim:

Provided further that any fine imposed under this sub-section shall be paid to the victim.

(*2*) Where a woman under eighteen years of age is raped by one or more persons constituting a group or acting in furtherance of a common intention, each of those persons shall be deemed to have committed the offence of rape and shall be punished with imprisonment for life, which shall mean imprisonment for the remainder of that person's natural life, and with fine, or with death:

Provided that such fine shall be just and reasonable to meet the medical expenses and rehabilitation of the victim:

Provided further that any fine imposed under this sub-section shall be paid to the victim.

71. Whoever has been previously convicted of an offence punishable under section 64 or section 65 or section 66 or section 70 and is subsequently convicted of an offence punishable under any of the said sections shall be punished with imprisonment for life which shall mean imprisonment for the remainder of that person's natural life, or with death.

72. (*1*) Whoever prints or publishes the name or any matter which may make known the identity of any person against whom an offence under section 64 or section 65 or section 66 or section 67 or section 68 or section 69 or section 70 or section 71 is alleged or found to have been committed (hereafter in this section referred to as the victim) shall be punished with imprisonment of either description for a term which may extend to two years and shall also be liable to fine.

(*2*) Nothing in sub-section (*1*) extends to any printing or publication of the name or any matter which may make known the identity of the victim if such printing or publication is—

(*a*) by or under the order in writing of the officer-in-charge of the police station or the police officer making the investigation into such offence acting in good faith for the purposes of such investigation; or

(*b*) by, or with the authorisation in writing of, the victim; or

(*c*) where the victim is dead or a child or of unsound mind, by, or with the authorisation in writing of, the next of kin of the victim:

Provided that no such authorisation shall be given by the next of kin to anybody other than the chairman or the secretary, by whatever name called, of any recognised welfare institution or organisation.

Explanation.—For the purposes of this sub-section, "recognised welfare institution or organisation" means a social welfare institution or organisation recognised in this behalf by the Central Government or the State Government.

73. Whoever prints or publishes any matter in relation to any proceeding before a Court with respect to an offence referred to in section 72 without the previous permission of such Court shall be punished with imprisonment of either description for a term which may extend to two years and shall also be liable to fine.

Explanation.—The printing or publication of the judgment of any High Court or the Supreme Court does not amount to an offence within the meaning of this section.

Of criminal force and assault against woman

74. Whoever assaults or uses criminal force to any woman, intending to outrage or knowing it to be likely that he will thereby outrage her modesty, shall be punished with imprisonment of either description for a term which shall not be less than one year but which may extend to five years, and shall also be liable to fine.

75. (*1*) A man committing any of the following acts:—

(*i*) physical contact and advances involving unwelcome and explicit sexual overtures; or

(*ii*) a demand or request for sexual favours; or

(*iii*) showing pornography against the will of a woman; or

(*iv*) making sexually coloured remarks, shall be guilty of the offence of sexual harassment.

(*2*)Any man who commits the offence specified in clause (*i*) or clause (*ii*) or clause (*iii*) of sub-section (*1*) shall be punished with rigorous imprisonment for a term which may extend to three years, or with fine, or with both.

(*3*) Any man who commits the offence specified in clause (*iv*) of sub-section (*1*) shall be punished with imprisonment of either description for a term which may extend to one year, or with fine, or with both.

76. Whoever assaults or uses criminal force to any woman or abets such act with the intention of disrobing or compelling her to be naked, shall be punished with imprisonment of either description for a term which shall not be less than three years but which may extend to seven years, and shall also be liable to fine.

77. Whoever watches, or captures the image of a woman engaging in a private act in circumstances where she would usually have the expectation of not being observed either by the perpetrator or by any other person at the behest of the perpetrator or disseminates such image shall be punished on first conviction with imprisonment of either description for a term which shall not be less than one year, but which may extend to three years, and shall also be liable to fine, and be punished on a second or subsequent conviction, with imprisonment of either description for a term which shall not be less than three years, but which may extend to seven years, and shall also be liable to fine.

40 *Explanation* 1.—For the purposes of this section, "private act" includes an act of watching carried out in a place which, in the circumstances, would reasonably be expected to provide privacy and where the victim's genitals, posterior or breasts are exposed or covered only in underwear; or the victim is using a lavatory; or the victim is doing a sexual act that is not of a kind ordinarily done in public.

Printing or publishing any matter

relating to Court proceedings without

permission.

Assault or use of criminal

force to woman with intent to outrage her modesty.

Sexual

harassment.

Assault or use of criminal

force to woman with intent to disrobe.

Voyeurism.

Stalking.

Word, gesture or act intended to

insult modesty of a woman.

Dowry death.

Cohabitation caused by man deceitfully inducing

belief of lawful marriage.

Marrying again during lifetime of husband or wife.

Explanation 2.—Where the victim consents to the capture of the images or any act, but not to their dissemination to third persons and where such image or act is disseminated, such dissemination shall be considered an offence under this section.

78. (*1*) Any man who—

(*i*) follows a woman and contacts, or attempts to contact such woman to foster personal interaction repeatedly despite a clear indication of disinterest by such woman; or

(*ii*) monitors the use by a woman of the internet, e-mail or any other form of electronic communication,

commits the offence of stalking:

Provided that such conduct shall not amount to stalking if the man who pursued it proves that—

(*i*) it was pursued for the purpose of preventing or detecting crime and the man accused of stalking had been entrusted with the responsibility of prevention and detection of crime by the State; or

(*ii*) it was pursued under any law or to comply with any condition or requirement imposed by any person under any law; or

(*iii*) in the particular circumstances such conduct was reasonable and justified. (*2*) Whoever commits the offence of stalking shall be punished on first conviction with imprisonment of either description for a term which may extend to three years, and shall also

be liable to fine; and be punished on a second or subsequent conviction, with imprisonment of either description for a term which may extend to five years, and shall also be liable to fine.

79. Whoever, intending to insult the modesty of any woman, utters any words, makes any sound or gesture, or exhibits any object in any form, intending that such word or sound shall be heard, or that such gesture or object shall be seen, by such woman, or intrudes upon the privacy of such woman, shall be punished with simple imprisonment for a term which may extend to three years, and also with fine.

Of offences relating to marriage

80. (*1*) Where the death of a woman is caused by any burns or bodily injury or occurs otherwise than under normal circumstances within seven years of her marriage and it is shown that soon before her death she was subjected to cruelty or harassment by her husband or any relative of her husband for, or in connection with, any demand for dowry, such death shall be called "dowry death", and such husband or relative shall be deemed to have caused her death.

Explanation.—For the purposes of this sub-section, "dowry" shall have the same meaning as in section 2 of the Dowry Prohibition Act, 1961.

(*2*) Whoever commits dowry death shall be punished with imprisonment for a term which shall not be less than seven years but which may extend to imprisonment for life.

81. Every man who by deceit causes any woman who is not lawfully married to him to believe that she is lawfully married to him and to cohabit or have sexual intercourse with him in that belief, shall be punished with imprisonment of either description for a term which may extend to ten years, and shall also be liable to fine.

82. (*1*) Whoever, having a husband or wife living, marries in any case in which such marriage is void by reason of its taking place during the life of such husband or wife, shall be punished with imprisonment of either description for a term which may extend to seven years, and shall also be liable to fine.

Exception.—This sub-section does not extend to any person whose marriage with such husband or wife has been declared void by a Court of competent jurisdiction, nor to any person who contracts a marriage during the life of a former husband or wife, if such husband or wife, at the time of the subsequent marriage, shall have been continually absent

from such person for the space of seven years, and shall not have been heard of by such person as being alive within that time provided the person contracting such subsequent marriage shall, before such marriage takes place, inform the person with whom such marriage is contracted of the real state of facts so far as the same are within his or her knowledge.

5 (*2*) Whoever commits the offence under sub-section (*1*) having concealed from the person with whom the subsequent marriage is contracted, the fact of the former marriage, shall be punished with imprisonment of either description for a term which may extend to ten years, and shall also be liable to fine.

83. Whoever, dishonestly or with a fraudulent intention, goes through the ceremony of being married, knowing that he is not thereby lawfully married, shall be punished with imprisonment of either description for a term which may extend to seven years, and shall also be liable to fine.

84. Whoever takes or entices away any woman who is and whom he knows or has reason to believe to be the wife of any other man, with intent that she may have illicit intercourse with any person, or conceals or detains with that intent any such woman, shall be punished with imprisonment of either description for a term which may extend to two years, or with fine, or with both.

85. Whoever, being the husband or the relative of the husband of a woman, subjects such woman to cruelty shall be punished with imprisonment for a term which may extend to three years and shall also be liable to fine.

86. For the purposes of section 85, "cruelty" means—

(*a*) any wilful conduct which is of such a nature as is likely to drive the woman to commit suicide or to cause grave injury or danger to life, limb or health (whether mental or physical) of the woman; or

(*b*) harassment of the woman where such harassment is with a view to coercing her or any person related to her to meet any unlawful demand for any property or valuable security or is on account of failure by her or any person related to her to meet such demand.

87. Whoever kidnaps or abducts any woman with intent that she may be compelled, or knowing it to be likely that she will be compelled, to marry any person against her will, or in order that she may be forced or seduced to illicit intercourse, or knowing it to be likely that she will be forced or seduced to illicit intercourse, shall be punished with imprisonment of either description for a term which may extend to ten years, and shall also be liable to fine; and whoever, by means of criminal intimidation as defined in this Sanhita or of abuse of authority or any other method of compulsion, induces any woman to go from any place with intent that she may be, or knowing that it is likely that she will be, forced or seduced to illicit intercourse with another person shall also be punishable as aforesaid.

Of causing miscarriage, etc.

88. Whoever voluntarily causes a woman with child to miscarry, shall, if such miscarriage be not caused in good faith for the purpose of saving the life of the woman, be punished with imprisonment of either description for a term which may extend to three years, or with fine, or with both; and, if the woman be quick with child, shall be punished with imprisonment of either description for a term which may extend to seven years, and shall also be liable to fine.

Explanation.—A woman who causes herself to miscarry, is within the meaning of this section.

Marriage

ceremony fraudulently gone through without lawful marriage.

Enticing or taking away or detaining with criminal

intent a married woman.

Husband or relative of husband of a woman subjecting her to cruelty.

Cruelty defined.

Kidnapping, abducting or inducing

woman to compel her marriage, etc.

Causing miscarriage.

Causing miscarriage

89. Whoever commits the offence under section 88 without the consent of the woman, whether the woman is quick with child or not, shall be punished with imprisonment for life, or consent.

without woman's with imprisonment of either description for a term which may extend to ten years, and shall

Death caused by act done

with intent to cause miscarriage.

Act done with intent to prevent child being born alive or to cause to die after birth.

Causing death of quick unborn child by act

amounting to culpable

homicide.

Exposure and abandonment of child under twelve years of age, by

parent or person having care of it.

Concealment of birth by secret disposal of dead body.

Hiring, employing or engaging a child to

commit an offence.

Procuration of child.

Kidnapping or abducting child under ten years of age with

intent to steal

from its person.

also be liable to fine.

90. (*1*) Whoever, with intent to cause the miscarriage of a woman with child, does any act which causes the death of such woman, shall be punished with imprisonment of either description for a term which may extend to ten years, and shall also be liable to fine.

(*2*) Where the act referred to in sub-section (*1*) is done without the consent of the woman, shall be punishable either with imprisonment for life, or with the punishment specified

in said sub-section.

Explanation.—It is not essential to this offence that the offender should know that the act is likely to cause death.

91. Whoever before the birth of any child does any act with the intention of thereby preventing that child from being born alive or causing it to die after its birth, and does by

such act prevent that child from being born alive, or causes it to die after its birth, shall, if such act be not caused in good faith for the purpose of saving the life of the mother, be punished with imprisonment of either description for a term which may extend to ten years,

or with fine, or with both.

92. Whoever does any act under such circumstances, that if he thereby caused death

he would be guilty of culpable homicide, and does by such act cause the death of a quick unborn child, shall be punished with imprisonment of either description for a term which may extend to ten years, and shall also be liable to fine.

Illustration.

A, knowing that he is likely to cause the death of a pregnant woman, does an act which, if it caused the death of the woman, would amount to culpable homicide. The woman is injured, but does not die; but the death of an unborn quick child with which she is pregnant is thereby caused. A is guilty of the offence defined in this section.

Of offences against child

93. Whoever being the father or mother of a child under the age of twelve years, or having the care of such child, shall expose or leave such child in any place with the intention of wholly abandoning such child, shall be punished with imprisonment of either description for a term which may extend to seven years, or with fine, or with both.

Explanation.—This section is not intended to prevent the trial of the offender for murder or culpable homicide, as the case may be, if the child die in consequence of the exposure.

94. Whoever, by secretly burying or otherwise disposing of the dead body of a child whether such child die before or after or during its birth, intentionally conceals or endeavours to conceal the birth of such child, shall be punished with imprisonment of either description for a term which may extend to two years, or with fine, or with both.

95. Whoever hires, employs or engages any child to commit an offence shall be punished with imprisonment of either description which shall not be less than three years but which may extend to ten years, and with fine; and if the offence be committed shall also be punished with the punishment provided for that offence as if the offence has been committed by such person himself.

Explanation.—Hiring, employing, engaging or using a child for sexual exploitation or pornography is covered within the meaning of this section.

96. Whoever, by any means whatsoever, induces any child to go from any place or to do any act with intent that such child may be, or knowing that it is likely that such child will be, forced or seduced to illicit intercourse with another person shall be punishable with imprisonment which may extend to ten years, and shall also be liable to fine.

97. Whoever kidnaps or abducts any child under the age of ten years with the intention of taking dishonestly any movable property from the person of such child, shall be punished with imprisonment of either description for a term which may extend to seven years, and shall also be liable to fine.

98. Whoever sells, lets to hire, or otherwise disposes of any child with intent that such child shall at any age be employed or used for the purpose of prostitution or illicit intercourse with any person or for any unlawful and immoral purpose, or knowing it to be likely that such child will at any age be employed or used for any such purpose, shall be punished with imprisonment of either description for a term which may extend to ten years, and shall also be liable to fine.

Explanation 1.—When a female under the age of eighteen years is sold, let for hire, or otherwise disposed of to a prostitute or to any person who keeps or manages a brothel, the person so disposing of such female shall, until the contrary is proved, be presumed to have disposed of her with the intent that she shall be used for the purpose of prostitution.

Explanation 2.—For the purposes of this section "illicit intercourse" means sexual intercourse between persons not united by marriage or by any union or tie which, though not amounting to a marriage, is recognised by the personal law or custom of the community to which they belong or, where they belong to different communities, of both such communities, as constituting between them a *quasi*-marital relation.

99. Whoever buys, hires or otherwise obtains possession of any child with intent that such child shall at any age be employed or used for the purpose of prostitution or illicit intercourse with any person or for any unlawful and immoral purpose, or knowing it to be likely that such child will at any age be employed or used for any such purpose, shall be punished with imprisonment of either description for a term which shall not be less than seven years but which may extend to fourteen years, and shall also be liable to fine.

Explanation 1.—Any prostitute or any person keeping or managing a brothel, who buys, hires or otherwise obtains possession of a female under the age of eighteen years shall, until the contrary is proved, be presumed to have obtained possession of such female with the intent that she shall be used for the purpose of prostitution.

Explanation 2.—"Illicit intercourse" has the same meaning as in section 98.

Chapter Six

OF OFFENCES AFFECTING THE HUMAN BODY

Of offences affecting life

30 **100.** Whoever causes death by doing an act with the intention of causing death, or with the intention of causing such bodily injury as is likely to cause death, or with the knowledge that he is likely by such act to cause death, commits the offence of culpable homicide.

Selling child for purposes of

prostitution, etc.

Buying child

for purposes of prostitution,

etc.

Culpable

homicide.

Illustrations.

(*a*) Alays sticks and turf over a pit, with the intention of thereby causing death, or with the knowledge that death is likely to be thereby caused. Z, believing the ground to be firm, treads on it, falls in and is killed. A has committed the offence of culpable homicide.

(*b*) A knows Z to be behind a bush. B does not know it. A, intending to cause, or knowing it to be likely to cause Z's death, induces B to fire at the bush. B fires and kills Z.

Here B may be guilty of no offence; but A has committed the offence of culpable homicide.

(*c*) A, by shooting at a fowl with intent to kill and steal it, kills B, who is behind a bush; A not knowing that he was there. Here, although A was doing an unlawful act, he was not guilty of culpable homicide, as he did not intend to kill B, or to cause death by doing an act that he knew was likely to cause death.

Explanation 1.—A person who causes bodily injury to another who is labouring under a disorder, disease or bodily infirmity, and thereby accelerates the death of that other, shall be deemed to have caused his death.

Murder.

Explanation 2.—Where death is caused by bodily injury, the person who causes such bodily injury shall be deemed to have caused the death, although by resorting to proper remedies and skilful treatment the death might have been prevented.

Explanation 3.—The causing of the death of a child in the mother's womb is not homicide. But it may amount to culpable homicide to cause the death of a living child, if any part of that child has been brought forth, though the child may not have breathed or been completely born.

101. Except in the cases hereinafter excepted, culpable homicide is murder,--

(*a*) if the act by which the death is caused is done with the intention of causing death; or

(*b*) if the act by which the death is caused is done with the intention of causing such bodily injury as the offender knows to be likely to cause the death of the person to whom the harm is caused; or

(*c*) if the act by which the death is caused is done with the intention of causing bodily injury to any person and the bodily injury intended to be inflicted is sufficient in the ordinary course of nature to cause death; or

(*d*) if the person committing the act by which the death is caused, knows that it is so imminently dangerous that it must, in all probability, cause death, or such bodily injury as is likely to cause death, and commits such act without any excuse for incurring

the risk of causing death or such injury as aforesaid.

Illustrations.

(*a*) A shoots Z with the intention of killing him. Z dies in consequence. A commits murder.

(*b*) A, knowing that Z is labouring under such a disease that a blow is likely to cause his death, strikes him with the intention of causing bodily injury. Z dies in consequence of the blow. A is guilty of murder, although the blow might not have been sufficient in the ordinary course of nature to cause the death of a person in a sound state of health. But if A, not knowing that Z is labouring under any disease, gives him such a blow as would not in the ordinary course of nature kill a person in a sound state of health, here A, although he may intend to cause bodily injury, is not guilty of murder, if he did not intend to cause death, or such bodily injury as in the ordinary course of nature would cause death.

(*c*) A intentionally gives Z a sword-cut or club-wound sufficient to cause the death of a man in the ordinary course of nature. Z dies in consequence. Here A is guilty of murder, although he may not have intended to cause Z's death.

(*d*) A without any excuse fires a loaded cannon into a crowd of persons and kills one of them.A is guilty of murder, although he may not have had a premeditated design to kill any particular individual.

Exception 1.—Culpable homicide is not murder if the offender, whilst deprived of the power of self-control by grave and sudden provocation, causes the death of the person who gave the provocation or causes the death of any other person by mistake or accident:

Provided that the provocation is not,--

(*a*) sought or voluntarily provoked by the offender as an excuse for killing or doing harm to any person;

(*b*) given by anything done in obedience to the law, or by a public servant in the lawful exercise of the powers of such public servant;

(*c*) given by anything done in the lawful exercise of the right of private defence.

Explanation.—Whether the provocation was grave and sudden enough to prevent the offence from amounting to murder is a question of fact.

Illustrations.

(*a*) A, under the influence of passion excited by a provocation given by Z, intentionally kills Y, Z's child. This is murder, in as much as the provocation was not given by the child, and the death of the child was not caused by accident or misfortune in doing an act caused by the provocation.

(*b*) Y gives grave and sudden provocation to A. A, on this provocation, fires a pistol at Y, neither intending nor knowing himself to be likely to kill Z, who is near him, but out of sight. A kills Z. HereAhas not committed murder, but merely culpable homicide.

(*c*) A is lawfully arrested by Z, a bailiff. A is excited to sudden and violent passion by the arrest, and kills Z. This is murder, in as much as the provocation was given by a thing done by a public servant in the exercise of his powers.

(*d*) A appears as a witness before Z, a Magistrate. Z says that he does not believe a word of A's deposition, and that A has perjured himself. A is moved to sudden passion by these words, and kills Z. This is murder.

(*e*) A attempts to pull Z's nose. Z, in the exercise of the right of private defence, lays hold of A to prevent him from doing so. A is moved to sudden and violent passion in consequence, and kills Z. This is murder, in as much as the provocation was giving by a thing done in the exercise of the right of private defence.

(*f*) Z strikes B. B is by this provocation excited to violent rage. A, a bystander, intending to take advantage of B's rage, and to cause him to kill Z, puts a knife into B's hand for that purpose. B kills Z with the knife. Here B may have committed only culpable homicide, but A is guilty of murder.

Exception 2.—Culpable homicide is not murder if the offender in the exercise in good faith of the right of private defence of person or property, exceeds the power given to him by law and causes the death of the person against whom he is exercising such right of defence without premeditation, and without any intention of doing more harm than is necessary for the purpose of such defence.

Illustration.

Z attempts to horsewhip A, not in such a manner as to cause grievous hurt to A. A draws out a pistol. Z persists in the assault. A believing in good faith that he can by no other means prevent himself from being horsewhipped, shoots Z dead. A has not committed murder, but only culpable homicide.

Exception 3.—Culpable homicide is not murder if the offender, being a public servant or aiding a public servant acting for the advancement of public justice, exceeds the powers given to him by law, and causes death by doing an act which he, in good faith, believes to be lawful and necessary for the due discharge of his duty as such public servant and without ill-will towards the person whose death is caused.

Exception 4.—Culpable homicide is not murder if it is committed without premeditation in a sudden fight in the heat of passion upon a sudden quarrel and without the offender's having taken undue advantage or acted in a cruel or unusual manner.

Explanation.—It is immaterial in such cases which party offers the provocation or commits the first assault.

Exception 5.—Culpable homicide is not murder when the person whose death is caused, being above the age of eighteen years, suffers death or takes the risk of death with his own consent.

Illustration.

A, by instigation, voluntarily causes Z, a child to commit suicide. Here, on account of Z's youth, he was incapable of giving consent to his own death; A has therefore abetted murder.

Culpable homicide by causing death of person

other than person whose death was intended.

Punishment for murder.

Punishment for murder by life-convict.

Punishment for culpable

homicide not amounting to murder.

Causing death by negligence.

Abetment of suicide of child or person of unsound mind.

Abetment of suicide.

Attempt to murder.

102. If a person, by doing anything which he intends or knows to be likely to cause death, commits culpable homicide by causing the death of any person, whose death he neither intends nor knows himself to be likely to cause, the culpable homicide committed by the offender is of the description of which it would have been if he had caused the death of

the person whose death he intended or knew himself to be likely to cause. 5

102. If a person, by doing anything which he intends or knows to be likely to cause death, commits culpable homicide by causing the death of any person, whose death he neither intends nor knows himself to be likely to cause, the culpable homicide committed by the offender is of the description of which it would have been if he had caused the death of the person whose death he intended or knew himself to be likely to cause.

103. (*1*) Whoever commits murder shall be punished with death or imprisonment for life, and shall also be liable to fine.

(*2*) When a group of five or more persons acting in concert commits murder on the ground of race, caste or community, sex, place of birth, language, personal belief or any other similar ground each member of such group shall be punished with death or with imprisonment for life, and shall also be liable to fine.

104. Whoever, being under sentence of imprisonment for life, commits murder, shall be punished with death or with imprisonment for life, which shall mean the remainder of that person's natural life.

105. Whoever commits culpable homicide not amounting to murder, shall be punished with imprisonment for life, or imprisonment of either description for a term which shall not be less than five years but which may extend to ten years, and shall also be liable to fine, if the act by which the death is caused is done with the intention of causing death, or of causing such bodily injury as is likely to cause death; or with imprisonment of either description for a term which may extend to ten years and with fine, if the act is done with the knowledge that it is likely to cause death, but without any intention to cause death, or to cause such bodily injury as is likely to cause death.

106. (*1*) Whoever causes death of any person by doing any rash or negligent act not amounting to culpable homicide, shall be punished with imprisonment of either description for a term which may extend to five years, and shall also be liable to fine.

(*2*) Whoever causes death of any person by rash and negligent driving of vehicle not amounting to culpable homicide, and escapes without reporting it to a police officer or a Magistrate soon after the incident, shall be punished with imprisonment of either description of a term which may extend to ten years, and shall also be liable to fine.

107. If any child, any person of unsound mind, any delirious person or any person in a state of intoxication, commits suicide, whoever abets the commission of such suicide, shall be punished with death or imprisonment for life, or imprisonment for a term not exceeding ten years, and shall also be liable to fine.

108. If any person commits suicide, whoever abets the commission of such suicide, shall be punished with imprisonment of either description for a term which may extend to ten years, and shall also be liable to fine.

109. (*1*) Whoever does any act with such intention or knowledge, and under such circumstances that, if he by that act caused death, he would be guilty of murder, shall be punished with imprisonment of either description for a term which may extend to ten years, and shall also be liable to fine; and if hurt is caused to any person by such act, the offender shall be liable either to imprisonment for life, or to such punishment as is hereinbefore mentioned.

(*2*) When any person offending under sub-section (*1*) is under sentence of imprisonment for life, he may, if hurt is caused, be punished with death or with imprisonment for life, which shall mean the remainder of that person's natural life.

Illustrations.

(*a*) A shoots at Z with intention to kill him, under such circumstances that, if death ensued, A would be guilty of murder. A is liable to punishment under this section.

(*b*) A, with the intention of causing the death of a child of tender years, exposes it in a desert place. A has committed the offence defined by this section, though the death of the child does not ensue.

(*c*) A, intending to murder Z, buys a gun and loads it. A has not yet committed the offence. A fires the gun at Z. He has committed the offence defined in this section, and, if by such firing he wounds Z, he is liable to the punishment provided by the latter part of sub-section (*1*).

(*d*) A, intending to murder Z by poison, purchases poison and mixes the same with food which remains in A's keeping; A has not yet committed the offence defined in this section. A places the food on Z's table or delivers it to Z's servants to place it on Z's table. A has committed the offence defined in this section.

110. Whoever does any act with such intention or knowledge and under such circumstances that, if he by that act caused death, he would be guilty of culpable homicide not amounting to murder, shall be punished with imprisonment of either description for a term which may extend to three years, or with fine, or with both; and, if hurt is caused to any person by such act, shall be punished with imprisonment of either description for a term which may extend to seven years, or with fine, or with both.

Illustration.

A, on grave and sudden provocation, fires a pistol at Z, under such circumstances that if he thereby caused death, he would be guilty of culpable homicide not amounting to murder. A has committed the offence defined in this section.

111. (*1*) Any continuing unlawful activity including kidnapping, robbery, vehicle theft, extortion, land grabbing, contract killing, economic offence, cyber-crimes, trafficking of persons, drugs, weapons or illicit goods or services, human trafficking for prostitution or ransom, by any person or a group of persons acting in concert, singly or jointly, either as a member of an organised crime syndicate or on behalf of such syndicate, by use of violence, threat of violence, intimidation, coercion, or by any other unlawful means to obtain direct or indirect material benefit including a financial benefit, shall constitute organised crime.

Explanation.—For the purposes of this sub-section,––

(*i*) "organised crime syndicate" means a group of two or more persons who, acting either singly or jointly, as a syndicate or gang indulge in any continuing unlawful activity;

(*ii*) "continuing unlawful activity" means an activity prohibited by law which is

a cognizable offence punishable with imprisonment of three years or more, undertaken by any person, either singly or jointly, as a member of an organised crime syndicate or

Attempt to commit culpable

homicide.

Organised crime.

Petty organised crime.

on behalf of such syndicate in respect of which more than one charge-sheets have been filed before a competent Court within the preceding period of ten years and that Court has taken cognizance of such offence, and includes economic offence;

(*iii*) "economic offence" includes criminal breach of trust, forgery, counterfeiting of currency-notes, bank-notes and Government stamps, *hawala* transaction, mass-marketing fraud or running any scheme to defraud several persons or doing any act in any manner with a view to defraud any bank or financial institution or any other institution or organisation for obtaining monetary benefits in any form.

(*2*) Whoever commits organised crime shall,—

(*a*) if such offence has resulted in the death of any person, be punished with death or imprisonment for life, and shall also be liable to fine which shall not be less than ten lakh rupees;

(*b*) in any other case, be punished with imprisonment for a term which shall not be less than five years but which may extend to imprisonment for life, and shall also be liable to fine which shall not be less than five lakh rupees.

(*3*) Whoever abets, attempts, conspires or knowingly facilitates the commission of an organised crime, or otherwise engages in any act preparatory to an organised crime, shall be punished with imprisonment for a term which shall not be less than five years but which may extend to imprisonment for life, and shall also be liable to fine which shall not be less than five lakh rupees.

(*4*) Any person who is a member of an organised crime syndicate shall be punished with imprisonment for a term which shall not be less than five years but which may extend to imprisonment for life, and shall also be liable to fine which shall not be less than five lakh rupees.

(*5*) Whoever, intentionally, harbours or conceals any person who has committed the offence of an organised crime shall be punished with imprisonment for a term which shall not be less than three years but which may extend to imprisonment for life, and shall also be liable to fine which shall not be less than five lakh rupees:

Provided that this sub-section shall not apply to any case in which the harbour or concealment is by the spouse of the offender.

(*6*) Whoever possesses any property derived or obtained from the commission of an organised crime or proceeds of any organised crime or which has been acquired through the organised crime, shall be punishable with imprisonment for a term which shall not be less than three years but which may extend to imprisonment for life and shall also be liable to fine which shall not be less than two lakh rupees.

(*7*) If any person on behalf of a member of an organised crime syndicate is, or at any time has been in possession of movable or immovable property which he cannot satisfactorily account for, shall be punishable with imprisonment for a term which shall not be less than three years but which may extend to imprisonment for ten years and shall also be liable to fine which shall not be less than one lakh rupees.

112. (*1*) Whoever, being a member of a group or gang, either singly or jointly, commits any act of theft, snatching, cheating, unauthorised selling of tickets, unauthorised betting or gambling, selling of public examination question papers or any other similar criminal act, is said to commit petty organised crime.

Explanation.—For the purposes of this sub-section "theft" includes trick theft, theft from vehicle, dwelling house or business premises, cargo theft, pick pocketing, theft through card skimming, shoplifting and theft of Automated Teller Machine.

(*2*) Whoever commits any petty organised crime shall be punished with imprisonment for a term which shall not be less than one year but which may extend to seven years, and shall also be liable to fine.

37 **113.** (*1*) Whoever does any act with the intent to threaten or likely to threaten the unity, integrity, sovereignty, security, or economic security of India or with the intent to strike terror or likely to strike terror in the people or any section of the people in India or in any foreign country,––

(*a*) by using bombs, dynamite or other explosive substance or inflammable substance or firearms or other lethal weapons or poisonous or noxious gases or other chemicals or by any other substance (whether biological, radioactive, nuclear or otherwise) of a hazardous nature or by any other means of whatever nature to cause or likely to cause,—

(*i*) death of, or injury to, any person or persons; or

(*ii*) loss of, or damage to, or destruction of, property; or

(*iii*) disruption of any supplies or services essential to the life of the community in India or in any foreign country; or

(*iv*) damage to, the monetary stability of India by way of production or smuggling or circulation of counterfeit Indian paper currency, coin or of any other material; or

(*v*) damage or destruction of any property in India or in a foreign country used or intended to be used for the defence of India or in connection with any other purposes of the Government of India, any State Government or any of their agencies; or

(*b*) overawes by means of criminal force or the show of criminal force or attempts to do so or causes death of any public functionary or attempts to cause death of any public functionary; or

(*c*) detains, kidnaps or abducts any person and threatening to kill or injure such person or does any other act in order to compel the Government of India, any State Government or the Government of a foreign country or an international or inter-governmental organisation or any other person to do or abstain from doing any act,

commit a terrorist act.

Explanation.—For the purpose of this sub-section,—

(*a*) "public functionary" means the constitutional authorities or any other functionary notified in the Official Gazette by the Central Government as public functionary;

(*b*) "counterfeit Indian currency" means the counterfeit currency as may be declared after examination by an authorised or notified forensic authority that such currency imitates or compromises with the key security features of Indian currency. (*2*) Whoever commits a terrorist act shall,—

(*a*) if such offence has resulted in the death of any person, be punished with death or imprisonment for life, and shall also be liable to fine;

(*b*) in any other case, be punished with imprisonment for a term which shall not be less than five years but which may extend to imprisonment for life, and shall also be liable to fine.

(*3*) Whoever conspires or attempts to commit, or advocates, abets, advises or incites, directly or knowingly facilitates the commission of a terrorist act or any act preparatory to the commission of a terrorist act, shall be punished with imprisonment for a term which shall not be less than five years but which may extend to imprisonment for life, and shall also be liable to fine.

Terrorist act.

Hurt.

Voluntarily causing hurt.

Grievous hurt.

Voluntarily causing grievous hurt.

(*4*) Whoever organises or causes to be organised any camp or camps for imparting training in terrorist act, or recruits or causes to be recruited any person or persons for commission of a terrorist act, shall be punished with imprisonment for a term which shall not be less than five years but which may extend to imprisonment for life, and shall also be liable to fine.

(*5*) Any person who is a member of an organisation which is involved in terrorist act, shall be punished with imprisonment for a term which may extend to imprisonment for life, and shall also be liable to fine.

(*6*) Whoever voluntarily harbours or conceals, or attempts to harbour or conceal any person knowing that such person has committed a terrorist act shall be punished with imprisonment for a term which shall not be less than three years but which may extend to imprisonment for life, and shall also be liable to fine:

Provided that this sub-section shall not apply to any case in which the harbour or concealment is by the spouse of the offender.

(*7*) Whoever knowingly possesses any property derived or obtained from commission of any terrorist act or acquired through the commission of any terrorist act shall be punished with imprisonment for a term which may extend to imprisonment for life, and shall also be liable to fine.

Explanation.—For the removal of doubts, it is hereby declared that the officer not below the rank of Superintendent of Police shall decide whether to register the case under this section or under the Unlawful Activities (Prevention) Act, 1967.

Of hurt

114. Whoever causes bodily pain, disease or infirmity to any person is said to cause hurt.

115. (*1*) Whoever does any act with the intention of thereby causing hurt to any person, or with the knowledge that he is likely thereby to cause hurt to any person, and does thereby cause hurt to any person, is said "voluntarily to cause hurt".

(*2*)Whoever, except in the case provided for by sub-section (*1*) of section 122 voluntarily causes hurt, shall be punished with imprisonment of either description for a term which may extend to one year, or with fine which may extend to ten thousand rupees, or with both.

116. The following kinds of hurt only are designated as "grievous", namely:-– (*a*) Emasculation;

(*b*) Permanent privation of the sight of either eye; (*c*) Permanent privation of the hearing of either ear; (*d*) Privation of any member or joint;

(*e*) Destruction or permanent impairing of the powers of any member or joint; (*f*) Permanent disfiguration of the head or face;

(*g*) Fracture or dislocation of a bone or tooth;

(*h*) Any hurt which endangers life or which causes the sufferer to be during the space of fifteen days in severe bodily pain, or unable to follow his ordinary pursuits.

117. (*1*) Whoever voluntarily causes hurt, if the hurt which he intends to cause or knows himself to be likely to cause is grievous hurt, and if the hurt which he causes is grievous hurt, is said "voluntarily to cause grievous hurt".

Explanation.—A person is not said voluntarily to cause grievous hurt except when he both causes grievous hurt and intends or knows himself to be likely to cause grievous hurt. But he is said voluntarily to cause grievous hurt, if intending or knowing himself to be likely to cause grievous hurt of one kind, he actually causes grievous hurt of another kind.

Illustration.

A, intending of knowing himself to be likely permanently to disfigure Z's face, gives Z a blow which does not permanently disfigure Z's face, but which causes Z to suffer severe bodily pain for the space of fifteen days. A has voluntarily caused grievous hurt.

(*2*) Whoever, except in the case provided for by sub-section (*2*) of section 122, voluntarily causes grievous hurt, shall be punished with imprisonment of either description for a term which may extend to seven years, and shall also be liable to fine.

(*3*) Whoever commits an offence under sub-section (*1*) and in the course of such commission causes any hurt to a person which causes that person to be in permanent disability or in persistent vegetative state, shall be punished with rigorous imprisonment for a term which shall not be less than ten years but which may extend to imprisonment for life, which shall mean imprisonment for the remainder of that person's natural life.

(*4*) When a group of five or more persons acting in concert, causes grievous hurt to a person on the ground of his race, caste or community, sex, place of birth, language, personal belief or any other similar ground, each member of such group shall be guilty of the offence of causing grievous hurt, and shall be punished with imprisonment of either description for a term which may extend to seven years, and shall also be liable to fine.

118. (*1*) Whoever, except in the case provided for by sub-section (*1*) of section 122, voluntarily causes hurt by means of any instrument for shooting, stabbing or cutting, or any instrument which, used as a weapon of offence, is likely to cause death, or by means of fire or any heated substance, or by means of any poison or any corrosive substance, or by means of any explosive substance, or by means of any substance which it is deleterious to the human body to inhale, to swallow, or to receive into the blood, or by means of any animal, shall be punished with imprisonment of either description for a term which may extend to three years, or with fine which may extend to twenty thousand rupees, or with both.

(*2*) Whoever, except in the case provided for by sub-section (*2*) of section 122, voluntarily causes grievous hurt by any means referred to in sub–section (*1*), shall be punished with imprisonment for life, or with imprisonment of either description for a term which shall not be less than one year but which may extend to ten years, and shall also be liable to fine.

119. (*1*) Whoever voluntarily causes hurt for the purpose of extorting from the sufferer, or from any person interested in the sufferer, any property or valuable security, or of constraining the sufferer or any person interested in such sufferer to do anything which is illegal or which may facilitate the commission of an offence, shall be punished with imprisonment of either description for a term which may extend to ten years, and shall also be liable to fine.

(*2*) Whoever voluntarily causes grievous hurt for any purpose referred to in sub-section (*1*), shall be punished with imprisonment for life, or imprisonment of either description for a term which may extend to ten years, and shall also be liable to fine.

120. (*1*) Whoever voluntarily causes hurt for the purpose of extorting from the sufferer or from any person interested in the sufferer, any confession or any information which may lead to the detection of an offence or misconduct, or for the purpose of constraining the sufferer or any person interested in the sufferer to restore or to cause the restoration of any property or valuable security or to satisfy any claim or demand, or to give information which may lead to the restoration of any property or valuable security, shall be punished with imprisonment of either description for a term which may extend to seven years, and shall also be liable to fine.

Voluntarily causing hurt or grievous hurt by dangerous weapons or

means.

Voluntarily causing hurt or grievous hurt

to extort

property, or to constrain to an illegal act.

Voluntarily causing hurt or grievous hurt

to extort confession, or to compel

restoration of property.

Voluntarily causing hurt or grievous hurt

to deter public servant from his duty.

Voluntarily causing hurt or grievous hurt

on

provocation.

Causing hurt by means of poison, etc.,

with intent to commit an

offence.

Voluntarily causing grievous hurt by use of acid, etc.

Illustrations.

(*a*) A, a police-officer, tortures Z in order to induce Z to confess that he committed a crime. A is guilty of an offence under this section.

(*b*) A, a police-officer, tortures B to induce him to point out where certain stolen property is deposited. A is guilty of an offence under this section.

(*c*) A, a revenue officer, tortures Z in order to compel him to pay certain arrears of revenue due from Z. A is guilty of an offence under this section.

(*2*) Whoever voluntarily causes grievous hurt for any purpose referred to in sub-section (*1*), shall be punished with imprisonment of either description for a term which may extend to ten years, and shall also be liable to fine.

121. (*1*) Whoever voluntarily causes hurt to any person being a public servant in the discharge of his duty as such public servant, or with intent to prevent or deter that person or any other public servant from discharging his duty as such public servant or in consequence of anything done or attempted to be done by that person in the lawful discharge of his duty as such public servant, shall be punished with imprisonment of either description for a term which may extend to five years, or with fine, or with both.

(*2*) Whoever voluntarily causes grievous hurt to any person being a public servant in the discharge of his duty as such public servant, or with intent to prevent or deter that person or any other public servant from discharging his duty as such public servant or in consequence of anything done or attempted to be done by that person in the lawful discharge of his duty as such public servant, shall be punished with imprisonment of either description for a term which shall not be less than one year but which may extend to ten years, and shall also be liable to fine.

122. (*1*) Whoever voluntarily causes hurt on grave and sudden provocation, if he neither intends nor knows himself to be likely to cause hurt to any person other than the person who gave the provocation, shall be punished with imprisonment of either description for a term which may extend to one month, or with fine which may extend to five thousand rupees, or with both.

(*2*) Whoever voluntarily causes grievous hurt on grave and sudden provocation, if he neither intends nor knows himself to be likely to cause grievous hurt to any person other than the person who gave the provocation, shall be punished with imprisonment of either description for a term which may extend to five years, or with fine which may extend to ten thousand rupees, or with both.

Explanation.—This section is subject to the same proviso as *Exception* 1 of section 101.

123. Whoever administers to or causes to be taken by any person any poison or any stupefying, intoxicating or unwholesome drug, or other thing with intent to cause hurt to such person, or with intent to commit or to facilitate the commission of an offence or knowing it to be likely that he will thereby cause hurt, shall be punished with imprisonment of either

description for a term which may extend to ten years, and shall also be liable to fine.

124. (*1*) Whoever causes permanent or partial damage or deformity to, or burns or maims or disfigures or disables, any part or parts of the body of a person or causes grievous hurt by throwing acid on or by administering acid to that person, or by using any other means with the intention of causing or with the knowledge that he is likely to cause such

injury or hurt or causes a person to be in a permanent vegetative state shall be punished with

imprisonment of either description for a term which shall not be less than ten years but which may extend to imprisonment for life, and with fine:

Provided that such fine shall be just and reasonable to meet the medical expenses of the treatment of the victim:

victim.

Provided further that any fine imposed under this sub-section shall be paid to the

(*2*) Whoever throws or attempts to throw acid on any person or attempts to administer acid to any person, or attempts to use any other means, with the intention of causing permanent or partial damage or deformity or burns or maiming or disfigurement or disability or grievous hurt to that person, shall be punished with imprisonment of either description for a term which shall not be less than five years but which may extend to seven years, and shall also be liable to fine.

Explanation 1.—For the purposes of this section, "acid" includes any substance which has acidic or corrosive character or burning nature, that is capable of causing bodily injury leading to scars or disfigurement or temporary or permanent disability.

Explanation 2.—For the purposes of this section, permanent or partial damage or deformity or permanent vegetative state shall not be required to be irreversible.

125. Whoever does any act so rashly or negligently as to endanger human life or the personal safety of others, shall be punished with imprisonment of either description for a term which may extend to three months or with fine which may extend to two thousand five hundred rupees, or with both, but—

(*a*) where hurt is caused, shall be punished with imprisonment of either description for a term which may extend to six months, or with fine which may extend to five thousand rupees, or with both;

(*b*) where grievous hurt is caused, shall be punished with imprisonment of either description for a term which may extend to three years, or with fine which may extend to ten thousand rupees, or with both.

Of wrongful restraint and wrongful confinement

126. (*1*) Whoever voluntarily obstructs any person so as to prevent that person from proceeding in any direction in which that person has a right to proceed, is said wrongfully to restrain that person.

Exception.—The obstruction of a private way over land or water which a person in good faith believes himself to have a lawful right to obstruct, is not an offence within the meaning of this section.

Illustration.

A obstructs a path along which Z has a right to pass, A not believing in good faith that he has a right to stop the path. Z is thereby prevented from passing. A wrongfully restrains Z.

(*2*) Whoever wrongfully restrains any person shall be punished with simple imprisonment for a term which may extend to one month, or with fine which may extend to five thousand rupees, or with both.

127. (*1*) Whoever wrongfully restrains any person in such a manner as to prevent that person from proceedings beyond certain circumscribing limits, is said "wrongfully to confine" that person.

Act endangering

life or personal safety of

others.

Wrongful restraint.

Wrongful

confinement.

Illustrations.

(*a*) A causes Z to go within a walled space, and locks Z in. Z is thus prevented from proceeding in any direction beyond the circumscribing line of wall.A wrongfully confines Z.

(*b*) Aplaces men with firearms at the outlets of a building, and tells Z that they will fire

at Z if Z attempts to leave the building. A wrongfully confines Z.

(*2*) Whoever wrongfully confines any person shall be punished with imprisonment of either description for a term which may extend to one year, or with fine which may extend to five thousand rupees, or with both.

(*3*) Whoever wrongfully confines any person for three days, or more, shall be punished with imprisonment of either description for a term which may extend to three years, or with fine which may extend to ten thousand rupees, or with both.

(*4*) Whoever wrongfully confines any person for ten days or more, shall be punished with imprisonment of either description for a term which may extend to five years, and shall also be liable to fine which shall not be less than ten thousand rupees.

(*5*) Whoever keeps any person in wrongful confinement, knowing that a writ for the liberation of that person has been duly issued, shall be punished with imprisonment of either description for a term which may extend to two years in addition to any term of imprisonment to which he may be liable under any other section of this Chapter and shall also be liable to fine.

(*6*) Whoever wrongfully confines any person in such manner as to indicate an intention that the confinement of such person may not be known to any person interested in the person so confined, or to any public servant, or that the place of such confinement may not be known to or discovered by any such person or public servant as hereinbefore mentioned, shall be punished with imprisonment of either description for a term which may extend to three years in addition to any other punishment to which he may be liable for such wrongful confinement and shall also be liable to fine.

(*7*) Whoever wrongfully confines any person for the purpose of extorting from the person confined, or from any person interested in the person confined, any property or valuable security or of constraining the person confined or any person interested in such person to do anything illegal or to give any information which may facilitate the commission of an offence, shall be punished with imprisonment of either description for a term which may extend to three years, and shall also be liable to fine.

(*8*) Whoever wrongfully confines any person for the purpose of extorting from the person confined or any person interested in the person confined any confession or any information which may lead to the detection of an offence or misconduct, or for the purpose of constraining the person confined or any person interested in the person confined to restore or to cause the restoration of any property or valuable security or to satisfy any claim or demand, or to give information which may lead to the restoration of any property or valuable security, shall be punished with imprisonment of either description for a term which may extend to three years, and shall also be liable to fine.

Of criminal force and assault

Force.

128. A person is said to use force to another if he causes motion, change of motion, or cessation of motion to that other, or if he causes to any substance such motion, or change of motion, or cessation of motion as brings that substance into contact with any part of that other's body, or with anything which that other is wearing or carrying, or with anything so situated that such contact affects that other's sense of feeling:

Provided that the person causing the motion, or change of motion, or cessation of motion, causes that motion, change of motion, or cessation of motion in one of the following three ways, namely:––

(*a*) by his own bodily power;

(*b*) by disposing any substance in such a manner that the motion or change or cessation of motion takes place without any further act on his part, or on the part of any other person;

(*c*) by inducing any animal to move, to change its motion, or to cease to move.

129. Whoever intentionally uses force to any person, without that person's consent, in order to the committing of any offence, or intending by the use of such force to cause, or knowing it to be likely that by the use of such force he will cause injury, fear or annoyance to the person to whom the force is used, is said to use criminal force to that other.

Illustrations.

(*a*) Z is sitting in a moored boat on a river. A unfastens the moorings, and thus intentionally causes the boat to drift down the stream. Here A intentionally causes motion to Z, and he does this by disposing substances in such a manner that the motion is produced without any other action on any person's part. A has therefore intentionally used force to Z; and if he has done so without Z's consent, in order to the committing of any offence, or intending or knowing it to be likely that this use of force will cause injury, fear or annoyance to Z, A has used criminal force to Z.

(*b*) Z is riding in a chariot. A lashes Z's horses, and thereby causes them to quicken their pace. Here A has caused change of motion to Z by inducing the animals to change their motion. A has therefore used force to Z; and if Ahas done this without Z's consent, intending or knowing it to be likely that he may thereby injure, frighten or annoy Z, A has used criminal force to Z.

(*c*) Z is riding in a palanquin. A, intending to rob Z, seizes the pole and stops the palanquin. Here A has caused cessation of motion to Z, and he has done this by his own bodily power. A has therefore used force to Z; and as A has acted thus intentionally, without Z's consent, in order to the commission of an offence. A has used criminal force to Z.

(*d*) A intentionally pushes against Z in the street. Here A has by his own bodily power moved his own person so as to bring it into contact with Z. He has therefore intentionally used force to Z; and if he has done so without Z's consent, intending or knowing it to be likely that he may thereby injure, frighten or annoy Z, he has used criminal force to Z.

(*e*) A throws a stone, intending or knowing it to be likely that the stone will be thus brought into contact with Z, or with Z's clothes, or with something carried by Z, or that it will strike water and dash up the water against Z's clothes or something carried by Z. Here, if the throwing of the stone produce the effect of causing any substance to come into contact with Z, or Z's clothes, A has used force to Z, and if he did so without Z's consent, intending thereby to injure, frighten or annoy Z, he has used criminal force to Z.

(*f*)A intentionally pulls up a woman's veil. HereAintentionally uses force to her, and if he does so without her consent intending or knowing it to be likely that he may thereby injure, frighten or annoy her, he has used criminal force to her.

(*g*) Z is bathing. A pours into the bath water which he knows to be boiling. Here A intentionally by his own bodily power causes such motion in the boiling water as brings that water into contact with Z, or with other water so situated that such contact must affect Z's sense of feeling; A has therefore intentionally used force to Z; and if he has done this without Z's consent intending or knowing it to be likely that he may thereby cause injury, fear or annoyance to Z, A has used criminal force.

(*h*) A incites a dog to spring upon Z, without Z's consent. Here, if A intends to cause injury, fear or annoyance to Z, he uses criminal force to Z.

130. Whoever makes any gesture, or any preparation intending or knowing it to be likely that such gesture or preparation will cause any person present to apprehend that he who makes that gesture or preparation is about to use criminal force to that person, is said to commit an assault.

Criminal force.

Assault.

Punishment for assault or criminal force otherwise than on grave

provocation.

Assault or criminal force to deter public servant from discharge of

his duty.

Assault or criminal force with intent to dishonour

person, otherwise than on grave

provocation.

Assault or criminal force in attempt to commit theft of property carried by a

person.

Assault or criminal force in attempt to wrongfully confine a

person.

Explanation.—Mere words do not amount to an assault. But the words which a person uses may give to his gestures or preparation such a meaning as may make those gestures or preparations amount to an assault.

Illustrations.

(*a*) Ashakes his fist at Z, intending or knowing it to be likely that he may thereby cause 5

Z to believe that A is about to strike Z. A has committed an assault.

(*b*) A begins to unloose the muzzle of a ferocious dog, intending or knowing it to be likely that he may thereby cause Z to believe that he is about to cause the dog to attack Z. A has committed an assault upon Z.

(*c*) A takes up a stick, saying to Z, "I will give you a beating". Here, though the words used byA could in no case amount to an assault, and though the mere gesture, unaccompanied by any other circumstances, might not amount to an assault, the gesture explained by the words may amount to an assault.

131. Whoever assaults or uses criminal force to any person otherwise than on grave and sudden provocation given by that person, shall be punished with imprisonment of either description for a term which may extend to three months, or with fine which may extend to one thousand rupees, or with both.

Explanation 1.—Grave and sudden provocation will not mitigate the punishment for an offence under this section,

(*a*) if the provocation is sought or voluntarily provoked by the offender as an excuse for the offence; or (*b*) if the provocation is given by anything done in obedience to the law, or by a public servant, in the lawful exercise of the powers of such public servant; or

(*c*) if the provocation is given by anything done in the lawful exercise of the right of private defence.

Explanation 2.—Whether the provocation was grave and sudden enough to mitigate the offence, is a question of fact.

132. Whoever assaults or uses criminal force to any person being a public servant in the execution of his duty as such public servant, or with intent to prevent or deter that person from discharging his duty as such public servant, or in consequence of anything done or attempted to be done by such person in the lawful discharge of his duty as such public servant, shall be punished with imprisonment of either description for a term which may extend to two years, or with fine, or with both.

133. Whoever assaults or uses criminal force to any person, intending thereby to dishonour that person, otherwise than on grave and sudden provocation given by that person, shall be punished with imprisonment of either description for a term which may extend to two years, or with fine, or with both.

134. Whoever assaults or uses criminal force to any person, in attempting to commit theft on any property which that person is then wearing or carrying, shall be punished with imprisonment of either description for a term which may extend to two years, or with fine, or with both.

135. Whoever assaults or uses criminal force to any person, in attempting wrongfully to confine that person, shall be punished with imprisonment of either description for a term which may extend to one year, or with fine which may extend to five thousand rupees, or with both.

136. Whoever assaults or uses criminal force to any person on grave and sudden provocation given by that person, shall be punished with simple imprisonment for a term which may extend to one month, or with fine which may extend to one thousand rupees, or with both.

Explanation.—This section is subject to the same *Explanation* as section 131.

Of kidnapping, abduction, slavery and forced labour

137. (*1*) Kidnapping is of two kinds: kidnapping from India, and kidnapping from lawful guardianship––

(*a*) whoever conveys any person beyond the limits of India without the consent of that person, or of some person legally authorised to consent on behalf of that person, is said to kidnap that person from India;

(*b*) whoever takes or entices any child or any person of unsound mind, out of the keeping of the lawful guardian of such child or person of unsound mind, without the consent of such guardian, is said to kidnap such child or person from lawful guardianship.

Explanation.––The words "lawful guardian" in this clause include any person lawfully entrusted with the care or custody of such child or other person.

Exception.—This clause does not extend to the act of any person who in good faith believes himself to be the father of an illegitimate child, or who in good faith believes himself to be entitled to the lawful custody of such child, unless such act is committed for an immoral or unlawful purpose.

(*2*) Whoever kidnaps any person from India or from lawful guardianship shall be punished with imprisonment of either description for a term which may extend to seven years, and shall also be liable to fine.

138. Whoever by force compels, or by any deceitful means induces, any person to go from any place, is said to abduct that person.

139. (*1*) Whoever kidnaps any child or, not being the lawful guardian of such child, obtains the custody of the child, in order that such child may be employed or used for the purposes of begging shall be punishable with rigorous imprisonment for a term which shall not be less than ten years but which may extend to imprisonment for life, and shall also be liable to fine.

(*2*) Whoever maims any child in order that such child may be employed or used for the purposes of begging shall be punishable with imprisonment which shall not be less than twenty years, but which may extend to life which shall mean imprisonment for the remainder of that person's natural life, and with fine.

(*3*) Where any person, not being the lawful guardian of a child employs or uses such child for the purposes of begging, it shall be presumed, unless the contrary is proved, that he kidnapped or otherwise obtained the custody of such child in order that such child might be employed or used for the purposes of begging.

(*4*) In this section "begging" means—

(*i*) soliciting or receiving alms in a public place, whether under the pretence of singing, dancing, fortune telling, performing tricks or selling articles or otherwise;

(*ii*) entering on any private premises for the purpose of soliciting or receiving

Assault or criminal force on grave

provocation.

Kidnapping.

Abduction. Kidnapping or

maiming a child for purposes of begging.

alms;

Kidnapping or abducting in order to murder or for

ransom, etc.

Importation of girl or boy from foreign country.

Wrongfully concealing or keeping in confinement, kidnapped or abducted person.

Trafficking of person.

(*iii*) exposing or exhibiting, with the object of obtaining or extorting alms, any sore, wound, injury, deformity or disease, whether of himself or of any other person or of an animal;

(*iv*) using such child as an exhibit for the purpose of soliciting or receiving alms.

140. (*1*) Whoever kidnaps or abducts any person in order that such person may be murdered or may be so disposed of as to be put in danger of being murdered, shall be punished with imprisonment for life or rigorous imprisonment for a term which may extend to ten years, and shall also be liable to fine.

Illustrations.

(*a*)Akidnaps Z from India, intending or knowing it to be likely that Z may be sacrificed to an idol. A has committed the offence defined in this section.

(*b*)Aforcibly carries or entices B away from his home in order that B may be murdered. A has committed the offence defined in this section.

(*2*) Whoever kidnaps or abducts any person or keeps a person in detention after such kidnapping or abduction, and threatens to cause death or hurt to such person, or by his conduct gives rise to a reasonable apprehension that such person may be put to death or hurt, or causes hurt or death to such person in order to compel the Government or any foreign State or international inter-governmental organisation or any other person to do or abstain from doing any act or to pay a ransom, shall be punishable with death, or imprisonment for life, and shall also be liable to fine.

(*3*) Whoever kidnaps or abducts any person with intent to cause that person to be secretly and wrongfully confined, shall be punished with imprisonment of either description for a term which may extend to seven years, and shall also be liable to fine.

(*4*) Whoever kidnaps or abducts any person in order that such person may be subjected, or may be so disposed of as to be put in danger of being subjected to grievous hurt, or slavery, or to the unnatural lust of any person, or knowing it to be likely that such person will be so subjected or disposed of, shall be punished with imprisonment of either description for a term which may extend to ten years, and shall also be liable to fine.

141. Whoever imports into India from any country outside India any girl under the age of twenty-one years or any boy under the age of eighteen years with intent that girl or boy may be, or knowing it to be likely that girl or boy will be, forced or seduced to illicit intercourse with another person, shall be punishable with imprisonment which may extend to ten years and shall also be liable to fine.

142. Whoever, knowing that any person has been kidnapped or has been abducted, wrongfully conceals or confines such person, shall be punished in the same manner as if he had kidnapped or abducted such person with the same intention or knowledge, or for the same purpose as that with or for which he conceals or detains such person in confinement.

143. (*1*)Whoever, for the purpose of exploitation recruits, transports, harbours, transfers, or receives a person or persons, by—

(*a*) using threats; or

(*b*) using force, or any other form of coercion; or

(*c*) by abduction; or

(*d*) by practising fraud, or deception; or

(*e*) by abuse of power; or

(*f*) by inducement, including the giving or receiving of payments or benefits, in order to achieve the consent of any person having control over the person recruited, transported, harboured, transferred or received, commits the offence of trafficking.

Explanation 1.—The expression "exploitation" shall include any act of physical exploitation or any form of sexual exploitation, slavery or practices similar to slavery, servitude, beggary or forced removal of organs.

Explanation 2.—The consent of the victim is immaterial in determination of the offence of trafficking.

(*2*) Whoever commits the offence of trafficking shall be punished with rigorous imprisonment for a term which shall not be less than seven years, but which may extend to ten years, and shall also be liable to fine.

(*3*) Where the offence involves the trafficking of more than one person, it shall be punishable with rigorous imprisonment for a term which shall not be less than ten years but which may extend to imprisonment for life, and shall also be liable to fine.

(*4*) Where the offence involves the trafficking of a child, it shall be punishable with rigorous imprisonment for a term which shall not be less than ten years, but which may extend to imprisonment for life, and shall also be liable to fine.

(*5*) Where the offence involves the trafficking of more than one child, it shall be punishable with rigorous imprisonment for a term which shall not be less than fourteen years, but which may extend to imprisonment for life, and shall also be liable to fine.

(*6*) If a person is convicted of the offence of trafficking of a child on more than one occasion, then such person shall be punished with imprisonment for life, which shall mean imprisonment for the remainder of that person's natural life, and shall also be liable to fine.

(*7*) When a public servant or a police officer is involved in the trafficking of any person then, such public servant or police officer shall be punished with imprisonment for life, which shall mean imprisonment for the remainder of that person's natural life, and shall also be liable to fine.

144. (*1*) Whoever, knowingly or having reason to believe that a child has been trafficked, engages such child for sexual exploitation in any manner, shall be punished with rigorous imprisonment for a term which shall not be less than five years, but which may extend to ten years, and shall also be liable to fine.

(*2*) Whoever, knowingly or having reason to believe that a person has been trafficked, engages such person for sexual exploitation in any manner, shall be punished with rigorous imprisonment for a term which shall not be less than three years, but which may extend to seven years, and shall also be liable to fine.

145. Whoever habitually imports, exports, removes, buys, sells, traffics or deals in slaves, shall be punished with imprisonment for life, or with imprisonment of either description for a term not exceeding ten years, and shall also be liable to fine.

146. Whoever unlawfully compels any person to labour against the will of that person, shall be punished with imprisonment of either description for a term which may extend to one year, or with fine, or with both.

Exploitation of a trafficked person.

Habitual dealing in slaves.

Unlawful

compulsory labour.

Waging, or

attempting to wage war, or

abetting waging of war, against

Government of India.

Conspiracy to commit

offences punishable by section 147.

Collecting arms, etc.,

with intention of waging war against

Government of India.

Concealing

with intent to facilitate design to wage war.

Assaulting

President,

Governor, etc., with intent to

compel or restrain

exercise of any lawful power.

Act endangering sovereignty, unity and

integrity of

India.

Waging war against

Government

of any foreign

State at peace with

Government of India.

Chapter Seven

OF OFFENCES AGAINST THE STATE

147. Whoever wages war against the Government of India, or attempts to wage such war, or abets the waging of such war, shall be punished with death, or imprisonment for life

and shall also be liable to fine.

Illustration.

A joins an insurrection against the Government of India. A has committed the offence defined in this section.

148. Whoever within or without and beyond India conspires to commit any of the offences punishable by section 147, or conspires to overawe, by means of criminal force or the show of criminal force, the Central Government or any State Government, shall be punished

with imprisonment for life, or with imprisonment of either description which may extend to ten years, and shall also be liable to fine.

Explanation.—To constitute a conspiracy under this section, it is not necessary that any act or illegal omission shall take place in pursuance thereof.

149. Whoever collects men, arms or ammunition or otherwise prepares to wage war with the intention of either waging or being prepared to wage war against the Government of India, shall be punished with imprisonment for life or imprisonment of either description for a term not exceeding ten years, and shall also be liable to fine.

150. Whoever by any act, or by any illegal omission, conceals the existence of a design to wage war against the Government of India, intending by such concealment to facilitate, or knowing it to be likely that such concealment will facilitate, the waging of such war, shall be punished with imprisonment of either description for a term which may extend to ten years, and shall also be liable to fine.

151. Whoever, with the intention of inducing or compelling the President of India, or Governor of any State, to exercise or refrain from exercising in any manner any of the lawful powers of such President or Governor, assaults or wrongfully restrains, or attempts wrongfully to restrain, or overawes, by means of criminal force or the show of criminal force, or attempts so to overawe, such President or Governor, shall be punished with imprisonment of either description for a term which may extend to seven years, and shall also be liable to fine.

152. Whoever, purposely or knowingly, by words, either spoken or written, or by signs, or by visible representation, or by electronic communication or by use of financial mean, or otherwise, excites or attempts to excite, secession or armed rebellion or subversive activities, or encourages feelings of separatist activities or endangers sovereignty or unity and integrity of India; or indulges in or commits any such act shall be punished with imprisonment for life or with imprisonment which may extend to seven years, and shall also be liable to fine.

Explanation.--Comments expressing disapprobation of the measures, or administrative or other action of the Government with a view to obtain their alteration by lawful means without exciting or attempting to excite the activities referred to in this section do not constitute an offence under this section.

153. Whoever wages war against the Government of any foreign State at peace with the Government of India or attempts to wage such war, or abets the waging of such war, shall be punished with imprisonment for life, to which fine may be added, or with imprisonment of either description for a term which may extend to seven years, to which fine may be added, or with fine.

154. Whoever commits depredation, or makes preparations to commit depredation, on the territories of any foreign State at peace with the Government of India, shall be punished with imprisonment of either description for a term which may extend to seven years, and shall also be liable to fine and to forfeiture of any property used or intended to be used in committing such depredation, or acquired by such depredation.

155. Whoever receives any property knowing the same to have been taken in the commission of any of the offences mentioned in sections 153 and 154, shall be punished with imprisonment of either description for a term which may extend to seven years, and shall also be liable to fine and to forfeiture of the property so received.

156. Whoever, being a public servant and having the custody of any State prisoner or prisoner of war, voluntarily allows such prisoner to escape from any place in which such prisoner is confined, shall be punished with imprisonment for life, or imprisonment of either description for a term which may extend to ten years, and shall also be liable to fine.

157. Whoever, being a public servant and having the custody of any State prisoner or prisoner of war, negligently suffers such prisoner to escape from any place of confinement in which such prisoner is confined, shall be punished with simple imprisonment for a term which may extend to three years, and shall also be liable to fine.

158. Whoever knowingly aids or assists any State prisoner or prisoner of war in escaping from lawful custody, or rescues or attempts to rescue any such prisoner, or harbours or conceals any such prisoner who has escaped from lawful custody, or offers or attempts to offer any resistance to the recapture of such prisoner, shall be punished with imprisonment for life, or with imprisonment of either description for a term which may extend to ten years, and shall also be liable to fine.

Explanation.—A State prisoner or prisoner of war, who is permitted to be at large on his parole within certain limits in India, is said to escape from lawful custody if he goes beyond the limits within which he is allowed to be at large.

Chapter Eight

OF OFFENCES RELATING TO THE ARMY, NAVY AND AIR FORCE

159. Whoever abets the committing of mutiny by an officer, soldier, sailor or airman, in the Army, Navy or Air Force of the Government of India or attempts to seduce any such officer, soldier, sailor or airman from his allegiance or his duty, shall be punished with imprisonment for life, or with imprisonment of either description for a term which may extend to ten years, and shall also be liable to fine.

160. Whoever abets the committing of mutiny by an officer, soldier, sailor or airman, in the Army, Navy or Air Force of the Government of India, shall, if mutiny be committed in consequence of that abetment, be punished with death or with imprisonment for life, or imprisonment of either description for a term which may extend to ten years, and shall also be liable to fine.

161. Whoever abets an assault by an officer, soldier, sailor or airman, in the Army, Navy or Air Force of the Government of India, on any superior officer being in the execution of his office, shall be punished with imprisonment of either description for a term which may extend to three years, and shall also be liable to fine.

Receiving

property taken by war or

depredation

mentioned in sections 153 and 154.

Public servant voluntarily allowing prisoner of State or war to escape.

Public servant negligently suffering such prisoner to escape.

Aiding escape of, rescuing or harbouring such prisoner.

Abetting mutiny, or

attempting to seduce a soldier, sailor or airman from his duty.

Abetment of mutiny, if mutiny is

committed in consequence

there of.

Abetment of assault by soldier, sailor or airman on his superior officer, when

in execution of his office.

Abetment of such assault, if assault

committed.

162. Whoever abets an assault by an officer, soldier, sailor or airman, in the Army, Navy or Air Force of the Government of India, on any superior officer being in the execution of his office, shall, if such assault be committed in consequence of that abetment be punished with imprisonment of either description for a term which may extend to seven years, and shall

also be liable to fine. 5

Abetment of desertion of soldier, sailor or airman.

Harbouring deserter.

Deserter concealed on board

merchant vessel through negligence of master.

Abetment of act of insubordination by soldier,

sailor or

airman.

Persons subject to certain

Acts.

Wearing garb or carrying token used by soldier, sailor or airman.

Candidate, electoral right defined.

Bribery.

163. Whoever abets the desertion of any officer, soldier, sailor or airman, in the Army, Navy orAir Force of the Government of India, shall be punished with imprisonment of either description for a term which may extend to two years, or with fine, or with both.

164. Whoever, except as hereinafter excepted, knowing or having reason to believe that an officer, soldier, sailor or airman, in the Army, Navy or Air Force of the Government of India, has deserted, harbours such officer, soldier, sailor or airman, shall be punished with imprisonment of either description for a term which may extend to two years, or with fine or with both.

Exception.—This provision does not extend to the case in which the harbour is given by the spouse of the deserter.

165. The master or person in charge of a merchant vessel, on board of which any deserter from the Army, Navy or Air Force of the Government of India is concealed, shall, though ignorant of such concealment, be liable to a penalty not exceeding three thousand rupees, if he might have known of such concealment but for some neglect of his duty as such master or person in charge, or but for some want of discipline on board of the vessel.

166. Whoever abets what he knows to be an act of insubordination by an officer, soldier, sailor or airman, in the Army, Navy orAir Force, of the Government of India, shall, if such act of insubordination be committed in consequence of that abetment, be punished with imprisonment of either description for a term which may extend to two years, or with fine, or with both.

167. No person subject to the Air Force Act, 1950, the Army Act, 1950 and the Navy Act, 1957, or shall be subject to punishment under this Sanhita for any of the offences defined in this Chapter.

168. Whoever, not being a soldier, sailor or airman in theArmy, Naval orAir service of the Government of India, wears any garb or carries any token resembling any garb or token used by such a soldier, sailor or airman with the intention that it may be believed that he is such a soldier, sailor or airman, shall be punished with imprisonment of either description for a term which may extend to three months, or with fine which may extend to two thousand rupees, or with both.

Chapter Nine

OF OFFENCES RELATING TO ELECTIONS

169. For the purposes of this Chapter—

(*a*) "candidate" means a person who has been nominated as a candidate at any election;

(*b*) "electoral right" means the right of a person to stand, or not to stand as, or to withdraw from being, a candidate or to vote or refrain from voting at an election.

170. (*1*) Whoever—

(*i*) gives a gratification to any person with the object of inducing him or any other person to exercise any electoral right or of rewarding any person for having exercised any such right; or

(*ii*) accepts either for himself or for any other person any gratification as a reward for exercising any such right or for inducing or attempting to induce any other person to exercise any such right, commits the offence of bribery:

Provided that a declaration of public policy or a promise of public action shall not be an offence under this section.

(*2*)Aperson who offers, or agrees to give, or offers or attempts to procure, a gratification shall be deemed to give a gratification.

(*3*) A person who obtains or agrees to accept or attempts to obtain a gratification shall be deemed to accept a gratification, and a person who accepts a gratification as a motive for doing what he does not intend to do, or as a reward for doing what he has not done, shall be deemed to have accepted the gratification as a reward.

171. (*1*) Whoever voluntarily interferes or attempts to interfere with the free exercise of any electoral right commits the offence of undue influence at an election.

(*2*) Without prejudice to the generality of the provisions of sub-section (*1*), whoever— (*a*) threatens any candidate or voter, or any person in whom a candidate or voter is interested, with injury of any kind; or

(*b*) induces or attempts to induce a candidate or voter to believe that he or any person in whom he is interested will become or will be rendered an object of Divine displeasure or of spiritual censure,

shall be deemed to interfere with the free exercise of the electoral right of such candidate or voter, within the meaning of sub-section (*1*).

(*3*) A declaration of public policy or a promise of public action or the mere exercise or a legal right without intent to interfere with an electoral right, shall not be deemed to be interference within the meaning of this section.

172. Whoever at an election applies for a voting paper on votes in the name of any other person, whether living or dead, or in a fictitious name, or who having voted once at such election applies at the same election for a voting paper in his own name, and whoever abets, procures or attempts to procure the voting by any person in any such way, commits the offence of personation at an election:

Provided that nothing in this section shall apply to a person who has been authorised to vote as proxy for an elector under any law for the time being in force in so far as he votes as a proxy for such elector.

173. Whoever commits the offence of bribery shall be punished with imprisonment of either description for a term which may extend to one year, or with fine, or with both: Provided that bribery by treating shall be punished with fine only.

Explanation.—"Treating" means that form of bribery where the gratification consists in food, drink, entertainment, or provision.

174. Whoever commits the offence of undue influence or personation at an election shall be punished with imprisonment of either description for a term which may extend to one year or with fine, or with both.

175. Whoever with intent to affect the result of an election makes or publishes any statement purporting to be a statement of fact which is false and which he either knows or believes to be false or does not believe to be true, in relation to the personal character or conduct of any candidate shall be punished with fine.

Undue influence at elections.

Personation at elections.

Punishment for bribery.

Punishment for undue influence or

personation at

an election.

False

statement in connection with an

election.

Illegal

payments in connection with an

election.

Failure to keep election

accounts.

176. Whoever without the general or special authority in writing of a candidate incurs or authorises expenses on account of the holding of any public meeting, or upon any advertisement, circular or publication, or in any other way whatsoever for the purpose of promoting or procuring the election of such candidate, shall be punished with fine which may extend to ten thousand rupees:

Provided that if any person having incurred any such expenses not exceeding the amount of ten rupees without authority obtains within ten days from the date on which such expenses were incurred the approval in writing of the candidate, he shall be deemed to have incurred such expenses with the authority of the candidate.

177. Whoever being required by any law for the time being in force or any rule having the force of law to keep accounts of expenses incurred at or in connection with an election fails to keep such accounts shall be punished with fine which may extend to five thousand rupees.

Counterfeiting coin,

Government stamps,

currency-notes or bank-notes.

Using as genuine, forged or counterfeit

coin,

Government stamp,

currency-notes

or bank-notes.

Possession of forged or

counterfeit coin,

Government stamp,

currency-notes

or bank-notes.

Chapter Ten

OF OFFENCES RELATING TO COIN, CURRENCY-NOTES, BANK-NOTES, AND GOVERNMENT STAMPS

178. Whoever counterfeits, or knowingly performs any part of the process of counterfeiting, any coin, stamp issued by Government for the purpose of revenue, currency-note or bank-note, shall be punished with imprisonment for life, or with imprisonment of either description for a term which may extend to ten years, and shall also be liable to fine.

Explanation.—For the purposes of this Chapter,—

(*1*) the expression "bank-note" means a promissory note or engagement for the payment of money to bearer on demand issued by any person carrying on the business of banking in any part of the world, or issued by or under the authority of any State or Sovereign Power, and intended to be used as equivalent to, or as a substitute for money;

(*2*) "coin" shall have the same meaning as assigned to it in section 2 of the Coinage Act, 2011 and includes metal used for the time being as money and is stamped and issued by or under the authority of any State or Sovereign Power intended to be so used;

(*3*) a person commits the offence of "counterfeiting Government stamp" who counterfeits by causing a genuine stamp of one denomination to appear like a genuine stamp of a different denomination;

(*4*) a person commits the offence of counterfeiting coin who intending to practise deception, or knowing it to be likely that deception will thereby be practised, causes a genuine coin to appear like a different coin; and

(*5*) the offence of "counterfeiting coin" includes diminishing the weight or alteration of the composition, or alteration of the appearance of the coin.

179. Whoever imports or exports, or sells or delivers to, or buys or receives from, any other person, or otherwise traffics or uses as genuine, any forged or counterfeit coin, stamp, currency-note or bank-note, knowing or having reason to believe the same to be forged or counterfeit, shall be punished with imprisonment for life, or with imprisonment of either description for a term which may extend to ten years, and shall also be liable to fine.

180. Whoever has in his possession any forged or counterfeit coin, stamp, currency-note or bank-note, knowing or having reason to believe the same to be forged or counterfeit and intending to use the same as genuine or that it may be used as genuine, shall be punished with imprisonment of either description for a term which may extend to seven years, or with fine, or with both.

Explanation.—If a person establishes the possession of the forged or counterfeit coin, stamp, currency-note or bank-note to be from a lawful source, it shall not constitute an offence under this section.

181. Whoever makes or mends, or performs any part of the process of making or mending, or buys or sells or disposes of, or has in his possession, any machinery, die, or instrument or material for the purpose of being used, or knowing or having reason to believe that it is intended to be used, for forging or counterfeiting any coin, stamp issued by Government for the purpose of revenue, currency-note or bank-note, shall be punished with imprisonment for life, or with imprisonment of either description for a term which may extend to ten years, and shall also be liable to fine.

182. (*1*) Whoever makes, or causes to be made, or uses for any purpose whatsoever, or delivers to any person, any document purporting to be, or in any way resembling, or so nearly resembling as to be calculated to deceive, any currency-note or bank-note shall be punished with fine which may extend to three hundred rupees.

(*2*) If any person, whose name appears on a document the making of which is an offence under sub-section (*1*), refuses, without lawful excuse, to disclose to a police officer on being so required the name and address of the person by whom it was printed or otherwise made, he shall be punished with fine which may extend to six hundred rupees.

(*3*) Where the name of any person appears on any document in respect of which any person is charged with an offence under sub-section (*1*) or on any other document used or distributed in connection with that document it may, until the contrary is proved, be presumed that the person caused the document to be made.

183. Whoever, fraudulently or with intent to cause loss to the Government, removes or effaces from any substance, bearing any stamp issued by Government for the purpose of revenue, any writing or document for which such stamp has been used, or removes from any writing or document a stamp which has been used for such writing or document, in order that such stamp may be used for a different writing or document, shall be punished with imprisonment of either description for a term which may extend to three years, or with fine, or with both.

184. Whoever, fraudulently or with intent to cause loss to the Government, uses for any purpose a stamp issued by Government for the purpose of revenue, which he knows to have been before used, shall be punished with imprisonment of either description for a term which may extend to two years, or with fine, or with both.

185. Whoever, fraudulently or with intent to cause loss to Government, erases or removes from a stamp issued by Government for the purpose of revenue, any mark, put or impressed upon such stamp for the purpose of denoting that the same has been used, or knowingly has in his possession or sells or disposes of any such stamp from which such mark has been erased or removed, or sells or disposes of any such stamp which he knows to have been used, shall be punished with imprisonment of either description for a term which may extend to three years, or with fine, or with both.

186. (*1*) Whoever—

(*a*) makes, knowingly utters, deals in or sells any fictitious stamp, or knowingly uses for any postal purpose any fictitious stamp; or

(*b*) has in his possession, without lawful excuse, any fictitious stamp; or

(*c*) makes or, without lawful excuse, has in his possession any die, plate, instrument or materials for making any fictitious stamp,

Making or possessing instruments or materials for forging or counterfeiting coin, Government stamp, currency-notes or bank-notes.

Making or using

documents

resembling

currency-notes

or bank-notes.

Effacing writing from substance bearing

Government stamp, or

removing from document a stamp used for it, with intent to cause loss to Government.

Using

Government

stamp known to have been before used.

Erasure of mark denoting that stamp has been used.

Prohibition of fictitious

stamps.

shall be punished with fine which may extend to two hundred rupees.

(*2*) Any such stamp, die, plate, instrument or materials in the possession of any person for making any fictitious stamp may be seized and, if seized shall be forfeited.

(*3*) In this section "fictitious stamp" means any stamp falsely purporting to be issued

by Government for the purpose of denoting a rate of postage, or any facsimile or imitation or representation, whether on paper or otherwise, of any stamp issued by Government for that purpose.

Person employed in mint causing coin to be of different weight or

composition

from that fixed by law.

Unlawfully taking coining instrument

from mint.

Unlawful assembly.

(*4*) In this section and also in sections 178 to 181 (both inclusive), and sections 183 to

185 (both inclusive) the word "Government", when used in connection with, or in reference

to any stamp issued for the purpose of denoting a rate of postage, shall, notwithstanding

anything in clause (*12*) of section 2, be deemed to include the person or persons authorised by law to administer executive Government in any part of India or in any foreign country.

187. Whoever, being employed in any mint lawfully established in India, does any act, or omits what he is legally bound to do, with the intention of causing any coin issued from

that mint to be of a different weight or composition from the weight or composition fixed by 15

law, shall be punished with imprisonment of either description for a term which may extend to seven years, and shall also be liable to fine.

188. Whoever, without lawful authority, takes out of any mint, lawfully established in

India, any coining tool or instrument, shall be punished with imprisonment of either description

for a term which may extend to seven years, and shall also be liable to fine.

Chapter Eleven

OF OFFENCES AGAINST THE PUBLIC TRANQUILLITY

189. (*1*) An assembly of five or more persons is designated an "unlawful assembly", if the common object of the persons composing that assembly is—

(*a*) to overawe by criminal force, or show of criminal force, the Central Government or any State Government or Parliament or the Legislature of any State, or any public servant in the exercise of the lawful power of such public servant; or

(*b*) to resist the execution of any law, or of any legal process; or

(*c*) to commit any mischief or criminal trespass, or other offence; or

(*d*) by means of criminal force, or show of criminal force, to any person, to take or obtain possession of any property, or to deprive any person of the enjoyment of a right of way, or of the use of water or other incorporeal right of which he is in possession or enjoyment, or to enforce any right or supposed right; or

(*e*) by means of criminal force, or show of criminal force, to compel any person to

do what he is not legally bound to do, or to omit to do what he is legally entitled to do.

Explanation.—An assembly which was not unlawful when it assembled, may subsequently become an unlawful assembly.

(*2*) Whoever, being aware of facts which render any assembly an unlawful assembly, intentionally joins that assembly, or continues in it, is said to be a member of an unlawful assembly and such member shall be punished with imprisonment of either description for a term which may extend to six months, or with fine, or with both.

(*3*) Whoever joins or continues in an unlawful assembly, knowing that such unlawful assembly has been commanded in the manner prescribed by law to disperse, shall be punished with imprisonment of either description for a term which may extend to two years, or with

fine, or with both.

(*4*) Whoever, being armed with any deadly weapon, or with anything which, used as a weapon of offence, is likely to cause death, is a member of an unlawful assembly, shall be punished with imprisonment of either description for a term which may extend to two years, or with fine, or with both.

(*5*) Whoever knowingly joins or continues in any assembly of five or more persons likely to cause a disturbance of the public peace, after such assembly has been lawfully commanded to disperse, shall be punished with imprisonment of either description for a term which may extend to six months, or with fine, or with both.

Explanation.—If the assembly is an unlawful assembly within the meaning of sub-section (*1*), the offender shall be punishable under sub-section (*3*).

(*6*) Whoever hires or engages, or employs, or promotes, or connives at the hiring, engagement or employment of any person to join or become a member of any unlawful assembly, shall be punishable as a member of such unlawful assembly, and for any offence which may be committed by any such person as a member of such unlawful assembly in pursuance of such hiring, engagement or employment, in the same manner as if he had been a member of such unlawful assembly, or himself had committed such offence.

(*7*) Whoever harbours, receives or assembles, in any house or premises in his occupation or charge, or under his control any persons knowing that such persons have been hired, engaged or employed, or are about to be hired, engaged or employed, to join or become members of an unlawful assembly, shall be punished with imprisonment of either description for a term which may extend to six months, or with fine, or with both.

(*8*) Whoever is engaged, or hired, or offers or attempts to be hired or engaged, to do or assist in doing any of the acts specified in sub-section

(*1*), shall be punished with imprisonment of either description for a term which may extend to six months, or with fine, or with both.

(*9*) Whoever, being so engaged or hired as referred to in sub-section (*8*), goes armed, or engages or offers to go armed, with any deadly weapon or with anything which used as a weapon of offence is likely to cause death, shall be punished with imprisonment of either description for a term which may extend to two years, or with fine, or with both.

190. If an offence is committed by any member of an unlawful assembly in prosecution

of the common object of that assembly, or such as the members of that assembly knew to be likely to be committed in prosecution of that object, every person who, at the time of the committing of that offence, is a member of the same assembly, is guilty of that offence.

191. (*1*) Whenever force or violence is used by an unlawful assembly, or by any member thereof, in prosecution of the common object of such assembly, every member of

such assembly is guilty of the offence of rioting.

(*2*) Whoever is guilty of rioting, shall be punished with imprisonment of either description for a term which may extend to two years, or with fine, or with both.

(*3*) Whoever is guilty of rioting, being armed with a deadly weapon or with anything which, used as a weapon of offence, is likely to cause death, shall be punished with imprisonment of either description for a term which may extend to five years, or with fine, or with both.

192. Whoever malignantly, or wantonly by doing anything which is illegal, gives provocation to any person intending or knowing it to be likely that such provocation will cause the offence of rioting to be committed, shall, if the offence of rioting be committed in

consequence of such provocation, be punished with imprisonment of either description for a term which may extend to one year, or with fine, or with both; and if the offence of rioting be not committed, with imprisonment of either description for a term which may extend to six months, or with fine, or with both.

Every member of unlawful assembly guilty of offence

committed in prosecution of

common object.

Rioting.

Wantonly giving

provocation

with intent to

cause riot-if rioting be committed; if not

committed.

Liability of owner, occupier, etc., of land on which an unlawful assembly or riot takes

place.

Affray.

Assaulting or obstructing public servant when suppressing

riot, etc.

Chapter Twelve

OF OFFENCES BY OR RELATING TO PUBLIC SERVANTS

198. Whoever, being a public servant, knowingly disobeys any direction of the law as 45 to the way in which he is to conduct himself as such public servant, intending to cause, or knowing it to be likely that he will by such disobedience, cause injury to any person, shall be punished with simple imprisonment for a term which may extend to one year, or with fine, or with both.

Public servant disobeying law, with intent to cause injury to any person.

Public servant disobeying direction under law.

Punishment for non-

treatment of

victim.

Public servant framing an

incorrect

document with intent to cause injury.

Public servant unlawfully engaging in

trade.

Public servant unlawfully buying or bidding for

property.

Personating a public servant.

Wearing garb or carrying token used by public servant with fraudulent intent.

Illustration.

A, being an officer directed by law to take property in execution, in order to satisfy a decree pronounced in Z's favour by a Court, knowingly disobeys that direction of law, with the knowledge that he is likely thereby to cause injury to Z. A has committed the offence

defined in this section.

199. Whoever, being a public servant,—

(*a*) knowingly disobeys any direction of the law which prohibits him from requiring the attendance at any place of any person for the purpose of investigation into an offence or any other matter; or

(*b*) knowingly disobeys, to the prejudice of any person, any other direction of the law regulating the manner in which he shall conduct such investigation; or

(*c*) fails to record any information given to him under sub-section (*1*) of section 173 of the Bharatiya Nagarik Suraksha Sanhita, 2023 in relation to cognizable offence punishable under section 64, section 65, section 66, section 67, section 68, section 70, section 71, section 74, section 76, section 77, section 79, section 124, section 143 or section 144,

shall be punished with rigorous imprisonment for a term which shall not be less than six months but which may extend to two years, and shall also be liable to fine.

200. Whoever, being in charge of a hospital, public or private, whether run by the Central Government, the State Government, local bodies or any other person, contravenes the provisions of section 397 of the Bharatiya Nagarik Suraksha Sanhita, 2023, shall be punished with imprisonment for a term which may extend to one year, or with fine, or with both.

201. Whoever, being a public servant, and being, as such public servant, charged with

the preparation or translation of any document or electronic record, frames, prepares or translates that document or electronic record in a manner which he knows or believes to be incorrect, intending thereby to cause or knowing it to be likely that he may thereby cause injury to any person, shall be punished with imprisonment of either description for a term which may extend to three years, or with fine, or with both.

202. Whoever, being a public servant, and being legally bound as such public servant not to engage in trade, engages in trade, shall be punished with simple imprisonment for a term which may extend to one year, or with fine, or with both or with community service.

203. Whoever, being a public servant, and being legally bound as such public servant, not to purchase or bid for certain property, purchases or bids for that property, either in his own name or in the name of another, or jointly, or in shares with others, shall be punished with simple imprisonment for a term which may extend to two years, or with fine, or with both;

and the property, if purchased, shall be confiscated.

204. Whoever pretends to hold any particular office as a public servant, knowing that he does not hold such office or falsely personates any other person holding such office, and in such assumed character does or attempts to do any act under colour of such office, shall be punished with imprisonment of either description for a term which shall not be less than six months but which may extend to three years and with fine.

205. Whoever, not belonging to a certain class of public servants, wears any garb or carries any token resembling any garb or token used by that class of public servants, with the intention that it may be believed, or with the knowledge that it is likely to be believed, that he belongs to that class of public servants, shall be punished with imprisonment of either description for a term which may extend to three months, or with fine which may extend to five thousand rupees, or with both.

Chapter Thirteen

OF CONTEMPTS OF THE LAWFUL AUTHORITY OF PUBLIC SERVANTS

206. Whoever absconds in order to avoid being served with a summons, notice or order proceeding from any public servant legally competent, as such public servant, to issue such summons, notice or order,––

(*a*) shall be punished with simple imprisonment for a term which may extend to one month, or with fine which may extend to five thousand rupees, or with both;

(*b*) where such summons or notice or order is to attend in person or by agent, or to produce a document or an electronic record in a Court shall be punished with simple imprisonment for a term which may extend to six months, or with fine which may extend to ten thousand rupees, or with both.

207. Whoever in any manner intentionally prevents the serving on himself, or on any other person, of any summons, notice or order proceeding from any public servant legally competent, as such public servant, to issue such summons, notice or order, or intentionally prevents the lawful affixing to any place of any such summons, notice or order or intentionally removes any such summons, notice or order from any place to which it is lawfully affixed or intentionally prevents the lawful making of any proclamation, under the authority of any public servant legally competent, as such public servant, to direct such proclamation to be made,––

(*a*) shall be punished with simple imprisonment for a term which may extend to one month, or with fine which may extend to five thousand rupees, or with both;

(*b*) where the summons, notice, order or proclamation is to attend in person or by agent, or to produce a document or electronic record in a Court, with simple imprisonment for a term which may extend to six months, or with fine which may extend to ten thousand rupees, or with both.

208. Whoever, being legally bound to attend in person or by an agent at a certain place and time in obedience to a summons, notice, order, or proclamation proceeding from any public servant legally competent, as such public servant, to issue the same, intentionally omits to attend at that place or time or departs from the place where he is bound to attend before the time at which it is lawful for him to depart,––

(*a*) shall be punished with simple imprisonment for a term which may extend to one month, or with fine which may extend to five thousand rupees, or with both;

(*b*) where the summons, notice, order or proclamation is to attend in person or by agent in a Court with simple imprisonment for a term which may extend to six months, or with fine which may extend to ten thousand rupees, or with both.

Illustrations.

(*a*) A, being legally bound to appear before a High Court, in obedience to a subpoena issuing from that Court, intentionally omits to appear. A has committed the offence defined in this section.

(*b*) A, being legally bound to appear before a District Judge, as a witness, in obedience to a summons issued by that District Judge intentionally omits to appear. A has committed the offence defined in this section.

209. Whoever fails to appear at the specified place and the specified time as required by a proclamation published under sub-section (*1*) of section 84 of the Bharatiya Nagarik Suraksha Sanhita, 2023, shall be punished with imprisonment for a term which may extend to three years, or with fine, or with both, or with community service, and where a declaration has been made under sub-section (*4*) of that section pronouncing him as a proclaimed offender, he shall be punished with imprisonment for a term which may extend to seven years and shall also be liable to fine.

Absconding to avoid service

of summons or

other proceeding.

Preventing service of summons or other

proceeding, or preventing publication

there of.

Non-

attendance in obedience to an order from

public servant.

Non- appearance in response to a proclamation under

section 84 of Bharatiya Nagarik Suraksha Sanhita, 2023.

Omission to produce document or electronic record to

public servant by person legally bound to produce it.

Omission to give notice or

information to public servant by person legally bound

to give it.

Furnishing false

information.

210. Whoever, being legally bound to produce or deliver up any document or electronic record to any public servant, as such, intentionally omits so to produce or deliver up the same,––

(*a*) shall be punished with simple imprisonment for a term which may extend to one month, or with fine which may extend to five thousand rupees, or with both;

(*b*) and where the document or electronic record is to be produced or delivered up to a Court with simple imprisonment for a term which may extend to six months, or with fine which may extend to ten thousand rupees, or with both.

Illustration.

A, being legally bound to produce a document before a District Court, intentionally omits to produce the same. A has committed the offence defined in this section.

211. Whoever, being legally bound to give any notice or to furnish information on any subject to any public servant, as such, intentionally omits to give such notice or to furnish such information in the manner and at the time required by law,––

(*a*) shall be punished with simple imprisonment for a term which may extend to one month, or with fine which may extend to five thousand rupees, or with both;

(*b*) where the notice or information required to be given respects the commission of an offence, or is required for the purpose of preventing the commission of an offence, or in order to the apprehension of an offender, with simple imprisonment for a term which may extend to six months, or with fine which may extend to ten thousand rupees, or with both;

(*c*) where the notice or information required to be given is required by an order passed under section 394 of the Bharatiya Nagarik Suraksha Sanhita, 2023 with imprisonment of either description for a term which may extend to six months, or with fine which may extend to one thousand rupees, or with both.

212. Whoever, being legally bound to furnish information on any subject to any public servant, as such, furnishes, as true, information on the subject which he knows or has reason to believe to be false,––

(*a*) shall be punished with simple imprisonment for a term which may extend to six months, or with fine which may extend to five thousand rupees, or with both;

(*b*) where the information which he is legally bound to give respects the commission of an offence, or is required for the purpose of preventing the commission of an offence, or in order to the apprehension of an offender, with imprisonment of either description for a term which may extend to two years, or with fine, or with both.

Illustrations.

(*a*) A, a landholder, knowing of the commission of a murder within the limits of his estate, wilfully misinforms the Magistrate of the district that the death has occurred by accident in consequence of the bite of a snake. A is guilty of the offence defined in this section.

(*b*) A, a village watchman, knowing that a considerable body of strangers has passed through his village in order to commit a dacoity in the house of Z, a wealthy merchant residing in a neighbouring place, and being legally bound to give early and punctual information of the above fact to the officer of the nearest police station, wilfully misinforms the police officer that a body of suspicious characters passed through the village with a view to commit dacoity in a certain distant place in a different direction. Here A is guilty of the offence defined in this section.

Explanation.—In section 211 and in this section the word "offence" include any act committed at any place out of India, which, if committed in India, would be punishable under any of the following sections, namely, 103, 105, 307, sub-sections (*2*), (*3*) and (*4*) of section 309, sub-sections (*2*), (*3*), (*4*) and (*5*) of section 310, 311, 312, clauses (*f*) and (*g*) of section 326, sub-sections (*4*), (*6*), (*7*) and (*8*) of section 331, clauses (*a*) and (*b*) of section 332 and the word "offender" includes any person who is alleged to have been guilty of any such act.

213. Whoever refuses to bind himself by an oath or affirmation to state the truth, when required so to bind himself by a public servant legally competent to require that he shall so bind himself, shall be punished with simple imprisonment for a term which may extend to six months, or with fine which may extend to five thousand rupees, or with both.

214. Whoever, being legally bound to state the truth on any subject to any public servant, refuses to answer any question demanded of him touching that subject by such public servant in the exercise of the legal powers of such public servant, shall be punished with simple imprisonment for a term which may extend to six months, or with fine which may extend to five thousand rupees, or with both.

215. Whoever refuses to sign any statement made by him, when required to sign that statement by a public servant legally competent to require that he shall sign that statement, shall be punished with simple imprisonment for a term which may extend to three months, or with fine which may extend to three thousand rupees, or with both.

216. Whoever, being legally bound by an oath or affirmation to state the truth on any subject to any public servant or other person authorised by law to administer such oath or affirmation, makes, to such public servant or other person as aforesaid, touching that subject, any statement which is false, and which he either knows or believes to be false or does not believe to be true, shall be punished with imprisonment of either description for a term which may extend to three years, and shall also be liable to fine.

217. Whoever gives to any public servant any information which he knows or believes to be false, intending thereby to cause, or knowing it to be likely that he will thereby cause, such public servant—

(*a*) to do or omit anything which such public servant ought not to do or omit if the true state of facts respecting which such information is given were known by him; or

(*b*) to use the lawful power of such public servant to the injury or annoyance of any person,

shall be punished with imprisonment of either description for a term which may extend to one year, or with fine which may extend to ten thousand rupees, or with both.

Illustrations.

(*a*) A informs a Magistrate that Z, a police officer, subordinate to such Magistrate, has been guilty of neglect of duty or misconduct, knowing such information to be false,

and knowing it to be likely that the information will cause the Magistrate to dismiss Z. A

has committed the offence defined in this section.

(*b*) A falsely informs a public servant that Z has contraband salt in a secret place, knowing such information to be false, and knowing that it is likely that the consequence of the information will be a search of Z's premises, attended with annoyance to Z. A has committed the offence defined in this section.

Refusing oath or affirmation when duly required by public servant to make it.

Refusing to answer public servant authorised to question.

Refusing to

sign statement.

False

statement on oath or

affirmation to public sevant or person authorised to administer an

oath or

affirmation.

False

information, with intent to cause public servant to use his lawful power to injury of

another person.

Resistance to taking of

property by lawful authority of a

public servant.

Obstructing sale of

property offered for sale by authority of public servant.

Illegal purchase or bid for

property offered for sale by authority of public servant.

Obstructing public servant in discharge of public

functions.

Omission to assist public servant when bound by law to give assistance.

Disobedience to order duly promulgated by public

servant.

(*c*) A falsely informs a policeman that he has been assaulted and robbed in the neighbourhood of a particular village. He does not mention the name of any person as one of his assailants, but knows it to be likely that in consequence of this information the police will make enquiries and institute searches in the village to the annoyance of the

villagers or some of them. A has committed an offence under this section. 5

218. Whoever offers any resistance to the taking of any property by the lawful authority of any public servant, knowing or having reason to believe that he is such public servant, shall be punished with imprisonment of either description for a term which may extend to six months, or with fine which may extend to ten thousand rupees, or with both.

219. Whoever intentionally obstructs any sale of property offered for sale by the lawful authority of any public servant, as such, shall be punished with imprisonment of either description for a term which may extend to one month, or with fine which may extend to five thousand rupees, or with both.

220. Whoever, at any sale of property held by the lawful authority of a public servant, as such, purchases or bids for any property on account of any person, whether himself or any other, whom he knows to be under a legal incapacity to purchase that property at that sale, or bids for such property not intending to perform the obligations under which he lays himself by such bidding, shall be punished with imprisonment of either description for a term which may extend to one month, or with fine which may extend to two hundred rupees, or with both.

221. Whoever voluntarily obstructs any public servant in the discharge of his public functions, shall be punished with imprisonment of either description for a term which may extend to three months, or with fine which may extend to two thousand and

five hundred rupees, or with both.

222. Whoever, being bound by law to render or furnish assistance to any public servant in the execution of his public duty, intentionally omits to give such assistance,––

(*a*) shall be punished with simple imprisonment for a term which may extend to one month, or with fine which may extend to two thousand and five hundred rupees, or with both;

(*b*) and where such assistance be demanded of him by a public servant legally competent to make such demand for the purposes of executing any process lawfully issued by a Court or of preventing the commission of an offence, or suppressing a riot, or affray, or of apprehending a person charged with or guilty of an offence, or of having escaped from lawful custody, shall be punished with simple imprisonment for a term which may extend to six months, or with fine which may extend to five thousand rupees, or with both.

223. Whoever, knowing that, by an order promulgated by a public servant lawfully empowered to promulgate such order, he is directed to abstain from a certain act, or to take certain order with certain property in his possession or under his management, disobeys such direction,--

(*a*) shall, if such disobedience causes or tends to cause obstruction, annoyance or injury, or risk of obstruction, annoyance or injury, to any person lawfully employed, be punished with simple imprisonment for a term which may extend to six months, or with fine which may extend to two thousand and five hundred rupees, or with both;

(*b*) and where such disobedience causes or tends to cause danger to human life, health or safety, or causes or tends to cause a riot or affray, shall be punished with imprisonment of either description for a term which may extend to one year, or with fine which may extend to five thousand rupees, or with both.

Explanation.—It is not necessary that the offender should intend to produce harm, or contemplate his disobedience as likely to produce harm. It is sufficient that he knows of the order which he disobeys, and that his disobedience produces, or is likely to produce, harm.

Illustration.

An order is promulgated by a public servant lawfully empowered to promulgate such order, directing that a religious procession shall not pass down a certain street. A knowingly disobeys the order, and thereby causes danger of riot. A has committed the offence defined in this section.

224. Whoever holds out any threat of injury to any public servant, or to any person in whom he believes that public servant to be interested, for the purpose of inducing that public servant to do any act, or to forbear or delay to do any act, connected with the exercise of the public functions of such public servant, shall be punished with imprisonment of either description for a term which may extend to two years, or with fine, or with both.

225. Whoever holds out any threat of injury to any person for the purpose of inducing that person to refrain or desist from making a legal application for protection against any injury to any public servant legally empowered as such to give such protection, or to cause such protection to be given, shall be punished with imprisonment of either description for a term which may extend to one year, or with fine, or with both.

226. Whoever attempts to commit suicide with the intent to compel or restrain any public servant from discharging his official duty shall be punished with simple imprisonment for a term which may extend to one year, or with fine, or with both, or with community service.

Chapter Fourteen

OF FALSE EVIDENCE AND OFFENCES AGAINST PUBLIC JUSTICE

227. Whoever, being legally bound by an oath or by an express provision of law to state the truth, or being bound by law to make a declaration upon any subject, makes any statement which is false, and which he either knows or believes to be false or does not believe to be true, is said to give false evidence.

Explanation 1.—A statement is within the meaning of this section, whether it is made verbally or otherwise.

Explanation 2.—A false statement as to the belief of the person attesting is within the meaning of this section, and a person may be guilty of giving false evidence by stating that he believes a thing which he does not believe, as well as by stating that he knows a thing which he does not know.

Illustrations.

(*a*) A, in support of a just claim which B has against Z for one thousand rupees, falsely swears on a trial that he heard Z admit the justice of B's claim. A has given false evidence.

Threat of injury to

public servant.

Threat of injury to induce person to refrain

from applying for protection to public

servant.

Attempt to commit suicide to compel or

restrain exercise of lawful power.

Giving false evidence.

(*b*) A, being bound by an oath to state the truth, states that he believes a certain signature to be the handwriting of Z, when he does not believe it to be the handwriting of Z. Here A states that which he knows to be false, and therefore gives false evidence.

(*c*) A, knowing the general character of Z's handwriting, states that he believes a certain signature to be the handwriting of Z; A in good faith believing it to be so. Here A's 5 statement is merely as to his belief, and is true as to his belief, and therefore, although the signature may not be the handwriting of Z, A has not given false evidence.

(*d*) A, being bound by an oath to state the truth, states that he knows that Z was at a particular place on a particular day, not knowing anything upon the subject. A gives false evidence whether Z was at that place on the day named or not.

(*e*) A, an interpreter or translator, gives or certifies as a true interpretation or translation of a statement or document which he is bound by oath to interpret or translate truly, that which is not and which he does not believe to be a true interpretation or translation. A has given false evidence.

Fabricating false evidence.

Punishment for false evidence.

228. Whoever causes any circumstance to exist or makes any false entry in any book or record, or electronic record or makes any document or electronic record containing a false statement, intending that such circumstance, false entry or false statement may appear in evidence in a judicial proceeding, or in a proceeding taken by law before a public servant as such, or before an arbitrator, and that such circumstance, false entry or false statement, so appearing in evidence, may cause any person who in such proceeding is to form an opinion upon the evidence, to entertain an erroneous opinion touching any point material to the result of such proceeding is said "to fabricate false evidence".

Illustrations.

(*a*) A puts jewels into a box belonging to Z, with the intention that they may be found in that box, and that this circumstance may cause Z to be convicted of theft. A has fabricated false evidence.

(*b*) A makes a false entry in his shop-book for the purpose of using it as corroborative evidence in a Court. A has fabricated false evidence.

(*c*) A, with the intention of causing Z to be convicted of a criminal conspiracy, writes a letter in imitation of Z's handwriting, purporting to be addressed to an accomplice in such criminal conspiracy, and puts the letter in a place which he knows that the officers of the police are likely to search. A has fabricated false evidence.

229. (*1*) Whoever intentionally gives false evidence in any stage of a judicial proceeding, or fabricates false evidence for the purpose of being used in any stage of a judicial proceeding, shall be punished with imprisonment of either description for a term which may extend to seven years, and shall also be liable to fine which may extend to ten thousand rupees.

(*2*) Whoever intentionally gives or fabricates false evidence in any case other than that referred to in sub-section (*1*), shall be punished with imprisonment of either description for a term which may extend to three years, and shall also be liable to fine which may extend to five thousand rupees.

Explanation 1.—A trial before a Court-martial is a judicial proceeding.

Explanation 2.—An investigation directed by law preliminary to a proceeding before a Court, is a stage of a judicial proceeding, though that investigation may not take place before a Court.

Illustration.

A, in an enquiry before a Magistrate for the purpose of ascertaining whether Z ought to be committed for trial, makes on oath a statement which he knows to be false. As this enquiry is a stage of a judicial proceeding, A has given false evidence.

Explanation 3.—An investigation directed by a Court according to law, and conducted under the authority of a Court, is a stage of a judicial proceeding, though that investigation may not take place before a Court.

Illustration.

A, in an enquiry before an officer deputed by a Court to ascertain on the spot the boundaries of land, makes on oath a statement which he knows to be false. As this enquiry is a stage of a judicial proceeding, A has given false evidence.

230. (*1*) Whoever gives or fabricates false evidence, intending thereby to cause, or knowing it to be likely that he will thereby cause, any person to be convicted of an offence which is capital by the law for the time being in force in India shall be punished with imprisonment for life, or with rigorous imprisonment for a term which may extend to ten years, and shall also be liable to fine which may extend to fifty thousand rupees.

(*2*) If an innocent person be convicted and executed in consequence of false evidence referred to in sub-section (*1*), the person who gives such false evidence shall be punished either with death or the punishment specified in sub-section (*1*).

231. Whoever gives or fabricates false evidence intending thereby to cause, or knowing it to be likely that he will thereby cause, any person to be convicted of an offence which by the law for the time being in force in India is not capital, but punishable with imprisonment for life, or imprisonment for a term of seven years or upwards, shall be punished as a person convicted of that offence would be liable to be punished.

Illustration.

A gives false evidence before a Court, intending thereby to cause Z to be convicted of a dacoity. The punishment of dacoity is imprisonment for life, or rigorous imprisonment for a term which may extend to ten years, with or without fine. A, therefore, is liable to imprisonment for life or imprisonment, with or without fine.

232. (*1*) Whoever threatens another with any injury to his person, reputation or property or to the person or reputation of any one in whom that person is interested, with intent to cause that person to give false evidence shall be punished with imprisonment of either description for a term which may extend to seven years, or with fine, or with both.

(*2*) If innocent person is convicted and sentenced in consequence of false evidence referred to in sub-section (*1*), with death or imprisonment for more than seven years, the

person who threatens shall be punished with the same punishment and sentence in the

same manner and to the same extent such innocent person is punished and sentenced.

Giving or fabricating false evidence with intent to procure

conviction of capital

offence.

Giving or fabricating

false evidence with intent to

procure

conviction of offence punishable with imprisonment for life or

imprisonment.

Threatening any person to give false evidence.

Using evidence known to be false.

Issuing or signing false certificate.

Using as true a certificate known to be false.

False

statement made in

declaration which is by law receivable as evidence.

Using as true such

declaration knowing it to be false.

Causing disappearance of evidence of offence, or giving false

information to screen

offender.

Intentional omission to give

information of offence by person bound to inform.

233. Whoever corruptly uses or attempts to use as true or genuine evidence any evidence which he knows to be false or fabricated, shall be punished in the same manner as if he gave or fabricated false evidence.

234. Whoever issues or signs any certificate required by law to be given or signed,

or relating to any fact of which such certificate is by law admissible in evidence, knowing or believing that such certificate is false in any material point, shall be punished in the same manner as if he gave false evidence.

235. Whoever corruptly uses or attempts to use any such certificate as a true certificate, knowing the same to be false in any material point, shall be punished in the same manner as if he gave false evidence.

236. Whoever, in any declaration made or subscribed by him, which declaration any Court or any public servant or other person, is bound or authorised by law to receive as evidence of any fact, makes any statement which is false, and which he either knows or believes to be false or does not believe to be true, touching any point material to the object for which the declaration is made or used, shall be punished in the same manner as if he gave false evidence.

237. Whoever corruptly uses or attempts to use as true any such declaration, knowing the same to be false in any material point, shall be punished in the same manner as if he gave false evidence.

Explanation.—A declaration which is inadmissible merely upon the ground of some informality, is a declaration within the meaning of section 236 and this section.

238. Whoever, knowing or having reason to believe that an offence has been committed, causes any evidence of the commission of that offence to disappear, with the intention of screening the offender from legal punishment, or with that intention gives any information respecting the offence which he knows or believes to be false shall,—

(*a*) if the offence which he knows or believes to have been committed is punishable with death, be punished with imprisonment of either description for a term which may extend to seven years, and shall also be liable to fine;

(*b*) if the offence is punishable with imprisonment for life, or with imprisonment which may extend to ten years, be punished with imprisonment of either description for a term which may extend to three years, and shall also be liable to fine;

(*c*) if the offence is punishable with imprisonment for any term not extending to ten years, be punished with imprisonment of the description provided for the offence, for a term which may extend to one-fourth part of the longest term of the imprisonment provided for the offence, or with fine, or with both.

Illustration.

A, knowing that B has murdered Z, assists B to hide the body with the intention of screening B from punishment. A is liable to imprisonment of either description for seven years, and also to fine.

239. Whoever, knowing or having reason to believe that an offence has been committed, intentionally omits to give any information respecting that offence which he is legally bound to give, shall be punished with imprisonment of either description for a term which may extend to six months, or with fine which may extend to five thousand rupees, or with both.

240. Whoever, knowing or having reason to believe that an offence has been committed, gives any information respecting that offence which he knows or believes to be false, shall be punished with imprisonment of either description for a term which may extend to two years, or with fine, or with both.

Explanation.—In sections 238 and 239 and in this section the word "offence" includes any act committed at any place out of India, which, if committed in India, would be punishable under any of the following sections, namely, 103, 105, 307, sub-sections (*2*), (*3*) and (*4*) of section

309, sub-sections (*2*), (*3*), (*4*) and (*5*) of section 310, 311, 312, clauses (*f*) and (*g*) of section 326, sub-sections (*4*), (*6*), (*7*) and (*8*) of section 331, clauses (*a*) and (*b*) of section 332.

241. Whoever secretes or destroys any document or electronic record which he may be lawfully compelled to produce as evidence in a Court or in any proceeding lawfully held before a public servant, as such, or obliterates or renders illegible the whole or any part of such document or electronic record with the intention of preventing the same from being produced or used as evidence before such Court or public servant as aforesaid, or after he shall have been lawfully summoned or required to produce the same for that purpose, shall be punished with imprisonment of either description for a term which may extend to three years, or with fine which may extend to five thousand rupees, or with both.

242. Whoever falsely personates another, and in such assumed character makes any admission or statement, or confesses judgment, or causes any process to be issued or becomes bail or security, or does any other act in any suit or criminal prosecution, shall be punished with imprisonment of either description for a term which may extend to three years, or with fine, or with both.

243. Whoever fraudulently removes, conceals, transfers or delivers to any person any property or any interest therein, intending thereby to prevent that property or interest therein from being taken as a forfeiture or in satisfaction of a fine, under a sentence which has been pronounced, or which he knows to be likely to be pronounced, by a

Court or other competent authority, or from being taken in execution of a decree or order which has been made, or which he knows to be likely to be made by a Court in a civil suit, shall be punished with imprisonment of either description for a term which may extend to three years, or with fine which may extend to five thousand rupees, or with both.

244. Whoever fraudulently accepts, receives or claims any property or any interest therein, knowing that he has no right or rightful claim to such property or interest, or practises any deception touching any right to any property or any interest therein, intending thereby to prevent that property or interest therein from being taken as a forfeiture or in satisfaction of a fine, under a sentence which has been pronounced, or which he knows to be likely to be pronounced by a Court or other competent authority, or from being taken in execution of a decree or order which has been made, or which he knows to be likely to be made by a Court in a civil suit, shall be punished with imprisonment of either description for a term which may extend to two years, or with fine, or with both.

245. Whoever fraudulently causes or suffers a decree or order to be passed against him at the suit of any person for a sum not due or for a larger sum than is due to such person or for any property or interest in property to which such person is not entitled, or fraudulently causes or suffers a decree or order to be executed against him after it has been satisfied, or for anything in respect of which it has been satisfied, shall be punished with imprisonment of either description for a term which may extend to two years, or with fine, or with both.

Giving false

information respecting an offence

committed.

Destruction of document or

electronic record to

prevent its production as evidence.

False

personation for purpose of act or proceeding in suit or

prosecution.

Fraudulent

removal or

concealment

of property to prevent its seizure as forfeited or in execution.

Fraudulent claim to

property to prevent its seizure as forfeited or in execution.

Fraudulently suffering

decree for sum not due.

Dishonestly making false claim in

Court.

Fraudulently obtaining decree for sum not due.

False charge of offence made with

intent to injure.

Harbouring offender.

Illustration.

A institutes a suit against Z. Z, knowing that A is likely to obtain a decree against him, fraudulently suffers a judgment to pass against him for a larger amount at the suit of B, who has no just claim against him, in order that B, either on his own account or for the

benefit of Z, may share in the proceeds of any sale of Z's property which may be made

under A's decree. Z has committed an offence under this section.

246. Whoever fraudulently or dishonestly, or with intent to injure or annoy any person, makes in a Court any claim which he knows to be false, shall be punished with imprisonment of either description for a term which may extend to two years, and shall also be liable to fine.

247. Whoever fraudulently obtains a decree or order against any person for a sum not due, or for a larger sum than is due or for any property or interest in property to which he is not entitled, or fraudulently causes a decree or order to be executed against any person after it has been satisfied or for anything in respect of which it has been satisfied,

or fraudulently suffers or permits any such act to be done in his name, shall be punished with imprisonment of either description for a term which may extend to two years, or with fine, or with both.

248. Whoever, with intent to cause injury to any person, institutes or causes to be instituted any criminal proceeding against that person, or falsely charges any person with having committed an offence, knowing that there is no just or lawful ground for such proceeding or charge against that person,—

(*a*) shall be punished with imprisonment of either description for a term which may extend to five years, or with fine which may extend to two lakh rupees, or with both;

(*b*) if such criminal proceeding be instituted on a false charge of an offence punishable with death, imprisonment for life, or imprisonment for ten years or upwards, shall be punishable with imprisonment of either description for a term which may extend to ten years, and shall also be liable to fine.

249. Whenever an offence has been committed, whoever harbours or conceals a person whom he knows or has reason to believe to be the offender, with the intention of screening him from legal punishment shall,—

(*a*) if the offence is punishable with death, be punished with imprisonment of either description for a term which may extend to five years, and shall also be liable to fine;

(*b*) if the offence is punishable with imprisonment for life, or with imprisonment which may extend to ten years, be punished with imprisonment of either description for a term which may extend to three years, and shall also be liable to fine;

(*c*) if the offence is punishable with imprisonment which may extend to one year, and not to ten years, be punished with imprisonment of the description provided for the offence for a term which may extend to one-fourth part of the longest term of imprisonment provided for the offence, or with fine, or with both.

Explanation.––"Offence" in this section includes any act committed at any place out of India, which, if committed in India, would be punishable under any of the following sections, namely 103, 105, 307, sub-sections (*2*), (*3*) and (*4*) of section 309, sub-sections (*2*), (*3*), (*4*) and (*5*) of section 310, 311, 312, clauses (*f*) and (*g*) of section 326, sub-sections (*4*), (*6*), (*7*) and (*8*) of section 331, clauses (*a*) and (*b*) of section 332 and every such act shall, for the purposes of this section, be deemed to be punishable as if the accused person had been guilty of it in India.

Exception.—This section shall not extend to any case in which the harbour or concealment is by the spouse of the offender.

Illustration.

A, knowing that B has committed dacoity, knowingly conceals B in order to screen him from legal punishment. Here, as B is liable to imprisonment for life, A is liable to imprisonment of either description for a term not exceeding three years, and is also liable to fine.

250. Whoever accepts or attempts to obtain, or agrees to accept, any gratification for himself or any other person, or any restitution of property to himself or any other person, in consideration of his concealing an offence or of his screening any person from legal punishment for any offence, or of his not proceeding against any person for the purpose of bringing him to legal punishment shall,––

(*a*) if the offence is punishable with death, be punished with imprisonment of either description for a term which may extend to seven years, and shall also be liable to fine;

(*b*) if the offence is punishable with imprisonment for life, or with imprisonment which may extend to ten years, be punished with imprisonment of either description for a term which may extend to three years, and shall also be liable to fine;

(*c*) if the offence is punishable with imprisonment not extending to ten years,

be punished with imprisonment of the description provided for the offence for a term which may extend to one-fourth part of the longest term of imprisonment provided for the offence, or with fine, or with both.

251. Whoever gives or causes, or offers or agrees to give or cause, any gratification to any person, or restores or causes the restoration of any property to any person, in consideration of that person's concealing an offence, or of his screening any person from legal punishment for any offence, or of his not proceeding against any person for the purpose of bringing him to legal punishment shall,––

(*a*) if the offence is punishable with death, be punished with imprisonment of either description for a term which may extend to seven years, and shall also be liable to fine;

(*b*) if the offence is punishable with imprisonment for life or with imprisonment which may extend to ten years, be punished with imprisonment of either description for a term which may extend to three years, and shall also be liable to fine;

(*c*) if the offence is punishable with imprisonment not extending to ten years,

be punished with imprisonment of the description provided for the offence for a term which may extend to one-fourth part of the longest term of imprisonment provided for the offence, or with fine, or with both.

Exception.—The provisions of this section and section 250 do not extend to any case in which the offence may lawfully be compounded.

252. Whoever takes or agrees or consents to take any gratification under pretence or on account of helping any person to recover any movable property of which he shall have been deprived by any offence punishable under this Sanhita, shall, unless he uses all means in his power to cause the offender to be apprehended and convicted of the

Taking gift, etc., to screen an offender

from

punishment.

Offering gift

or restoration of property in consideration of screening

offender.

Taking gift to help to

recover stolen property, etc.

offence, be punished with imprisonment of either description for a term which may extend to two years, or with fine, or with both.

Harbouring offender who has escaped from custody or whose

apprehension has been ordered.

Penalty for harbouring robbers or dacoits.

Public servant disobeying direction of law with

intent to save person from

punishment or property from forfeiture.

253. Whenever any person convicted of or charged with an offence, being in lawful custody for that offence, escapes from such custody, or whenever a public servant, in the exercise of the lawful powers of such public servant, orders a certain person to be apprehended for an offence, whoever, knowing of such escape or order for apprehension, harbours or conceals that person with the intention of preventing him from being apprehended, shall be punished in the manner following, namely:––

(*a*) if the offence for which the person was in custody or is ordered to be apprehended is punishable with death, he shall be punished with imprisonment of either description for a term which may extend to seven years, and shall also be liable to fine;

(*b*) if the offence is punishable with imprisonment for life or imprisonment for ten years, he shall be punished with imprisonment of either description for a term which may extend to three years, with or without fine;

(*c*) if the offence is punishable with imprisonment which may extend to one year and not to ten years, he shall be punished with imprisonment of the description provided for the offence for a term which may extend to one-fourth part of the longest term of the imprisonment provided for such offence, or with fine, or with both.

Explanation.––"Offence" in this section includes also any act or omission of which a person is alleged to have been guilty out of India, which, if he had been guilty of it in India, would have been punishable as an offence, and for which he is, under any law relating to extradition, or otherwise, liable to be apprehended or detained in custody in India, and every such act or omission shall, for the purposes of this section, be deemed to be punishable as if the accused person had been guilty of it in India.

Exception.—The provisions of this section do not extend to the case in which the harbour or concealment is by the spouse of the person to be apprehended.

254. Whoever, knowing or having reason to believe that any persons are about to commit or have recently committed robbery or dacoity, harbours them or any of them, with the intention of facilitating the commission of such robbery or dacoity, or of screening

them or any of them from punishment, shall be punished with rigorous imprisonment for a

term which may extend to seven years, and shall also be liable to fine.

Explanation.—For the purposes of this section it is immaterial whether the robbery

or dacoity is intended to be committed, or has been committed, within or without India.

Exception.—The provisions of this section do not extend to the case in which the harbour is by the spouse of the offender.

255. Whoever, being a public servant, knowingly disobeys any direction of the law as to the way in which he is to conduct himself as such public servant, intending thereby

to save, or knowing it to be likely that he will thereby save, any person from legal punishment, or subject him to a less punishment than that to which he is liable, or with intent to save, or knowing that he is likely thereby to save, any property from forfeiture or

any charge to which it is liable by law, shall be punished with imprisonment of either description for a term which may extend to two years, or with fine, or with both.

256. Whoever, being a public servant, and being as such public servant, charged with the preparation of any record or other writing, frames that record or writing in a manner which he knows to be incorrect, with intent to cause, or knowing it to be likely that he will thereby cause, loss or injury to the public or to any person, or with intent thereby

to save, or knowing it to be likely that he will thereby save, any person from legal

punishment, or with intent to save, or knowing that he is likely thereby to save, any property from forfeiture or other charge to which it is liable by law, shall be punished with imprisonment of either description for a term which may extend to three years, or with fine, or with both.

257. Whoever, being a public servant, corruptly or maliciously makes or pronounces in any stage of a judicial proceeding, any report, order, verdict, or decision which he knows to be contrary to law, shall be punished with imprisonment of either description for a term which may extend to seven years, or with fine, or with both.

258. Whoever, being in any office which gives him legal authority to commit persons for trial or to confinement, or to keep persons in confinement, corruptly or maliciously commits any person for trial or to confinement, or keeps any person in confinement, in the exercise of that authority knowing that in so doing he is acting contrary to law, shall be punished with imprisonment of either description for a term which may extend to seven years, or with fine, or with both.

259. Whoever, being a public servant, legally bound as such public servant to apprehend or to keep in confinement any person charged with or liable to be apprehended for an offence, intentionally omits to apprehend such person, or intentionally suffers such person to escape, or intentionally aids such person in escaping or attempting to escape from such confinement, shall be punished,––

(*a*) with imprisonment of either description for a term which may extend to seven years, with or without fine, if the person in confinement, or who ought to have been apprehended, was charged with, or liable to be apprehended for, an offence punishable with death; or

(*b*) with imprisonment of either description for a term which may extend to three years, with or without fine, if the person in confinement, or who ought to have been apprehended, was charged with, or liable to be apprehended for, an offence punishable with imprisonment for life or imprisonment for a term which may extend to ten years; or

(*c*) with imprisonment of either description for a term which may extend to two

years, with or without fine, if the person in confinement, or who ought to have been apprehended, was charged with, or liable to be apprehended for, an offence punishable with imprisonment for a term less than ten years.

260. Whoever, being a public servant, legally bound as such public servant to apprehend or to keep in confinement any person under sentence of a Court for any

offence or lawfully committed to custody, intentionally omits to apprehend such person,

or intentionally suffers such person to escape or intentionally aids such person in escaping or attempting to escape from such confinement, shall be punished,—

(*a*) with imprisonment for life or with imprisonment of either description for a term which may extend to fourteen years, with or without fine, if the person in

confinement, or who ought to have been apprehended, is under sentence of death; or

Public servant framing

incorrect record or writing with

intent to save person from

punishment or property from forfeiture.

Public servant in judicial proceeding

corruptly making report, etc., contrary to law.

Commitment for trial or confinement by person having

authority who knows that he is acting contrary to law.

Intentional omission to

apprehend on part of public servant bound to apprehend.

Chapter Fifteen

OF OFFENCES AFFECTING THE PUBLIC HEALTH, SAFETY, CONVENIENCE, DECENCY AND MORALS

(*i*) any ancient monument within the meaning of the Ancient Monuments and Archaeological Sites and Remains Act, 1958; or

(*ii*) any temple, or on any car used for the conveyance of idols, or kept or used for any religious purpose.

295. Whoever sells, lets to hire, distributes, exhibits or circulates to any child any such obscene object as is referred to in section 294, or offers or attempts so to do, shall be punished on first conviction with imprisonment of either description for a term which may extend to three years, and with fine which may extend to two thousand rupees, and, in the event of a second or subsequent conviction, with imprisonment of either description for a term which may extend to seven years, and also with fine which may extend to five thousand rupees.

296. Whoever, to the annoyance of others,—

(*a*) does any obscene act in any public place; or

(*b*) sings, recites or utters any obscene song, ballad or words, in or near any public place,

shall be punished with imprisonment of either description for a term which may extend to three months, or with fine which may extend to one thousand rupees, or with both.

297. (*1*) Whoever keeps any office or place for the purpose of drawing any lottery not being a State lottery or a lottery authorised by the State Government, shall be punished with imprisonment of either description for a term which may extend to six months, or with fine, or with both.

(*2*) Whoever publishes any proposal to pay any sum, or to deliver any goods, or to do or forbear from doing anything for the benefit of any person, on any event or contingency relative or applicable to the drawing of any ticket, lot, number or figure in any such lottery, shall be punished with fine which may extend to five thousand rupees.

Chapter Sixteen

OF OFFENCES RELATING TO RELIGION

298. Whoever destroys, damages or defiles any place of worship, or any object held sacred by any class of persons with the intention of thereby insulting the religion of any class of persons or with the knowledge that any class of persons is likely to consider such destruction, damage or defilement as an insult to their religion, shall be punished with imprisonment of either description for a term which may extend to two years, or with fine, or with both.

299. Whoever, with deliberate and malicious intention of outraging the religious feelings of any class of citizens of India, by words, either spoken or written, or by signs or by visible representations or through electronic means or otherwise, insults or attempts to insult the religion or the religious beliefs of that class, shall be punished with imprisonment of either description for a term which may extend to three years, or with fine, or with both.

300. Whoever voluntarily causes disturbance to any assembly lawfully engaged in the performance of religious worship, or religious ceremonies, shall be punished with imprisonment of either description for a term which may extend to one year, or with fine, or with both.

Sale, etc., of obscene objects to child.

Obscene acts and songs.

Keeping

lottery office.

Injuring or defiling place of worship

with intent to insult religion of any class.

Deliberate and malicious acts, intended to outrage religious feelings of any class by insulting its religion or religious beliefs.

Disturbing religious assembly.

Trespassing on burial places, etc.

Uttering words, etc., with deliberate

intent to wound religious feelings of any person.

Theft.

301. Whoever, with the intention of wounding the feelings of any person, or of insulting the religion of any person, or with the knowledge that the feelings of any person are likely to be wounded, or that the religion of any person is likely to be insulted thereby, commits any trespass in any place of worship or on any place of sepulchre, or any place set apart for the performance of funeral rites or as a depository for the remains of the dead, or offers any indignity to any human corpse, or causes disturbance to any persons assembled for the performance of funeral ceremonies, shall be punished with imprisonment of either description

for a term which may extend to one year, or with fine, or with both.

302. Whoever, with the deliberate intention of wounding the religious feelings of any person, utters any word or makes any sound in the hearing of that person or makes any gesture in the sight of that person or places any object in the sight of that person, shall be punished with imprisonment of either description for a term which may extend to one year, or with fine, or with both.

Chapter Seventeen

OF OFFENCES AGAINST PROPERTY Of theft

303. (*1*) Whoever, intending to take dishonestly any movable property out of the possession of any person without that person's consent, moves that property in order to such taking, is said to commit theft.

Explanation 1.—A thing so long as it is attached to the earth, not being movable property, is not the subject of theft; but it becomes capable of being the subject of theft as soon as it is severed from the earth.

Explanation 2.—A moving effected by the same act which affects the severance may be a theft.

Explanation 3.—A person is said to cause a thing to move by removing an obstacle which prevented it from moving or by separating it from any other thing, as well as by actually moving it.

Explanation 4.—A person, who by any means causes an animal to move, is said to move that animal, and to move everything which, in consequence of the motion so caused, is moved by that animal.

Explanation 5.—The consent mentioned in this section may be express or implied, and may be given either by the person in possession, or by any person having for that purpose authority either express or implied.

Illustrations.

(*a*) A cuts down a tree on Z's ground, with the intention of dishonestly taking the tree out of Z's possession without Z's consent. Here, as soon as A has severed the tree in order to such taking, he has committed theft.

(*b*) A puts a bait for dogs in his pocket, and thus induces Z's dog to follow it. Here, if A's intention be dishonestly to take the dog out of Z's possession without Z's consent. A has committed theft as soon as Z's dog has begun to follow A.

(*c*) A meets a bullock carrying a box of treasure. He drives the bullock in a certain direction, in order that he may dishonestly take the treasure. As soon as the bullock begins to move, A has committed theft of the treasure.

(*d*) A being Z's servant, and entrusted by Z with the care of Z's plate, dishonestly runs away with the plate, without Z's consent. A has committed theft.

(*e*) Z, going on a journey, entrusts his plate to A, the keeper of a warehouse, till Z shall return. Acarries the plate to a goldsmith and sells it. Here the plate was not in Z's possession. It could not therefore be taken out of Z's possession, and A has not committed theft, though he may have committed criminal breach of trust.

(*f*) Afinds a ring belonging to Z on a table in the house which Z occupies. Here the ring is in Z's possession, and if A dishonestly removes it, A commits theft.

(*g*) A finds a ring lying on the highroad, not in the possession of any person. A, by taking it, commits no theft, though he may commit criminal misappropriation of property.

(*h*) A sees a ring belonging to Z lying on a table in Z's house. Not venturing to misappropriate the ring immediately for fear of search and detection, A hides the ring in a place where it is highly improbable that it will ever be found by Z, with the intention of taking the ring from the hiding place and selling it when the loss is forgotten. Here A, at the time of first moving the ring, commits theft.

(*i*) A delivers his watch to Z, a jeweler, to be regulated. Z carries it to his shop. A, not owing to the jeweler any debt for which the jeweler might lawfully detain the watch as a security, enters the shop openly, takes his watch by force out of Z's hand, and carries it away. Here A, though he may have committed criminal trespass and assault, has not committed theft, in as much as what he did was not done dishonestly.

(*j*) If A owes money to Z for repairing the watch, and if Z retains the watch lawfully as a security for the debt, and A takes the watch out of Z's possession, with the intention of depriving Z of the property as a security for his debt, he commits theft, in as much as he takes it dishonestly.

(*k*) Again, if A, having pawned his watch to Z, takes it out of Z's possession without Z's consent, not having paid what he borrowed on the watch, he commits theft, though the watch is his own property in as much as he takes it dishonestly.

(*l*) A takes an article belonging to Z out of Z's possession without Z's consent, with the intention of keeping it until he obtains money from Z as a reward for its restoration. Here A takes dishonestly; A has therefore committed theft.

(*m*) A, being on friendly terms with Z, goes into Z's library in Z's absence, and takes away a book without Z's express consent for the purpose merely of reading it, and with the intention of returning it. Here, it is probable that A may have conceived that he had Z's implied consent to use Z's book. If this was A's impression, A has not committed theft.

(*n*) A asks charity from Z's wife. She givesA money, food and clothes, whichA knows to belong to Z her husband. Here it is probable that Amay conceive that Z's wife is authorised to give away alms. If this was A's impression, A has not committed theft.

(*o*) A is the paramour of Z's wife. She gives a valuable property, which A knows to belong to her husband Z, and to be such property as she has no authority from Z to give. If A takes the property dishonestly, he commits theft.

(*p*) A, in good faith, believing property belonging to Z to be A's own property, takes that property out of Z's possession. Here, as A does not take dishonestly, he does not commit theft.

(*2*) Whoever commits theft shall be punished with imprisonment of either description for a term which may extend to three years, or with fine, or with both and in case of second or subsequent conviction of any person under this section, he shall be punished with rigorous imprisonment for a term which shall not be less than one year but which may extend to five years and with fine:

Provided that in cases of theft where the value of the stolen property is less than five thousand rupees, and a person is convicted for the first time, shall upon return of the value of property or restoration of the stolen property, shall be punished with community service.

Snatching.

Theft in a dwelling house, or means of transportation or place of worship, etc.

Theft by clerk or servant of property in possession of master.

Theft after preparation made for causing death, hurt or restraint in order to committing of theft.

Extortion.

304. (*1*) Theft is snatching if, in order to commit theft, the offender suddenly or quickly or forcibly seizes or secures or grabs or takes away from any person or from his possession any movable property.

(*2*) Whoever commits snatching, shall be punished with imprisonment of either description for a term which may extend to three years, and shall also be liable to fine.

305. Whoever commits theft—

(*a*) in any building, tent or vessel used as a human dwelling or used for the custody of property; or

(*b*) of any means of transport used for the transport of goods or passengers; or

(*c*) of any article or goods from any means of transport used for the transport of goods or passengers; or

(*d*) of idol or icon in any place of worship; or

(*e*) of any property of the Government or of a local authority,

shall be punished with imprisonment of either description for a term which may extend to seven years, and shall also be liable to fine.

306. Whoever, being a clerk or servant, or being employed in the capacity of a clerk or servant, commits theft in respect of any property in the possession of his master or employer, shall be punished with imprisonment of either description for a term which may extend to seven years, and shall also be liable to fine.

307. Whoever commits theft, having made preparation for causing death, or hurt, or restraint, or fear of death, or of hurt, or of restraint, to any person, in order to the committing of such theft, or in order to the effecting of his escape after the committing of such theft, or in order to the retaining of property taken by such theft, shall be punished with rigorous imprisonment for a term which may extend to ten years, and shall also be liable to fine.

Illustrations.

(*a*) A commits theft on property in Z's possession; and while committing this theft, he has a loaded pistol under his garment, having provided this pistol for the purpose of hurting Z in case Z should resist. A has committed the offence defined in this section.

(*b*) A picks Z's pocket, having posted several of his companions near him, in order that they may restrain Z, if Z should perceive what is passing and should resist, or should attempt to apprehend A. A has committed the offence defined in this section.

Of extortion

308. (*1*) Whoever intentionally puts any person in fear of any injury to that person, or to any other, and thereby dishonestly induces the person so put in fear to deliver to any person any property, or valuable security or anything signed or sealed which may be converted into a valuable security, commits extortion.

Illustrations.

(*a*) A threatens to publish a defamatory libel concerning Z unless Z gives him money. He thus induces Z to give him money. A has committed extortion.

(*b*)Athreatens Z that he will keep Z's child in wrongful confinement, unless Z will sign and deliver to Aa promissory note binding Z to pay certain monies to A. Z signs and delivers the note. A has committed extortion.

(*c*) A threatens to send club-men to plough up Z's field unless Z will sign and deliver to B a bond binding Z under a penalty to deliver certain produce to B, and thereby induces Z to sign and deliver the bond. A has committed extortion.

(*d*) A, by putting Z in fear of grievous hurt, dishonestly induces Z to sign or affix his seal to a blank paper and deliver it to A. Z signs and delivers the paper to A. Here, as the paper so signed may be converted into a valuable security. A has committed extortion.

(*e*) A threatens Z by sending a message through an electronic device that "Your child is in my possession, and will be put to death unless you send me one lakh rupees." A thus induces Z to give him money. A has committed extortion.

(*2*) Whoever commits extortion shall be punished with imprisonment of either description for a term which may extend to seven years, or with fine, or with both.

(*3*) Whoever, in order to the committing of extortion, puts any person in fear, or attempts to put any person in fear, of any injury, shall be punished with imprisonment of either description for a term which may extend to two years, or with fine, or with both.

(*4*) Whoever, in order to the committing of extortion, puts or attempts to put any person in fear of death or of grievous hurt to that person or to any other, shall be punished with imprisonment of either description for a term which may extend to seven years, and shall also be liable to fine.

(*5*) Whoever commits extortion by putting any person in fear of death or of grievous hurt to that person or to any other, shall be punished with imprisonment of either description for a term which may extend to ten years, and shall also be liable to fine.

(*6*) Whoever, in order to the committing of extortion, puts or attempts to put any person in fear of an accusation, against that person or any other, of having committed, or attempted to commit, an offence punishable with death or with imprisonment for life, or with imprisonment for a term which may extend to ten years, shall be punished with imprisonment of either description for a term which may extend to ten years, and shall also be liable to fine.

(*7*) Whoever commits extortion by putting any person in fear of an accusation against that person or any other, of having committed or attempted to commit any offence punishable with death, or with imprisonment for life, or with imprisonment for a term which may extend to ten years, or of having attempted to induce any other person to commit such offence, shall be punished with imprisonment of either description for a term which may extend to ten years, and shall also be liable to fine.

Of robbery and dacoity

309. (*1*) In all robbery there is either theft or extortion.

(*2*) Theft is robbery if, in order to the committing of the theft, or in committing the theft, or in carrying away or attempting to carry away property obtained by the theft, the offender, for that end voluntarily causes or attempts to cause to any person death or hurt or wrongful restraint, or fear of instant death or of instant hurt, or of instant wrongful restraint.

(*3*) Extortion is robbery if the offender, at the time of committing the extortion, is in the presence of the person put in fear, and commits the extortion by putting that person in fear of instant death, of instant hurt, or of instant wrongful restraint to that person or to some other person, and, by so putting in fear, induces the person so put in fear then and there to deliver up the thing extorted.

Explanation.—The offender is said to be present if he is sufficiently near to put the other person in fear of instant death, of instant hurt, or of instant wrongful restraint.

Illustrations.

(*a*) A holds Z down, and fraudulently takes Z's money and jewels from Z's clothes, without Z's consent. HereA has committed theft, and, in order to the committing of that theft, has voluntarily caused wrongful restraint to Z. A has therefore committed robbery.

Robbery.

Dacoity.

Robbery, or dacoity, with attempt to

cause death or grievous hurt.

Attempt to commit robbery or dacoity when armed with deadly weapon.

(*b*) A meets Z on the high road, shows a pistol, and demands Z's purse. Z, in consequence, surrenders his purse. Here A has extorted the purse from Z by putting him in fear of instant hurt, and being at the time of committing the extortion in his presence. A has therefore committed robbery.

(*c*) A meets Z and Z's child on the high road. A takes the child, and threatens to fling it

down a precipice, unless Z delivers his purse. Z, in consequence, delivers his purse. Here A has extorted the purse from Z, by causing Z to be in fear of instant hurt to the child who is there present. A has therefore committed robbery on Z.

(*d*) A obtains property from Z by saying—"Your child is in the hands of my gang, and

will be put to death unless you send us ten thousand rupees". This is extortion, and punishable as such; but it is not robbery, unless Z is put in fear of the instant death of his child.

(*4*) Whoever commits robbery shall be punished with rigorous imprisonment for a term which may extend to ten years, and shall also be liable to fine; and, if the robbery be committed on the highway between sunset and sunrise, the imprisonment may be extended to fourteen years.

(*5*) Whoever attempts to commit robbery shall be punished with rigorous imprisonment for a term which may extend to seven years, and shall also be liable to fine.

(*6*) If any person, in committing or in attempting to commit robbery, voluntarily causes hurt, such person, and any other person jointly concerned in committing or attempting to commit such robbery, shall be punished with imprisonment for life, or with rigorous imprisonment for a term which may extend to ten years, and shall also be liable to fine.

310. (*1*) When five or more persons conjointly commit or attempt to commit a robbery, or where the whole number of persons conjointly committing or attempting to commit a robbery, and persons present and aiding such commission or attempt, amount to five or more, every person so committing, attempting or aiding, is said to commit dacoity.

(*2*) Whoever commits dacoity shall be punished with imprisonment for life, or with rigorous imprisonment for a term which may extend to ten years, and shall also be liable to fine.

(*3*) If any one of five or more persons, who are conjointly committing dacoity, commits murder in so committing dacoity, every one of those persons shall be punished with death, or imprisonment for life, or rigorous imprisonment for a term which shall not be less than ten years, and shall also be liable to fine.

(*4*) Whoever makes any preparation for committing dacoity, shall be punished with rigorous imprisonment for a term which may extend to ten years, and shall also be liable to fine.

(*5*) Whoever is one of five or more persons assembled for the purpose of committing dacoity, shall be punished with rigorous imprisonment for a term which may extend to seven years, and shall also be liable to fine.

(*6*) Whoever belongs to a gang of persons associated for the purpose of habitually committing dacoity, shall be punished with imprisonment for life, or with rigorous imprisonment for a term which may extend to ten years, and shall also be liable to fine.

311. If, at the time of committing robbery or dacoity, the offender uses any deadly weapon, or causes grievous hurt to any person, or attempts to cause death or grievous hurt to any person, the imprisonment with which such offender shall be punished shall not be less than seven years.

312. If, at the time of attempting to commit robbery or dacoity, the offender is armed with any deadly weapon, the imprisonment with which such offender shall be punished shall not be less than seven years.

313. Whoever belongs to any gang of persons associated in habitually committing theft or robbery, and not being a gang of dacoits, shall be punished with rigorous imprisonment for a term which may extend to seven years, and shall also be liable to fine.

Of criminal misappropriation of property

314. Whoever dishonestly misappropriates or converts to his own use any movable property, shall be punished with imprisonment of either description for a term which shall not be less than six months but which may extend to two years and with fine.

Illustrations.

(*a*) A takes property belonging to Z out of Z's possession, in good faith believing at the time when he takes it, that the property belongs to himself. A is not guilty of theft; but if A, after discovering his mistake, dishonestly appropriates the property to his own use, he is guilty of an offence under this section.

(*b*) A, being on friendly terms with Z, goes into Z's library in Z's absence, and takes away a book without Z's express consent. Here, if A was under the impression that he had Z's implied consent to take the book for the purpose of reading it, Ahas not committed theft. But, ifA afterwards sells the book for his own benefit, he is guilty of an offence under this section.

(*c*) A and B, being, joint owners of a horse. A takes the horse out of B's possession, intending to use it. Here, as A has a right to use the horse, he does not dishonestly misappropriate it. But, if A sells the horse and appropriates the whole proceeds to his own use, he is guilty of an offence under this section.

Explanation 1.—A dishonest misappropriation for a time only is a misappropriation within the meaning of this section.

Punishment for belonging to gang of robbers, etc.

Dishonest misappropria- tion of property.

Illustration.

A finds a Government promissory note belonging to Z, bearing a blank endorsement. A, knowing that the note belongs to Z, pledges it with a banker as a security for a loan, intending at a future time to restore it to Z. A has committed an offence under this section.

Explanation 2.—A person who finds property not in the possession of any other person, and takes such property for the purpose of protecting it for, or of restoring it to, the owner, does not take or misappropriate it dishonestly, and is not guilty of an offence; but he is guilty of the offence above defined, if he appropriates it to his own use, when he knows or has the means of discovering the owner, or before he has used reasonable means to discover and give notice to the owner and has kept the property a reasonable time to enable the owner to claim it.

What are reasonable means or what is a reasonable time in such a case, is a question of fact.

It is not necessary that the finder should know who is the owner of the property, or that any particular person is the owner of it; it is sufficient if, at the time of appropriating it, he does not believe it to be his own property, or in good faith believe that the real owner cannot be found.

Illustrations.

(*a*) A finds a rupee on the high road, not knowing to whom the rupee belongs, A picks up the rupee. Here A has not committed the offence defined in this section.

(*b*) Afinds a letter on the road, containing a bank-note. From the direction and contents of the letter he learns to whom the note belongs. He appropriates the note. He is guilty of an offence under this section.

(*c*) Afinds a cheque payable to bearer. He can form no conjecture as to the person who has lost the cheque. But the name of the person, who has drawn the cheque, appears. A

Dishonest misappropria- tion of property possessed by deceased person at the time of his death.

Criminal breach of trust.

knows that this person can direct him to the person in whose favour the cheque was drawn. A appropriates the cheque without attempting to discover the owner. He is guilty of an offence under this section.

(*d*) A sees Z drop his purse with money in it. A picks up the purse with the intention of restoring it to Z, but afterwards appropriates it to his own use. A has committed an offence under this section.

(*e*) Afinds a purse with money, not knowing to whom it belongs; he afterwards discovers that it belongs to Z, and appropriates it to his own use. A is guilty of an offence under this section.

(*f*) A finds a valuable ring, not knowing to whom it belongs. A sells it immediately without attempting to discover the owner. A is guilty of an offence under this section.

315. Whoever dishonestly misappropriates or converts to his own use any property, knowing that such property was in the possession of a deceased person at the time of that person's decease, and has not since been in the possession of any person legally entitled to such possession, shall be punished with imprisonment of either description for a term which may extend to three years, and shall also be liable to fine, and if the offender at the time of such person's decease was employed by him as a clerk or servant, the imprisonment may extend to seven years.

Illustration.

Z dies in possession of furniture and money. His servant A, before the money comes into the possession of any person entitled to such possession, dishonestly misappropriates it. A has committed the offence defined in this section.

Of criminal breach of trust

316. (*1*) Whoever, being in any manner entrusted with property, or with any dominion over property, dishonestly misappropriates or converts to his own use that property, or dishonestly uses or disposes of that property in violation of any direction of law prescribing the mode in which such trust is to be discharged, or of any legal contract, express or implied, which he has made touching the discharge of such trust, or wilfully suffers any other person so to do, commits criminal breach of trust.

Explanation 1.—A person, being an employer of an establishment whether exempted under section 17 of the Employees' Provident Funds and Miscellaneous Provisions Act, 1952 or not who deducts the employee's contribution from the wages payable to the employee for credit to a Provident Fund or Family Pension Fund established by any law for the time being in force, shall be deemed to have been entrusted with the amount of the contribution so deducted by him and if he makes default in the payment of such contribution to the said Fund in violation of the said law, shall be deemed to have dishonestly used the amount of the said contribution in violation of a direction of law as aforesaid.

Explanation 2.—A person, being an employer, who deducts the employees' contribution from the wages payable to the employee for credit to the Employees' State Insurance Fund held and administered by the Employees' State Insurance Corporation established under the Employees' State Insurance Act, 1948 shall be deemed to have been entrusted with the amount of the contribution so deducted by him and if he makes default in the payment of such contribution to the said

Fund in violation of the said Act, shall be deemed to have dishonestly used the amount of the said contribution in violation of a direction of law as aforesaid.

Illustrations.

(*a*) A, being executor to the will of a deceased person, dishonestly disobeys the law which directs him to divide the effects according to the will, and appropriates them to his own use. A has committed criminal breach of trust.

(*b*) A is a warehouse-keeper Z going on a journey, entrusts his furniture to A, under a contract that it shall be returned on payment of a stipulated sum for warehouse room. A dishonestly sells the goods. A has committed criminal breach of trust.

(*c*) A, residing in Kolkata, is agent for Z, residing at Delhi. There is an express or implied contract between A and Z, that all sums remitted by Z to A shall be invested by A, according to Z's direction. Z remits one lakh of rupees to A, with directions to A to invest the same in Company's paper. A dishonestly disobeys the directions and employs the money in his own business. A has committed criminal breach of trust.

(*d*) But if A, in illustration (*c*), not dishonestly but in good faith, believing that it will be more for Z's advantage to hold shares in the Bank of Bengal, disobeys Z's directions, and buys shares in the Bank of Bengal, for Z, instead of buying Company's paper, here, though Z should suffer loss, and should be entitled to bring a civil action against A, on account of that loss, yet A, not having acted dishonestly, has not committed criminal breach of trust.

(*e*) A, a revenue-officer, is entrusted with public money and is either directed by law, or bound by a contract, express or implied, with the Government, to pay into a certain treasury all the public money which he holds. Adishonestly appropriates the money. Ahas committed criminal breach of trust.

(*f*) A, a carrier, is entrusted by Z with property to be carried by land or by water. A dishonestly misappropriates the property. A has committed criminal breach of trust.

(*2*) Whoever commits criminal breach of trust shall be punished with imprisonment of either description for a term which may extend to five years, or with fine, or with both.

(*3*) Whoever, being entrusted with property as a carrier, wharfinger or warehouse- keeper, commits criminal breach of trust in respect of such property, shall be punished with imprisonment of either description for a term which may extend to seven years, and shall also be liable to fine.

(*4*) Whoever, being a clerk or servant or employed as a clerk or servant, and being in any manner entrusted in such capacity with property, or with any dominion over property, commits criminal breach of trust in respect of that property, shall be punished with imprisonment of either description for a term which may extend to seven years, and shall also be liable to fine.

(*5*) Whoever, being in any manner entrusted with property, or with any dominion over property in his capacity of a public servant or in the way of his business as a banker, merchant, factor, broker, attorney or agent commits criminal breach of trust in respect of that property, shall be punished with imprisonment for life, or with imprisonment of either description for a term which may extend to ten years, and shall also be liable to fine.

Of receiving stolen property

317. (*1*) Property, the possession whereof has been transferred by theft or extortion or robbery or cheating, and property which has been criminally misappropriated or in respect of which criminal breach of trust has been committed, is designated as stolen property, whether the transfer has been made, or the misappropriation or breach of trust has been committed, within or without India, but, if such property subsequently comes into the possession of a person legally entitled to the possession thereof, it then ceases to be stolen property.

(*2*) Whoever dishonestly receives or retains any stolen property, knowing or having reason to believe the same to be stolen property, shall be punished with imprisonment of either description for a term which may extend to three years, or with fine, or with both.

(*3*) Whoever dishonestly receives or retains any stolen property, the possession whereof he knows or has reason to believe to have been transferred by the commission of

Stolen property.

dacoity, or dishonestly receives from a person, whom he knows or has reason to believe to belong or to have belonged to a gang of dacoits, property which he knows or has reason to believe to have been stolen, shall be punished with imprisonment for life, or with rigorous imprisonment for a term which may extend to ten years, and shall also be liable to fine.

(*4*) Whoever habitually receives or deals in property which he knows or has reason to believe to be stolen property, shall be punished with imprisonment for life, or with imprisonment of either description for a term which may extend to ten years, and shall also be liable to fine.

(*5*) Whoever voluntarily assists in concealing or disposing of or making away with property which he knows or has reason to believe to be stolen property, shall be punished with imprisonment of either description for a term which may extend to three years, or with fine, or with both.

Cheating.

Of cheating

318. (*1*) Whoever, by deceiving any person, fraudulently or dishonestly induces the person so deceived to deliver any property to any person, or to consent that any person shall retain any property, or intentionally induces the person so deceived to do or omit to do anything which he would not do or omit if he were not so deceived, and which act or omission causes or is likely to cause damage or harm to that person in body, mind, reputation or property, is said to cheat.

Explanation.—A dishonest concealment of facts is a deception within the meaning of this section.

Illustrations.

(*a*) A, by falsely pretending to be in the Civil Service, intentionally deceives Z, and thus dishonestly induces Z to let him have on credit goods for which he does not mean to pay. A cheats.

(*b*) A, by putting a counterfeit mark on an article, intentionally deceives Z into a belief that this article was made by a certain celebrated manufacturer, and thus dishonestly induces Z to buy and pay for the article. A cheats.

(*c*) A, by exhibiting to Z a false sample of an article intentionally deceives Z into believing that the article corresponds with the sample, and thereby dishonestly induces Z to buy and pay for the article. A cheats.

(*d*) A, by tendering in payment for an article a bill on a house with which A keeps no money, and by which A expects that the bill will be dishonoured, intentionally deceives Z, and thereby dishonestly induces Z to deliver the article, intending not to pay for it. A cheats.

(*e*)A, by pledging as diamonds articles which he knows are not diamonds, intentionally deceives Z, and thereby dishonestly induces Z to lend money. A cheats.

(*f*) A intentionally deceives Z into a belief that A means to repay any money that Z may lend to him and thereby dishonestly induces Z to lend him money, A not intending to repay it. A cheats.

(*g*) A intentionally deceives Z into a belief that A means to deliver to Z a certain quantity of indigo plant which he does not intend to deliver, and thereby dishonestly induces Z to advance money upon the faith of such delivery. A cheats; but if A, at the time of obtaining the money, intends to deliver the indigo plant, and afterwards breaks his contract and does not deliver it, he does not cheat, but is liable only to a civil action for breach of contract.

(*h*) Aintentionally deceives Z into a belief that A has performedA's part of a contract made with Z, which he has not performed, and thereby dishonestly induces Z to pay money. A cheats.

(*i*) A sells and conveys an estate to B. A, knowing that in consequence of such sale he has no right to the property, sells or mortgages the same to Z, without disclosing the fact of the previous sale and conveyance to B, and receives the purchase or mortgage money from Z. A cheats.

(*2*) Whoever cheats shall be punished with imprisonment of either description for a term which may extend to three years, or with fine, or with both.

(*3*) Whoever cheats with the knowledge that he is likely thereby to cause wrongful loss to a person whose interest in the transaction to which the cheating relates, he was bound, either by law, or by a legal contract, to protect, shall be punished with imprisonment of either description for a term which may extend to five years, or with fine, or with both.

(*4*) Whoever cheats and thereby dishonestly induces the person deceived to deliver any property to any person, or to make, alter or destroy the whole or any part of a valuable security, or anything which is signed or sealed, and which is capable of being converted into a valuable security, shall be punished with imprisonment of either description for a term which may extend to seven years, and shall also be liable to fine.

319. (*1*) A person is said to cheat by personation if he cheats by pretending to be some other person, or by knowingly substituting one person for or another, or representing that he or any other person is a person other than he or such other person really is.

Explanation.—The offence is committed whether the individual personated is a real or imaginary person.

Illustrations.

(*a*) A cheats by pretending to be a certain rich banker of the same name. A cheats by personation.

(*b*) A cheats by pretending to be B, a person who is deceased. A cheats by personation.

(*2*) Whoever cheats by personation shall be punished with imprisonment of either description for a term which may extend to five years, or with fine, or with both.

Of fraudulent deeds and dispositions of property

320. Whoever dishonestly or fraudulently removes, conceals or delivers to any person, or transfers or causes to be transferred to any person, without adequate consideration, any property, intending thereby to prevent, or knowing it to be likely that he will thereby prevent, the distribution of that property according to law among his creditors or the creditors of any other person, shall be punished with imprisonment of either description for a term which shall not be less than six months but which may extend to two years, or with fine, or with both.

321. Whoever dishonestly or fraudulently prevents any debt or demand due to himself or to any other person from being made available according to law for payment of his debts or the debts of such other person, shall be punished with imprisonment of either description for a term which may extend to two years, or with fine, or with both.

322. Whoever dishonestly or fraudulently signs, executes or becomes a party to any deed or instrument which purports to transfer or subject to any charge any property, or any interest therein, and which contains any false statement relating to the consideration for such transfer or charge, or relating to the person or persons for whose use or benefit it is really intended to operate, shall be punished with imprisonment of either description for a term which may extend to three years, or with fine, or with both.

Cheating by personation.

Dishonest or fraudulent

removal or

concealment

of property to prevent distribution

among creditors.

Dishonestly or fraudulently

preventing debt being available for creditors.

Dishonest or fraudulent execution of deed of transfer containing false statement of

consideration.

Dishonest or fraudulent

removal or

concealment of property.

Mischief.

323. Whoever dishonestly or fraudulently conceals or removes any property of himself or any other person, or dishonestly or fraudulently assists in the concealment or removal thereof, or dishonestly releases any demand or claim to which he is entitled, shall be punished with imprisonment of either description for a term which may extend to three years, or with fine, or with both.

Of mischief

324. (*1*) Whoever with intent to cause, or knowing that he is likely to cause, wrongful loss or damage to the public or to any person, causes the destruction of any property, or any such change in any property or in the situation thereof as destroys or diminishes its value or utility, or affects it injuriously, commits mischief.

Explanation 1.—It is not essential to the offence of mischief that the offender should intend to cause loss or damage to the owner of the property injured or destroyed. It is sufficient if he intends to cause, or knows that he is likely to cause, wrongful loss or damage to any person by injuring any property, whether it belongs to that person or not.

Explanation 2.—Mischief may be committed by an act affecting property belonging to the person who commits the act, or to that person and others jointly.

Illustrations.

(*a*) A voluntarily burns a valuable security belonging to Z intending to cause wrongful loss to Z. A has committed mischief.

(*b*) A introduces water into an ice-house belonging to Z and thus causes the ice to melt, intending wrongful loss to Z. A has committed mischief.

(*c*)A voluntarily throws into a river a ring belonging to Z, with the intention of thereby causing wrongful loss to Z. A has committed mischief.

(*d*) A, knowing that his effects are about to be taken in execution in order to satisfy a debt due from him to Z, destroys those effects, with the intention of thereby preventing Z from obtaining satisfaction of the debt, and of thus causing damage to Z. A has committed mischief.

(*e*) A having insured a ship, voluntarily causes the same to be cast away, with the intention of causing damage to the underwriters. A has committed mischief.

(*f*) A causes a ship to be cast away, intending thereby to cause damage to Z who has lent money on bottomry on the ship. A has committed mischief.

(*g*) A, having joint property with Z in a horse, shoots the horse, intending thereby to cause wrongful loss to Z. A has committed mischief.

(*b*) A causes cattle to enter upon a field belonging to Z, intending to cause and knowing that he is likely to cause damage to Z's crop. A has committed mischief.

(*2*) Whoever commits mischief shall be punished with imprisonment of either description for a term which may extend to six months, or with fine, or with both.

(*3*) Whoever commits mischief and thereby causes loss or damage to any property including the property of Government or LocalAuthority shall be punished with imprisonment of either description for a term which may extend to one year, or with fine, or with both.

(*4*) Whoever commits mischief and thereby causes loss or damage to the amount of twenty thousand rupees and more but less than one lakh rupees shall be punished with imprisonment of either description for a term which may extend to two years, or with fine, or with both.

(*5*) Whoever commits mischief and thereby causes loss or damage to the amount of one lakh rupees or upwards, shall be punished with imprisonment of either description for a term which may extend to five years, or with fine, or with both.

(*6*) Whoever commits mischief, having made preparation for causing to any person death, or hurt, or wrongful restraint, or fear of death, or of hurt, or of wrongful restraint, shall be punished with imprisonment of either description for a term which may extend to five years, and shall also be liable to fine.

325. Whoever commits mischief by killing, poisoning, maiming or rendering useless any animal shall be punished with imprisonment of either description for a term which may extend to five years, or with fine, or with both.

326. Whoever commits mischief by,—

(*a*) doing any act which causes, or which he knows to be likely to cause, a diminution of the supply of water for agricultural purposes, or for food or drink for human beings or for animals which are property, or for cleanliness or for carrying on any manufacture, shall be punished with imprisonment of either description for a term which may extend to five years, or with fine, or with both;

(*b*) doing any act which renders or which he knows to be likely to render any public road, bridge, navigable river or navigable channel, natural or artificial, impassable or less safe for travelling or conveying property, shall be punished with imprisonment of either description for a term which may extend to five years, or with fine, or with both;

(*c*) doing any act which causes or which he knows to be likely to cause an inundation or an obstruction to any public drainage attended with injury or damage, shall be punished with imprisonment of either description for a term which may extend to five years, or with fine, or with both;

(*d*) destroying or moving any sign or signal used for navigation of rail, aircraft or ship or other thing placed as a guide for navigators, or by any act which renders any such sign or signal less useful as a guide for navigators, shall be punished with imprisonment of either description for a term which may extend to seven years, or with fine, or with both;

(*e*) destroying or moving any land-mark fixed by the authority of a public servant, or by any act which renders such land-mark less useful as such, shall be punished with imprisonment of either description for a term which may extend to one year, or with fine, or with both;

(*f*) fire or any explosive substance intending to cause, or knowing it to be likely that he will thereby cause, damage to any property including agricultural produce, shall be punished with imprisonment of either description for a term which may extend to seven years, and shall also be liable to fine;

(*g*) fire or any explosive substance, intending to cause, or knowing it to be likely that he will thereby cause, the destruction of any building which is ordinarily used as a place of worship or as a human dwelling or as a place for the custody of property, shall be punished with imprisonment for life, or with imprisonment of either description for a term which may extend to ten years, and shall also be liable to fine.

327. (*1*) Whoever commits mischief to any rail, aircraft, or a decked vessel or any vessel of a burden of twenty tons or upwards, intending to destroy or render unsafe, or knowing it to be likely that he will thereby destroy or render unsafe, that rail, aircraft or vessel, shall be punished with imprisonment of either description for a term which may extend to ten years, and shall also be liable to fine.

(*2*) Whoever commits, or attempts to commit, by fire or any explosive substance, such mischief as is described in sub-section (*1*), shall be punished with imprisonment for life or with imprisonment of either description for a term which may extend to ten years, and shall also be liable to fine.

Mischief by killing or

maiming animal.

Mischief by injury, inundation, fire or explosive substance, etc.

Mischief with intent to destroy or make unsafe a rail, aircraft, decked vessel or one of

twenty tons burden.

Punishment for intentionally running vessel aground or ashore with

intent to

commit theft, etc.

Criminal trespass and house-trespass.

House-trespass and house- breaking.

328. Whoever intentionally runs any vessel aground or ashore, intending to commit theft of any property contained therein or to dishonestly misappropriate any such property, or with intent that such theft or misappropriation of property may be committed, shall be punished with imprisonment of either description for a term which may extend to ten years, and shall also be liable to fine.

Of criminal trespass

329. (*1*) Whoever enters into or upon property in the possession of another with intent to commit an offence or to intimidate, insult or annoy any person in possession of such property or having lawfully entered into or upon such property, unlawfully remains there with intent thereby to intimidate, insult or annoy any such person or with intent to commit an offence is said to commit criminal trespass.

(*2*) Whoever commits criminal trespass by entering into or remaining in any building, tent or vessel used as a human dwelling or any building used as a place for worship, or as a place for the custody of property, is said to commit house-trespass.

Explanation.—The introduction of any part of the criminal trespasser's body is entering sufficient to constitute house-trespass.

(*3*) Whoever commits criminal trespass shall be punished with imprisonment of either description for a term which may extend to three months, or with fine which may extend to five thousand rupees, or with both.

(*4*) Whoever commits house-trespass shall be punished with imprisonment of either description for a term which may extend to one year, or with fine which may extend to five thousand rupees, or with both.

330. (*1*) Whoever commits house-trespass having taken precautions to conceal such house-trespass from some person who has a right to exclude or eject the trespasser from the building, tent or vessel which is the subject of the trespass, is said to commit lurking house-trespass.

(*2*) A person is said to commit house-breaking who commits house-trespass if he effects his entrance into the house or any part of it in any of the six ways hereinafter described; or if, being in the house or any part of it for the purpose of committing an offence, or having committed an offence therein, he quits the house or any part of it in any of the following ways, namely:––

(*a*) if he enters or quits through a passage made by himself, or by any abettor of the house-trespass, in order to the committing of the house-trespass;

(*b*) if he enters or quits through any passage not intended by any person, other than himself or an abettor of the offence, for human entrance; or through any passage to which he has obtained access by scaling or climbing over any wall or building;

(*c*) if he enters or quits through any passage which he or any abettor of the house-trespass has opened, in order to the committing of the house-trespass by any means by which that passage was not intended by the occupier of the house to be opened;

(*d*) if he enters or quits by opening any lock in order to the committing of the house-trespass, or in order to the quitting of the house after a house-trespass;

(*e*) if he effects his entrance or departure by using criminal force or committing an assault, or by threatening any person with assault;

(*f*) if he enters or quits by any passage which he knows to have been fastened against such entrance or departure, and to have been unfastened by himself or by an abettor of the house-trespass.

Explanation.—Any out-house or building occupied with a house, and between which and such house there is an immediate internal communication, is part of the house within the meaning of this section.

Illustrations.

(*a*) A commits house-trespass by making a hole through the wall of Z's house, and putting his hand through the aperture. This is house-breaking.

(*b*) A commits house-trespass by creeping into a ship at a port-hole between decks. This is house-breaking.

(*c*) A commits house-trespass by entering Z's house through a window. This is house-breaking.

(*d*) A commits house-trespass by entering Z's house through the door, having opened a door which was fastened. This is house-breaking.

(*e*) A commits house-trespass by entering Z's house through the door, having lifted a latch by putting a wire through a hole in the door. This is house-breaking.

(*f*) A finds the key of Z's house door, which Z had lost, and commits house-trespass by entering Z's house, having opened the door with that key. This is house-breaking.

(*g*) Z is standing in his doorway. Aforces a passage by knocking Z down, and commits house-trespass by entering the house. This is house-breaking.

(*h*) Z, the door-keeper of Y, is standing in Y's doorway. A commits house-trespass by entering the house, having deterred Z from opposing him by threatening to beat him. This is house-breaking.

331. (*1*) Whoever commits lurking house-trespass or house-breaking, shall be punished with imprisonment of either description for a term which may extend to two years, and shall also be liable to fine.

(*2*) Whoever commits lurking house-trespass or house-breaking after sunset and before sunrise, shall be punished with imprisonment of either description for a term which may extend to three years, and shall also be liable to fine.

(*3*) Whoever commits lurking house-trespass or house-breaking, in order to the committing of any offence punishable with imprisonment, shall be punished with imprisonment of either description for a term which may extend to three years, and shall also be liable to fine; and if the offence intended to be committed is theft, the term of the imprisonment may be extended to ten years.

(*4*) Whoever commits lurking house-trespass or house-breaking after sunset and before sunrise, in order to the committing of any offence punishable with imprisonment, shall be punished with imprisonment of either description for a term which may extend to five years, and shall also be liable to fine; and, if the offence intended to be committed is theft, the term of the imprisonment may be extended to fourteen years.

(*5*) Whoever commits lurking house-trespass, or house-breaking, having made preparation for causing hurt to any person, or for assaulting any person, or for wrongfully restraining any person, or for putting any person in fear of hurt or of assault or of wrongful restraint, shall be punished with imprisonment of either description or a term which may extend to ten years, and shall also be liable to fine.

(*6*) Whoever commits lurking house-trespass or house-breaking after sunset and before sunrise, having made preparation for causing hurt to any person or for assaulting any

45 person, or for wrongfully restraining any person, or for putting any person in fear of hurt, or of assault, or of wrongful restraint, shall be punished with imprisonment of either description for a term which may extend to fourteen years, and shall also be liable to fine.

Punishment for house-trespass or house- breaking.

House-trespass in order to

commit offence.

House-trespass after preparation for hurt, assault or wrongful

restraint.

Dishonestly breaking open receptacle

containing property.

Making a false document.

(*7*) Whoever, whilst committing lurking house-trespass or house-breaking, causes grievous hurt to any person or attempts to cause death or grievous hurt to any person, shall be punished with imprisonment for life, or imprisonment of either description for a term which may extend to ten years, and shall also be liable to fine.

(*8*) If, at the time of the committing of lurking house-trespass or house-breaking after 5 sunset and before sunrise, any person guilty of such offence shall voluntarily cause or attempt to cause death or grievous hurt to any person, every person jointly concerned in committing such lurking house-trespass or house-breaking after sunset and before sunrise, shall be punished with imprisonment for life, or with imprisonment of either description for a term which may extend to ten years, and shall also be liable to fine.

332. Whoever commits house-trespass in order to the committing of any offence–– (*a*) punishable with death, shall be punished with imprisonment for life, or with rigorous imprisonment for a term not exceeding ten years, and shall also be liable to fine;

(*b*) punishable with imprisonment for life, shall be punished with imprisonment of either description for a term not exceeding ten years, and shall also be liable to fine;

(*c*) punishable with imprisonment, shall be punished with imprisonment of either description for a term which may extend to two years, and shall also be liable to fine:

Provided that if the offence intended to be committed is theft, the term of the imprisonment may be extended to seven years.

333. Whoever commits house-trespass, having made preparation for causing hurt to any person or for assaulting any person, or for wrongfully restraining any person, or for putting any person in fear of hurt, or of assault, or of wrongful restraint, shall be punished with imprisonment of either description for a term which may extend to seven years, and shall also be liable to fine.

334. (*1*) Whoever dishonestly or with intent to commit mischief, breaks open or unfastens any closed receptacle which contains or which he believes to contain property, shall be punished with imprisonment of either description for a term which may extend to two years, or with fine, or with both.

(*2*) Whoever, being entrusted with any closed receptacle which contains or which he 30 believes to contain property, without having authority to open the same, dishonestly, or with intent to commit mischief, breaks open or unfastens that receptacle, shall be punished with imprisonment of either description for a term which may extend to three years, or with fine, or with both.

Chapter Eighteen

OF OFFENCES RELATING TO DOCUMENTS AND TO PROPERTY MARKS

335. A person is said to make a false document or false electronic record— (*A*) Who dishonestly or fraudulently—

(*i*) makes, signs, seals or executes a document or part of a document;

(*ii*) makes or transmits any electronic record or part of any electronic record;

(*iii*) affixes any electronic signature on any electronic record;

(*iv*) makes any mark denoting the execution of a document or the authenticity of the electronic signature,

with the intention of causing it to be believed that such document or part of document,

electronic record or electronic signature was made, signed, sealed, executed, transmitted or affixed by or by the authority of a person by whom or by whose authority he knows that it was not made, signed, sealed, executed or affixed; or

(*B*) Who without lawful authority, dishonestly or fraudulently, by cancellation or otherwise, alters a document or an electronic record in any material part thereof, after it has been made, executed or affixed with electronic signature either by himself or by any other person, whether such person be living or dead at the time of such alteration; or

(*C*) Who dishonestly or fraudulently causes any person to sign, seal, execute or alter a document or an electronic record or to affix his electronic signature on any electronic record knowing that such person by reason of unsoundness of mind or intoxication cannot, or that by reason of deception practised upon him, he does not know the contents of the document or electronic record or the nature of the alteration.

Illustrations.

(*a*)Ahas a letter of credit upon B for rupees 10,000, written by Z. A, in order to defraud B, adds cipher to the 10,000, and makes the sum 1,00,000 intending that it may be believed by B that Z so wrote the letter. A has committed forgery.

(*b*)A, without Z's authority, affixes Z's seal to a document purporting to be a conveyance of an estate from Z to A, with the intention of selling the estate to B and thereby of obtaining from B the purchase-money. A has committed forgery.

(*c*) A picks up a cheque on a banker signed by B, payable to bearer, but without any sum having been inserted in the cheque. A fraudulently fills up the cheque by inserting the sum of ten thousand rupees. A commits forgery.

(*d*) A leaves with B, his agent, a cheque on a banker, signed byA, without inserting the sum payable and authorises B to fill up the cheque by inserting a sum not exceeding ten thousand rupees for the purpose of making certain payments. B fraudulently fills up the cheque by inserting the sum of twenty thousand rupees. B commits forgery.

(*e*) A draws a bill of exchange on himself in the name of B without B's authority, intending to discount it as a genuine bill with a banker and intending to take up the bill on its maturity. Here, as A draws the bill with intent to deceive the banker by leading him to suppose that he had the security of B, and thereby to discount the bill, A is guilty of forgery.

(*f*) Z's will contains these words—"I direct that all my remaining property be equally divided between A, B and C." A dishonestly scratches out B's name, intending that it may be believed that the whole was left to himself and C. A has committed forgery.

(*g*) A endorses a Government promissory note and makes it payable to Z or his order by writing on the bill the words "Pay to Z or his order" and signing the endorsement. B dishonestly erases the words "Pay to Z or his order", and thereby converts the special endorsement into a blank endorsement. B commits forgery.

(*h*) A sells and conveys an estate to Z. A afterwards, in order to defraud Z of his estate, executes a conveyance of the same estate to B, dated six months earlier than the date of the conveyance to Z, intending it to be believed that he had conveyed the estate to B before he conveyed it to Z. A has committed forgery.

(*i*) Z dictates his will to A. A intentionally writes down a different legatee from the legatee named by Z, and by representing to Z that he has prepared the will according to his instructions, induces Z to sign the will. A has committed forgery.

(*j*) Awrites a letter and signs it with B's name without B's authority, certifying thatA is a man of good character and in distressed circumstances from unforeseen misfortune, intending by means of such letter to obtain alms from Z and other persons. Here, as A made a false document in order to induce Z to part with property, A has committed forgery.

Forgery.

(*k*) A without B's authority writes a letter and signs it in B's name certifying to A's character, intending thereby to obtain employment under Z. A has committed forgery in as much as he intended to deceive

Z by the forged certificate, and thereby to induce Z to enter into an express or implied contract for service.

Explanation 1.—A man's signature of his own name may amount to forgery.

Illustrations.

(*a*) A signs his own name to a bill of exchange, intending that it may be believed that the bill was drawn by another person of the same name. A has committed forgery.

(*b*) A writes the word "accepted" on a piece of paper and signs it with Z's name, in order that B may afterwards write on the paper a bill of exchange drawn by B upon Z, and negotiate the bill as though it had been accepted by Z. A is guilty of forgery; and if B, knowing the fact, draws the bill upon the paper pursuant to A's intention, B is also guilty of forgery.

(*c*) A picks up a bill of exchange payable to the order of a different person of the same name. A endorses the bill in his own name, intending to cause it to be believed that it was endorsed by the person to whose order it was payable; here A has committed forgery.

(*d*) A purchases an estate sold under execution of a decree against B. B, after the seizure of the estate, in collusion with Z, executes a lease of the estate, to Z at a nominal rent and for a long period and dates the lease six months prior to the seizure, with intent to defraud A, and to cause it to be believed that the lease was granted before the seizure. B, though he executes the lease in his own name, commits forgery by antedating it.

(*e*) A, a trader, in anticipation of insolvency, lodges effects with B for A's benefit, and with intent to defraud his creditors; and in order to give a colour to the transaction, writes a promissory note binding himself to pay to B a sum for value received, and antedates the note, intending that it may be believed to have been made before A was on the point of insolvency. A has committed forgery under the first head of the definition.

Explanation 2.—The making of a false document in the name of a fictitious person, intending it to be believed that the document was made by a real person, or in the name of a deceased person, intending it to be believed that the document was made by the person in his lifetime, may amount to forgery.

Illustration.

A draws a bill of exchange upon a fictitious person, and fraudulently accepts the bill in the name of such fictitious person with intent to negotiate it. A commits forgery.

Explanation 3.—For the purposes of this section, the expression "affixing electronic signature" shall have the meaning assigned to it in clause (*d*) of sub-section (*1*) of section 2 of the Information Technology Act, 2000.

336. (*1*) Whoever makes any false document or false electronic record or part of a document or electronic record, with intent to cause damage or injury, to the public or to any person, or to support any claim or title, or to cause any person to part with property, or to enter into any express or implied contract, or with intent to commit fraud or that fraud may be committed, commits forgery.

(*2*) Whoever commits forgery shall be punished with imprisonment of either description for a term which may extend to two years, or with fine, or with both.

(*3*) Whoever commits forgery, intending that the document or electronic record forged shall be used for the purpose of cheating, shall be punished with imprisonment of either description for a term which may extend to seven years, and shall also be liable to fine.

(*4*) Whoever commits forgery, intending that the document or electronic record forged shall harm the reputation of any party, or knowing that it is likely to be used for that purpose, shall be punished with imprisonment of either description for a term which may extend to three years, and shall also be liable to fine.

337. Whoever forges a document or an electronic record, purporting to be a record or proceeding of or in a Court or an identity document issued by Government including voter identity card or Aadhaar Card, or a register of birth, marriage or burial, or a register kept by a public servant as such, or a certificate or document purporting to be made by a public servant in his official capacity, or an authority to institute or defend a suit, or to take any proceedings therein, or to confess judgment, or a power of attorney, shall be punished with imprisonment of either description for a term which may extend to seven years, and shall also be liable to fine.

Explanation.—For the purposes of this section, "register" includes any list, data or record of any entries maintained in the electronic form as defined in clause (*r*) of sub-section (*1*) of section 2 of the Information Technology Act, 2000.

338. Whoever forges a document which purports to be a valuable security or a will, or an authority to adopt a son, or which purports to give authority to any person to make or transfer any valuable security, or to receive the principal, interest or dividends thereon, or to receive or deliver any money, movable property, or valuable security, or any document purporting to be an acquittance or receipt acknowledging the payment of money, or an acquittance or receipt for the delivery of any movable property or valuable security, shall be punished with imprisonment for life, or with imprisonment of either description for a term which may extend to ten years, and shall also be liable to fine.

339. Whoever has in his possession any document or electronic record, knowing the same to be forged and intending that the same shall fraudulently or dishonestly be used as genuine, shall, if the document or electronic record is one of the description mentioned in section 337 of this Sanhita, be punished with imprisonment of either description for a term which may extend to seven years, and shall also be liable to fine; and if the document is one of the description mentioned in section 338, shall be punished with imprisonment for life, or with imprisonment of either description, for a term which may extend to seven years, and shall also be liable to fine.

340. (*1*) A false document or electronic record made wholly or in part by forgery is designated a forged document or electronic record.

(*2*) Whoever fraudulently or dishonestly uses as genuine any document or electronic record which he knows or has reason to believe to be a forged document or electronic record, shall be punished in the same manner as if he had forged such document or electronic record.

341. (*1*) Whoever makes or counterfeits any seal, plate or other instrument for making an impression, intending that the same shall be used for the purpose of committing any forgery which would be punishable under section 338 of this Sanhita, or, with such intent, has in his possession any such seal, plate or other instrument, knowing the same to be counterfeit, shall be punished with imprisonment for life, or with imprisonment of either description for a term which may extend to seven years, and shall also be liable to fine.

(*2*) Whoever makes or counterfeits any seal, plate or other instrument for making an impression, intending that the same shall be used for the purpose of committing any forgery which would be punishable under any section of this Chapter other than section 338, or, with such intent, has in his possession any such seal, plate or other instrument, knowing the same to be counterfeit, shall be punished with imprisonment of either description for a term which may extend to seven years, and shall also be liable to fine.

(*3*) Whoever possesses any seal, plate or other instrument knowing the same to be counterfeit, shall be punished with imprisonment of either description for a term which may extend to three years, and shall also be liable to fine.

Forgery of record of Court or of

public register, etc.

Forgery of valuable security, will, etc.

Having possession of document described in

section 337 or section 338, knowing it to be forged and intending to use it as genuine.

Forged document or electronic record and using it as genuine.

Making or possessing

counterfeit seal, etc., with intent to

commit forgery punishable under section 338.

Counterfeiting device or

mark used for

authenticating documents described in

section 338, or possessing counterfeit

marked

material.

Fraudulent

cancellation, destruction, etc., of will,

authority to adopt, or valuable security.

Falsification of accounts.

Property mark.

(*4*) Whoever fraudulently or dishonestly uses as genuine any seal, plate or other instrument knowing or having reason to believe the same to be counterfeit, shall be punished in the same manner as if he had made or counterfeited such seal, plate or other instrument.

342. (*1*) Whoever counterfeits upon, or in the substance of, any material, any device or mark used for the purpose of authenticating any document described in section 338, intending that such device or mark shall be used for the purpose of giving the appearance of authenticity to any document then forged or thereafter to be forged on such material, or who, with such intent, has in his possession any material upon or in the substance of which any such device or mark has been counterfeited, shall be punished with imprisonment for life, or with imprisonment of either description for a term which may extend to seven years, and shall also be liable to fine.

(*2*) Whoever counterfeits upon, or in the substance of, any material, any device or mark used for the purpose of authenticating any document or electronic record other than the documents described in section 338, intending that such device or mark shall be used for the purpose of giving the appearance of authenticity to any document then forged or thereafter to be forged on such material, or who with such intent, has in his possession any material upon or in the substance of which any such device or mark has been counterfeited, shall be punished with imprisonment of either description for a term which may extend to seven years, and shall also be liable to fine.

343. Whoever fraudulently or dishonestly, or with intent to cause damage or injury to the public or to any person, cancels, destroys or defaces, or attempts to cancel, destroy or deface, or secretes or attempts to secrete any document which is or purports to be a will, or an authority to adopt a son, or any valuable security, or commits mischief in respect of such document, shall be punished with imprisonment for life, or with imprisonment of either description for a term which may extend to seven years, and shall also be liable to fine.

344. Whoever, being a clerk, officer or servant, or employed or acting in the capacity of a clerk, officer or servant, wilfully, and with intent to defraud, destroys, alters, mutilates or falsifies any book, electronic record, paper, writing, valuable security or account which belongs to or is in the possession of his employer, or has been received by him for or on behalf of his employer, or wilfully, and with intent to defraud, makes or abets the making of any false entry in, or omits or alters or abets the omission or alteration of any material particular from or in, any such book, electronic record, paper, writing, valuable security or account, shall be punished with imprisonment of either description for a term which may extend to seven years, or with fine, or with both.

Explanation.—It shall be sufficient in any charge under this section to allege a general

intent to defraud without naming any particular person intended to be defrauded or specifying

any particular sum of money intended to be the subject of the fraud, or any particular day on which the offence was committed. *Of property marks*

345. (*1*)Amark used for denoting that movable property belongs to a particular person is called a property mark.

(*2*) Whoever marks any movable property or goods or any case, package or other receptacle containing movable property or goods, or uses any case, package or other receptacle having any mark thereon, in a manner reasonably calculated to cause it to be believed that the property or goods so marked, or any property or goods contained in any such receptacle so marked, belong to a person to whom they do not belong, is said to use a false property mark.

(*3*) Whoever uses any false property mark shall, unless he proves that he acted without intent to defraud, be punished with imprisonment of either description for a term which may extend to one year, or with fine, or with both.

346. Whoever removes, destroys, defaces or adds to any property mark, intending or knowing it to be likely that he may thereby cause injury to any person, shall be punished with imprisonment of either description for a term which may extend to one year, or with fine, or with both.

347. (*1*) Whoever counterfeits any property mark used by any other person shall be punished with imprisonment of either description for a term which may extend to two years, or with fine, or with both.

(*2*) Whoever counterfeits any property mark used by a public servant, or any mark used by a public servant to denote that any property has been manufactured by a particular person or at a particular time or place, or that the property is of a particular quality or has passed through a particular office, or that it is entitled to any exemption, or uses as genuine any such mark knowing the same to be counterfeit, shall be punished with imprisonment of either description for a term which may extend to three years, and shall also be liable to fine.

348. Whoever makes or has in his possession any die, plate or other instrument for the purpose of counterfeiting a property mark, or has in his possession a property mark for the purpose of denoting that any goods belong to a person to whom they do not belong, shall be punished with imprisonment of either description for a term which may extend to three years, or with fine, or with both.

349. Whoever sells, or exposes, or has in possession for sale, any goods or things with a counterfeit property mark affixed to or impressed upon the same or to or upon any case, package or other receptacle in which such goods are contained, shall, unless he proves—

(*a*) that, having taken all reasonable precautions against committing an offence against this section, he had at the time of the commission of the alleged offence no reason to suspect the genuineness of the mark; and

(*b*) that, on demand made by or on behalf of the prosecutor, he gave all the information in his power with respect to the persons from whom he obtained such goods or things; or

(*c*) that otherwise he had acted innocently,

be punished with imprisonment of either description for a term which may extend to one year, or with fine, or with both.

350. (*1*) Whoever makes any false mark upon any case, package or other receptacle containing goods, in a manner reasonably calculated to cause any public servant or any other person to believe that such receptacle contains goods which it does not contain or that it does not contain goods which it does contain, or that the goods contained in such receptacle are of a nature or quality different from the real nature or quality thereof, shall, unless he proves that he acted without intent to defraud, be punished with imprisonment of either description for a term which may extend to three years, or with fine, or with both.

(*2*) Whoever makes use of any false mark in any manner prohibited under sub-section (*1*) shall, unless he proves that he acted without intent to defraud, be punished as if he had committed the offence under sub-section (*1*).

Chapter Nineteen

OF CRIMINAL INTIMIDATION, INSULT, ANNOYANCE, DEFAMATION, ETC.

351. (*1*) Whoever threatens another by any means, with any injury to his person, reputation or property, or to the person or reputation of any one in whom that person is

interested, with intent to cause alarm to that person, or to cause that person to do any act

which he is not legally bound to do, or to omit to do any act which that person is legally entitled to do, as the means of avoiding the execution of such threat, commits criminal intimidation.

Tampering

with property mark with intent to cause injury.

Counterfeiting a property

mark.

Making or possession of any instru-

ment for

counterfeiting a property

mark.

Selling goods marked with a counterfeit

property mark.

Making a false mark upon

any receptacle containing goods.

Criminal

intimidation.

Intentional insult with

intent to provoke breach of peace.

Statements conducing to public mischief.

Explanation.—A threat to injure the reputation of any deceased person in whom the person threatened is interested, is within this section.

Illustration.

A, for the purpose of inducing B to resist from prosecuting a civil suit, threatens to

burn B's house. A is guilty of criminal intimidation. 5

(*2*) Whoever commits the offence of criminal intimidation shall be punished with imprisonment of either description for a term which may extend to two years, or with fine, or with both.

(*3*) Whoever commits the offence of criminal intimidation by threatening to cause death or grievous hurt, or to cause the destruction of any property by fire, or to cause an offence punishable with death or imprisonment for life, or with imprisonment for a term which may extend to seven years, or to impute unchastity to a woman, shall be punished with imprisonment of either description for a term which may extend to seven years, or with fine, or with both.

(*4*) Whoever commits the offence of criminal intimidation by an anonymous communication, or having taken precaution to conceal the name or abode of the person from whom the threat comes, shall be punished with imprisonment of either description for a term which may extend to two years, in addition to the punishment provided for the offence under sub-section (*1*).

352. Whoever intentionally insults in any manner, and thereby gives provocation to any person, intending or knowing it to be likely that such provocation will cause him to break the public peace, or to commit any other offence, shall be punished with imprisonment of either description for a term which may extend to two years, or with fine, or with both.

353. (*1*) Whoever makes, publishes or circulates any statement, false information, rumour, or report, including through electronic means—

(*a*) with intent to cause, or which is likely to cause, any officer, soldier, sailor or airman in the Army, Navy or Air Force of India to mutiny or otherwise disregard or fail in his duty as such; or

(*b*) with intent to cause, or which is likely to cause, fear or alarm to the public, or

to any section of the public whereby any person may be induced to commit an offence against the State or against the public tranquility; or

(*c*) with intent to incite, or which is likely to incite, any class or community of persons to commit any offence against any other class or community,

shall be punished with imprisonment which may extend to three years, or with fine, or with both.

(*2*) Whoever makes, publishes or circulates any statement or report containing false information, rumour or alarming news, including through electronic means, with intent to create or promote, or which is likely to create or promote, on grounds of religion, race, place of birth, residence, language, caste or community or any other ground whatsoever, feelings of enmity, hatred or ill will between different religious, racial, language or regional groups or castes or communities, shall be punished with imprisonment which may extend to three years, or with fine, or with both.

(*3)* Whoever commits an offence specified in sub-section (*2*) in any place of worship or in any assembly engaged in the performance of religious worship or religious ceremonies,

shall be punished with imprisonment which may extend to five years and shall also be liable to fine.

Exception.—It does not amount to an offence, within the meaning of this section, when the person making, publishing or circulating any such statement, false information, rumour or report, has reasonable grounds for believing that such statement, false information, rumour or report is true and makes, publishes or circulates it in good faith and without any such intent as aforesaid.

354. Whoever voluntarily causes or attempts to cause any person to do anything which that person is not legally bound to do, or to omit to do anything which he is legally entitled to do, by inducing or attempting to induce that person to believe that he or any person in whom he is interested will become or will be rendered by some act of the offender an object of Divine displeasure if he does not do the thing which it is the object of the offender to cause him to do, or if he does the thing which it is the object of the offender to cause him to omit, shall be punished with imprisonment of either description for a term which may extend to one year, or with fine, or with both.

Illustrations.

(*a*) A sits dharna at Z's door with the intention of causing it to be believed that, by so sitting, he renders Z an object of Divine displeasure. A has committed the offence defined in this section.

(*b*) A threatens Z that, unless Z performs a certain act, A will kill one of A's own children, under such circumstances that the killing would be believed to render Z an object of Divine displeasure. A has committed the offence defined in this section.

355. Whoever, in a state of intoxication, appears in any public place, or in any place which it is a trespass in him to enter, and there conducts himself in such a manner as to cause annoyance to any person, shall be punished with simple imprisonment for a term which may extend to twenty-four hours, or with fine which may extend to one thousand rupees, or with both or with community service.

Of defamation

356. (*1*) Whoever, by words either spoken or intended to be read, or by signs or by visible representations, makes or publishes in any manner, any imputation concerning any person intending to harm, or knowing or having reason to believe that such imputation will harm, the reputation of such person, is said, except in the cases hereinafter excepted, to defame that person.

Explanation 1.—It may amount to defamation to impute anything to a deceased person, if the imputation would harm the reputation of that person if living, and is intended to be hurtful to the feelings of his family or other near relatives.

Explanation 2.—It may amount to defamation to make an imputation concerning a company or an association or collection of persons as such.

Explanation 3.—An imputation in the form of an alternative or expressed ironically, may amount to defamation.

Explanation 4.—No imputation is said to harm a person's reputation, unless that imputation directly or indirectly, in the estimation of others, lowers the moral or intellectual character of that person, or lowers the character of that person in respect of his caste or of his calling, or lowers the credit of that person, or causes it to be believed that the body of that person is in a loathsome state, or in a state generally considered as disgraceful.

Illustrations.

(*a*) A says— "Z is an honest man; he never stole B's watch"; intending to cause it to be believed that Z did steal B's watch. This is defamation, unless it falls within one of the exceptions.

(*b*) A is asked who stole B's watch. A points to Z, intending to cause it to be believed that Z stole B's watch. This is defamation, unless it falls within one of the exceptions.

Act caused by inducing person to

believe that he will be rendered an object of

Divine displeasure.

Misconduct in public by a

drunken person.

Defamation.

(*c*)A draws a picture of Z running away with B's watch, intending it to be believed that Z stole B's watch. This is defamation, unless it falls within one of the exceptions.

Exception 1.—It is not defamation to impute anything which is true concerning any person, if it be for the public good that the imputation should be made or published. Whether or not it is for the public good is a question of fact.

Exception 2.—It is not defamation to express in good faith any opinion whatever respecting the conduct of a public servant in the discharge of his public functions, or respecting his character, so far as his character appears in that conduct, and no further.

Exception 3.—It is not defamation to express in good faith any opinion whatever respecting the conduct of any person touching any public question, and respecting his character, so far as his character appears in that conduct, and no further.

Illustration.

It is not defamation in A to express in good faith any opinion whatever respecting Z's conduct in petitioning Government on a public question, in signing a requisition for a meeting on a public question, in presiding or attending at such meeting, in forming or joining any society which invites the public support, in voting or canvassing for a particular candidate for any situation in the efficient discharge of the duties of which the public is interested.

Exception 4.––It is not defamation to publish substantially true report of the proceedings of a Court, or of the result of any such proceedings.

Explanation.—A Magistrate or other officer holding an inquiry in open Court preliminary to a trial in a Court, is a Court within the meaning of the above section.

Exception 5.—It is not defamation to express in good faith any opinion whatever respecting the merits of any case, civil or criminal, which has been decided by a Court, or respecting the conduct of any person as a party, witness or agent, in any such case, or respecting the character of such person, as far as his character appears in that conduct, and no further.

Illustrations.

(*a*) A says—"I think Z's evidence on that trial is so contradictory that he must be stupid or dishonest". A is within this exception if he says this in good faith, in as much as the opinion which he expresses respects Z's character as it appears in Z's conduct as a witness, and no further.

(*b*) But if A says—"I do not believe what Z asserted at that trial because I know him to be a man without veracity"; A is not within this exception, in as much as the opinion which expresses of Z's character, is an opinion not founded on Z's conduct as a witness.

Exception 6.—It is not defamation to express in good faith any opinion respecting the merits of any performance which its author has submitted to the judgment of the public, or respecting the character of the author so far as his character appears in such performance, and no further.

Explanation.—A performance may be submitted to the judgment of the public expressly or by acts on the part of the author which imply such submission to the judgment of the public.

Illustrations.

(*a*) A person who publishes a book, submits that book to the judgment of the public. (*b*) A person who makes a speech in public, submits that speech to the judgment of the public.

(*c*) An actor or singer who appears on a public stage, submits his acting or singing to the judgment of the public.

(*d*) A says of a book published by Z—"Z's book is foolish; Z must be a weak man. Z's book is indecent; Z must be a man of impure mind." A is within the exception, if he says this in good faith, in as much as the opinion which he expresses of Z respects Z's character only so far as it appears in Z's book, and no further.

(*e*) But if A says "I am not surprised that Z's book is foolish and indecent, for he is a weak man and a libertine." A is not within this exception, inasmuch as the opinion which he expresses of Z's character is an opinion not founded on Z's book.

Exception 7.—It is not defamation in a person having over another any authority, either conferred by law or arising out of a lawful contract made with that other, to pass in good faith any censure on the conduct of that other in matters to which such lawful authority relates.

Illustration.

A Judge censuring in good faith the conduct of a witness, or of an officer of the Court; a head of a department censuring in good faith those who are under his orders, a parent censuring in good faith a child in the presence of other children; a schoolmaster, whose authority is derived from a parent, censuring in good faith a pupil in the presence of other pupils; a master censuring a servant in good faith for remissness in service; a banker censuring in good faith the cashier of his bank for the conduct of such cashier as such cashier are within this exception.

Exception 8.—It is not defamation to prefer in good faith an accusation against any person to any of those who have lawful authority over that person with respect to the subject-matter of accusation.

Illustration.

If A in good faith accuses Z before a Magistrate; if A in good faith complains of the conduct of Z, a servant, to Z's master; if A in good faith complains of the conduct of Z, a child, to Z's father-A is within this exception.

Exception 9.— It is not defamation to make an imputation on the character of another provided that the imputation be made in good faith for the protection of the interests of the person making it, or of any other person, or for the public good.

Illustrations.

(*a*) A, a shopkeeper, says to B, who manages his business—"Sell nothing to Z unless he pays you ready money, for I have no opinion of his honesty." A is within the exception, if he has made this imputation on Z in good faith for the protection of his own interests.

(*b*) A, a Magistrate, in making a report to his own superior officer, casts an imputation on the character of Z. Here, if the imputation is made in good faith, and for the public good, A is within the exception.

Exception 10.— It is not defamation to convey a caution, in good faith, to one person against another, provided that such caution be intended for the good of the person to whom it is conveyed, or of some person in whom that person is interested, or for the public good.

(*2*) Whoever defames another shall be punished with simple imprisonment for a term which may extend to two years, or with fine, or with both or with community service.

(*3*) Whoever prints or engraves any matter, knowing or having good reason to believe that such matter is defamatory of any person, shall be punished with simple imprisonment for a term which may extend to two years, or with fine, or with both.

45 (*4*) Whoever sells or offers for sale any printed or engraved substance containing defamatory matter, knowing that it contains such matter, shall be punished with simple imprisonment for a term which may extend to two years, or with fine, or with both.

Breach of

contract to attend on and supply wants of helpless

person.

Of breach of contract to attend on and supply wants of helpless person

357. Whoever, being bound by a lawful contract to attend on or to supply the wants of any person who, by reason of youth, or of unsoundness of mind, or of a disease or bodily weakness, is helpless or incapable of providing for his own safety or of supplying his own wants, voluntarily omits so to do, shall be punished with imprisonment of either description 5 for a term which may extend to three months, or with fine which may extend to five thousand rupees, or with both.

Repeal and savings.

Chapter Twenty

REPEAL AND SAVINGS

358. (*1*) The Indian Penal Code is hereby repealed.

(*2*) Notwithstanding the repeal of the Code referred to in sub-section (*1*), it shall not affect,— 10 45 of 1860.

(*a*) the previous operation of the Code so repealed or anything duly done or suffered thereunder; or

(*b*) any right, privilege, obligation or liability acquired, accrued or incurred under the Code so repealed; or

(*c*) any penalty, or punishment incurred in respect of any offences committed against the Code so repealed; or

(*d*) any investigation or remedy in respect of any such penalty, or punishment; or

(*e*) any proceeding, investigation or remedy in respect of any such penalty or punishment as aforesaid, and any such proceeding or remedy may be instituted, continued or enforced, and any such penalty may be imposed as if that Code had not been repealed.

(*3*) Notwithstanding such repeal, anything done or any action taken under the said Code shall be deemed to have been done or taken under the corresponding provisions of this Sanhita.

(*4*) The mention of particular matters in sub-section (*2*) shall not be held to prejudice or affect the general application of section 6 of the General Clauses Act,1897 with regard to the effect of the repeal.

STATEMENT OF OBJECTS AND REASONS

In the year 1834, the first Indian Law Commission was constituted under the Chairmanship of Lord Thomas Babington Macaulay to examine the jurisdiction, power and rules of the existing Courts as well as the police establishments and the laws in force in India.

2. The Commission suggested various enactments to the Government. One of the important recommendations made by the Commission was on, the Indian Penal Code, which was enacted in 1860 and the said Code is still continuing in the country with some amendments made thereto from time to time.

3. The Government considered it expedient and necessary to review the existing criminal laws with an aim to strengthen law and order and also focus on simplifying legal procedure so that ease of living is ensured to the common man. The Government also considered to make existing laws relevant to the contemporary situation and provide speedy justice to common man. Accordingly, various stakeholders were consulted keeping in mind contemporary needs and aspirations of the people with a view to create a legal structure which is citizen centric and to secure life and liberty of the citizens.

4. It is proposed to enact a new law, by repealing the Indian Penal Code, to streamline provisions relating to offences and penalties. It is proposed to provide first time community service as one of the punishments for petty offences. The offences against women and children, murder and offences against the State have been given precedence. Some offences have been made gender neutral. In order to deal effectively with the problem of organised crimes and terrorist activities, new offences of terrorist acts and organised crime have been added in the Bill with deterrent punishments. A new offence on acts of armed rebellion, subversive activities, separatist activities or endangering sovereignty or unity and integrity of India has also been added. The fines and punishments for various offences have also been suitably enhanced.

5. Accordingly, a Bill, namely, the Bharatiya Nyaya Sanhita, 2023 was introduced in the Lok Sabha on 11th August, 2023. The Bill was referred to the Department-related Parliamentary Standing Committee on Home Affairs for its consideration and report. The Committee after deliberations made its recommendations in its report submitted on

10th November, 2023. The recommendations made by the Committee have been considered by the Government and it has been decided to withdraw the Bill pending in Lok Sabha and introduce a new Bill incorporating therein those recommendations made by the Committee that have been accepted by the Government.

6. The Notes on Clauses explains the various provisions of the Bill.

7. The Bill seeks to achieve the above objectives.

NEW DELHI;

The 9th December, 2023. AMIT SHAH.

NOTES ON CLAUSES

Clause 1 of the Bill seeks to provide short title, commencement and application of the proposed legislation.

Clause 2 of the Bill seeks to define certain words and expressions used in the proposed legislation such as act, omission, counterfeit, dishonestly, gender, good faith, offence, voluntarily, etc.

Clause 3 of the Bill seeks to provide general *Explanations* and expressions enumerated in the proposed legislation subject to the exceptions contained in the "General Exceptions" Chapter.

Clause 4 of the Bill seeks to provide punishments such as death, imprisonment of life, Forfeiture of property, fine and Community Service for offences provided under the provisions of the proposed Bill.

Clause 5 of the Bill relates to commutation of sentence.

This clause seeks to provide that the appropriate Government may, without the consent of the offender, commute any punishment under this Sanhita to any other punishment in accordance with section 474 of the Bharatiya Nagarik Suraksha Sanhita, 2023.

It further explains the term "appropriate Government".

Clause 6 of the Bill seeks to provide fractions of terms of punishment of imprisonment for life shall be reckoned as equivalent to twenty years unless otherwise provided.

Clause 7 of the Bill seeks to provide for sentence which may be either wholly or partly rigorous or simple.

It provides that in every case in which an offender is punishable with imprisonment which may be of either description, it shall be competent to the Court which sentences such offender to direct in the sentence that such imprisonment shall be wholly rigorous, or that such imprisonment shall be wholly simple, or that any part of such imprisonment shall be rigorous and the rest simple.

Clause 8 of the Bill seeks to provide for amount of fine in default of payment of fine and imprisonment in default of payment of fine.

It provides that where no sum is expressed to which a fine may extend, the amount of fine to which the offender is liable is unlimited, but shall not be excessive and also provides the term or type of imprisonment under given circumstances.

It further provides that the fine, or any part thereof which remains unpaid, may be levied at any time within six years after the passing of the sentence, and if, under the sentence, the offender be liable to imprisonment for a longer period than six years, then at any time previous to the expiration of that period; and the death of the offender does not discharge from the liability any property which would, after his death, be legally liable for his debts.

Clause 9 of the Bill seeks to provide for the limit of punishment for several offences. It provides that where anything which is an offence is made up of parts, any of which

parts is itself an offence, the offender shall not be punished with the punishment of more

than one of such his offences, unless it be so expressly provided.

Clause 10 of the Bill seeks to provide that in all cases in which judgment is given that a person is guilty of one of several offences specified in the judgment, but that it is doubtful 104 of which of these offences he is guilty, the offender shall be punished for the offence for which the lowest punishment is provided if the same punishment is not provided for all.

Clause 11 of the Bill seeks to provide the power to court for solitary confinement.

It provides that whenever any person is convicted of an offence for which under this Sanhita the Court has power to sentence him to rigorous imprisonment, the Court may, by its sentence, order that the offender shall be kept in solitary confinement for any portion or portions of the imprisonment to which he is sentenced, not exceeding three months in the whole, according to the given scale under this clause.

Clause 12 of the Bill seeks to provide for limit of solitary confinement in certain cases. It provides that in executing a sentence of solitary confinement, such confinement shall in no case exceed fourteen days at a time, with intervals between the periods of solitary

confinement of not less duration than such periods; and when the imprisonment awarded shall exceed three months, the solitary confinement shall not exceed seven days in any one month of the whole imprisonment awarded, with intervals between the periods of solitary confinement of not less duration than such periods.

Clause 13 of the Bill seeks to provide for enhanced punishment for certain offences after previous conviction.

Clause 14 of the Bill seeks to exempt a person who acts by mistake of fact and not by mistake of law in good faith believing himself to be bound by law to do it.

Clause 15 of the Bill seeks to provide that nothing is an offence which is done by a Judge when acting judicially in the exercise of any power which is, or which in good faith he believes to be, given to him by law.

Clause 16 of the Bill seeks to exempt a person from an offence when acting under a judgment or order notwithstanding that the Court had no jurisdiction to pass such judgment or order, provided the person doing the act in good faith believes that the Court had such jurisdiction.

Clause 17 of the Bill seeks to provide that nothing is an offence which is done by any person who is justified by law, or who by reason of a mistake of fact and not by reason of a mistake of law in good faith, believes himself to be justified by law, in doing it.

Clause 18 of the Bill seeks to provide that nothing is an offence which is done by accident or misfortune, and without any criminal intention or knowledge in the doing of a lawful act in a lawful manner by lawful means and with proper care and caution.

Clause 19 of the Bill seeks to provide that nothing is an offence merely by reason of its being done with the knowledge that it is likely to cause harm, if it be done without any criminal intention to cause harm, and in good faith for the purpose of preventing or avoiding other harm to person or property.

Clause 20 of the Bill seeks to provide that nothing is an offence which is done by a child under seven years of age.

Clause 21 of the Bill seeks to provide that nothing is an offence which is done by a child above seven years of age and under twelve, who has not attained sufficient maturity of understanding to judge of the nature and consequences of his conduct on that occasion.

Clause 22 of the Bill seeks to provide that nothing is an offence which is done by a person who, at the time of doing it, by reason of unsoundness of mind, is incapable of knowing the nature of the act, or that he is doing what is either wrong or contrary to law.

Clause 23 of the Bill seeks to provide that nothing is an offence which is done by a person under intoxication provided that the thing which intoxicated him was administered to him without his knowledge or against his will.

Clause 24 of the Bill seeks to provide that in cases where an act done is not an offence unless done with a particular knowledge or intent, a person who does the act in a state of intoxication shall be liable to be dealt with as if he had the same knowledge as he would have had if he had not been intoxicated, unless the thing which intoxicated him was administered to him without his knowledge or against his will.

Clause 25 of the Bill seeks to provide that nothing is an offence which is not intendent to cause death, or grievous hurt when the harm done with consent of a person above eighteen years of age whether express or implied, to suffer that harm; or by reason of any harm which it may be known by the doer to be likely to cause to any such person who has consented to take the risk of that harm.

Clause 26 of the Bill seeks to provide that nothing is an offence when the act not intended to cause death done by consent in good faith and for persons' benefit.

Clause 27 of the Bill seeks to provide that nothing is an offence when an act is done in good faith for benefit of child or person with unsound mind, by or by consent of guardian.

Clause 28 of the Bill seeks to provide that the consent is not a consent as intended by the proposed legislation when it is given under fear of injury or misconception of facts or unsoundness of mind, intoxication or by a person under twelve years of age.

Clause 29 of the Bill seeks to provide that *Exceptions* in clauses 25, 26 and 27 do not extend to acts which are offences independently of any harm which they may cause, or be intended to cause, or be known to be likely to cause, to the person giving the consent, or on whose behalf the consent is given.

Clause 30 of the Bill seeks to provide that nothing is an offence when act done in good faith for benefit of a person without consent if the circumstances are such that it is impossible for that person to signify consent, or if that person is incapable of giving consent, and has no guardian or other person in lawful charge of him from whom it is possible to obtain consent in time for the thing to be done with benefit.

It further provides that these exception shall not extend under given circumstances. It also explains that mere pecuniary benefit is not benefit within the meaning of clauses 26, 27 and this clause.

Clause 31 of the Bill seeks to provide that no communication made in good faith is an offence by reason of any harm to the person to whom it is made, if it is made for the benefit of that person.

Clause 32 of the Bill seeks to provide that nothing is an offence done by a person except murder, and offences against the State punishable with death, which is done by a person who is compelled to do it by threats, which, at the time of doing it, reasonably cause the apprehension that instant death to that person will otherwise be the consequence.

It further explains that a person who, of his own accord, or by reason of a threat of being beaten, joins a gang of dacoits, knowing their character, is not entitled to the benefit of this exception, on the ground of his having been compelled by his associates to do anything that is an offence by law and A person seized by a gang of dacoits, and forced, by threat of instant death, to do a thing which is an offence by law; for example, a smith compelled to take his tools and to force the door of a house for the dacoits to enter and plunder it, is entitled to the benefit of this exception.

Clause 33 of the Bill seeks to provide that nothing is an offence by reason that it causes, or that it is intended to cause, or that it is known to be likely to cause, any harm, if that harm is so slight that no person of ordinary sense and temper would complain of such harm.

Clause 34 of the Bill seeks to provide that nothing is an offence which is done in the exercise of the right of private defence.

Clause 35 of the Bill seeks to provide that every person has a right of private defence of the body and of property subject to the restrictions contained in clause 37.

Clause 36 of the Bill seeks to provide that nothing is an offence, when an act is done in exercise of right of private defence, due to want of maturity of understanding, the unsoundness of mind or the intoxication of the person doing that act, or by reason of any misconception on the part of that person, however, every person has the same right of private defence against that act which he would have if the act were that offence.

Clause 37 of the Bill seeks to provide certain acts against which the right of private defence does not extend.

It further explains that A person is not deprived of the right of private defence against an act done, or attempted to be done, by a public servant, as such, unless he knows or has reason to believe, that the person doing the act is such public servant and a person is not deprived of the right of private defence against an act done, or attempted to be done, by the direction of a public servant, unless he knows, or has reason to believe, that the person doing the act is acting by such direction, or unless such person states the authority under which he acts, or if he has authority in writing, unless he produces such authority, if demanded.

Clause 38 of the Bill seeks to provide for certain circumstances where the right of private defence of the body extends to causing death.

Clause 39 of the Bill seeks to provide that if the offence be not of any of the descriptions specified in clause 38, the right of private defence of the body does not extend to the voluntary causing of death to the assailant, but does extend, under the restrictions specified in clause 37, to the voluntary causing to the assailant of any harm other than death.

Clause 40 of the Bill seeks to provide that the right of private defence of the body commences as soon as a reasonable apprehension of danger to the body arises from an attempt or threat to commit the offence though the offence may not have been committed; and it continues as long as such apprehension of danger to the body continues.

Clause 41 of the Bill seeks to provides that the right of private defence of property extends, under the restrictions specified in clause 37, to the voluntary causing of death or of any other harm to the wrong-doer, if the offence, the committing of which, or the attempting to commit which, occasions the exercise of the right, be an offence of any of the descriptions provided under this clause.

Clause 42 of the Bill seeks to provide the circumstances when the right of private defence of property extends to causing any harm other than death.

Clause 43 of the Bill seeks to provide that the right of private defence of property starts as soon as reasonable apprehension of danger to the property commences and continues as long as such apprehension continues under given circumstances under this clause.

Clause 44 of the Bill seeks to provide that if in the exercise of the right of private defence against an assault which reasonably causes the apprehension of death and the defender be so situated that he cannot effectually exercise that right without risk of harm to an innocent person, his right of private defence extends to the running of that risk.

Clause 45 of the Bill seeks to provide the meaning of abetment to mean that instigation by any person to do a thing, or engages with one or more other person or persons in any conspiracy for the doing of that thing, if an act or illegal omission takes place in pursuance of that conspiracy, and in order to the doing of that thing, or intentionally aids, by any act or illegal omission, the doing of that thing.

It further explains that a person who, by wilful misrepresentation, or by wilful concealment of a material fact which he is bound to disclose, voluntarily causes or procures, or attempts to cause or procure, a thing to be done, is said to instigate the doing of that thing and Whoever, either prior to or at the time of the commission of an act, does anything in order to facilitate the commission of that act, and thereby facilitates the commission thereof, is said to aid the doing of that act.

Clause 46 of the Bill seeks to provide that a person abets an offence, who abets either the commission of an offence, or the commission of an act which would be an offence, if committed by a person capable by law of committing an offence with the same intention or knowledge as that of the abettor.

It further explains the essentials of abetment.

Clause 47 of the Bill seeks to provide that a person abets an offence within the meaning of this Sanhita who, in India, abets the commission of any act without and beyond India which would constitute an offence if committed in India.

Clause 48 of the Bill seeks to provide that a person abets an offence within the meaning of this Sanhita who, without and beyond India, abets the commission of any act in India which would constitute an offence if committed in India.

Clause 49 of the Bill seeks to provide for the punishment of abetment if the act abetted is committed in consequence and where no express provision is made for its punishment.

It further explains an act or offence is said to be committed in consequence of abetment, when it is committed in consequence of the instigation, or in pursuance of the conspiracy, or with the aid which constitutes the abetment.

Clause 50 of the Bill seeks to provide that punishment of abetment if person abetted does act with different intention from that of abettor.

Clause 51 of the Bill seeks to provide that when an Act is abetted and a different act is done, the abettor is liable for the act done, in the same manner and to the same extent as if he had directly abetted it, provided that the act done was a probable consequence of the abetment, and was committed under the influence of the instigation, or with the aid or in pursuance of the conspiracy which constituted the abetment.

Clause 52 of the Bill seeks to provide that if the act for which the abettor is liable under clause 51 is committed in addition to the act abetted, and constitute a distinct offence, the abettor is liable to punishment for each of the offences.

Clause 53 of the Bill seeks to provide that when an act is abetted with the intention on the part of the abettor of causing a particular effect, and an act for which the abettor is liable in consequence of the abetment, causes a different effect from that intended by the abettor, the abettor is liable for the effect caused, in the same manner and to the same extent as if he had abetted the act with the intention of causing that effect, provided he knew that the act abetted was likely to cause that effect.

Clause 54 of the Bill seeks to provide that whenever any person, who is absent would be liable to be punished as an abettor, is present when the act or offence for which he would be punishable in consequence of the abetment is committed, he shall be deemed to have committed such act or offence.

Clause 55 of the Bill seeks to provide that whoever abets the commission of an offence punishable with death or imprisonment for life, shall, if that offence be not committed in consequence of the abetment, and no express provision is made under this Sanhita for the punishment of such abetment, be punished with imprisonment of either description for a term which may extend to seven years, and shall also be liable to fine; and if any act for which the abettor is liable in consequence of the abetment, and which causes hurt to any person, is done, the abettor shall be liable to imprisonment of either description for a term which may extend to fourteen years, and shall also be liable to fine.

Clause 56 of the Bill seeks to provide *inter alia,* that whoever abets an offence punishable with imprisonment shall, if that offence be not committed in consequence of the

abetment, and no express provision is made under this Sanhita for the punishment of such abetment, be punished with imprisonment of any description provided for that offence for a term which may extend to one-fourth part of the longest term provided for that offence; or with such fine as is provided for that offence, or with both.

Clause 57 of the Bill seeks to provide that whoever abets the commission of an offence by the public generally or by any number or class of persons exceeding ten, shall be punished with imprisonment of either description for a term which may extend to seven years and with fine.

Clause 58 of the Bill seeks to provide punishment for three years and seven years with fine stating whoever intending to facilitate or knowing it to be likely that he will thereby facilitate the commission of an offence punishable with death or imprisonment for life, voluntarily conceals by any act or omission, or by the use of encryption or any other information hiding tool, the existence of a design to commit such offence or makes any representation which he knows to be false respecting such design .

Clause 59 of the Bill seeks to provide for punishment to the public servant for concealing design of offence and thereby intending to facilitate such offence which it is his duty as such public servant to prevent the said offence.

Clause 60 of the Bill seeks to provide for punishment where a person intending to facilitate or knowing it to be likely that he will thereby facilitate the commission of an offence punishable with imprisonment, voluntarily conceals, by any act or illegal omission, the existence of a design to commit such offence, or makes any representation which he knows to be false respecting such design.

Clause 61 of the Bill seeks to provide that when two or more persons agree to do, or cause to be done an illegal act, or an act which is not illegal by illegal means, such an agreement is designated a criminal conspiracy.

It further explains that it is immaterial whether the illegal act is the ultimate object of such agreement, or is merely incidental to that object. It also provides punishment for being a party to a criminal conspiracy.

Clause 62 of the Bill seeks to provide for punishment for attempting to commit offences, which is punishable with imprisonment for life or other imprisonment, for a term which may extend to one-half of the imprisonment for life or, as the case may be, one half of the longest term of imprisonment provided for that offence, or with such fine as is provided for the offence, or with both.

Clause 63 of the Bill seeks to provide for definition of rape and such circumstances under which the offence shall be treated as rape.

It further explains the "vagina" and "consent" for the purposes of this clause.

It further provides in *Exceptions* 1 and 2 that a medical procedure or intervention shall not constitute rape and sexual intercourse or sexual acts by a man with his own wife, the wife not being under eighteen years of age, is not rape.

Clause 64 of the Bill seeks to provide punishment with rigorous imprisonment of either description for a term which shall not be less than ten years, but which may extend to imprisonment for life, and shall also be liable to fine.

It also provides punishment with rigorous imprisonment for rape when committed by persons such as police officer, public servant, being a member of armed forces, staff of jail etc., which may extend to for a term which shall not be less than ten years but which may extend to imprisonment for life, which shall mean imprisonment for the remainder of that person's natural life, and shall also be liable to fine.

It further explains the terms "armed forces", "hospitals" "police officer" and "women's or children's institution".

Clause 65 of the Bill seeks to provide that whoever, commits rape on a woman under sixteen years of age shall be punished with rigorous imprisonment for a term which shall not be less than twenty years, but which may extend to imprisonment for life, which shall mean imprisonment for the remainder of that person's natural life, and shall also be liable to fine.

It further provides that whoever, commits rape on a woman under twelve years of age shall be punished with rigorous imprisonment for a term which shall not be less than twenty years, but which may extend to imprisonment for life, which shall mean imprisonment for the remainder of that person's natural life, and with fine or with death.

It also provides that such fine shall be just and reasonable to meet the medical expenses and rehabilitation of the victim and any fine imposed under sub-clause (*2*) shall be paid to the victim.

Clause 66 of the Bill seeks to provide for punishment for rape, if in the course of commission of rape inflicts an injury which causes the death of the woman or causes the woman to be in a persistent vegetative state, with rigorous imprisonment for a term which shall not be less than twenty years, but which may extend to imprisonment for life, which shall mean imprisonment for the remainder of that person's natural life, or with death.

Clause 67 of the Bill seeks to provide for punishment of a person to two years which may extend to seven years and also liable for fine if such person commits sexual intercourse with his own wife during separation whether under a decree of separation or otherwise, without her consent.

It further explains the term "sexual intercourse".

Clause 68 of the Bill seeks to provide for punishment of rape, when committed by a person who is in a position of authority or in a fiduciary relationship such as public servant, superintendent or manager of jail, staff under the management of hospital etc., for term which shall not less than five years but may extend to ten years and also with fine.

It further explains the terms "sexual intercourse", "vagina" "Superintendent" and

"hospitals, women's or children's institution".

Clause 69 of the Bill seeks to provide that whoever, by deceitful means or making by promise to marry to a woman without any intention of fulfilling the same, and has sexual intercourse with her, such sexual intercourse not amounting to the offence of rape, shall be punished with imprisonment of either description for a term which may extend to ten years and shall also be liable to fine.

It further explains the term "deceitful means".

Clause 70 of the Bill seeks to provide for punishment for gang rape, by one or more persons, to rigorous imprisonment for a term which shall not be less than twenty years, but which may extend to life which shall mean imprisonment for the remainder of that person's natural life, and with fine and also provide for punishment for imprisonment for life or with death when a gang rape is committed with a woman under eighteen years of age.

It further proposed that such fine shall be just and reasonable to meet the medical expenses and rehabilitation of the victim and any fine imposed under this sub-clause shall be paid to the victim.

Clause 71 of the Bill seeks to provide for punishment for a repeat offender, previously convicted of an offence punishable under clauses 64, 65, 66 or clause 67 and is subsequently convicted for said clauses, with imprisonment for life which shall mean imprisonment for the remainder of that person's natural life, or with death.

Clause 72 of the Bill seeks to provide for punishment to offender who prints or publishes, the name or any matter which may make known the identity of any person against whom an offence under clauses 64, 65, 66, 67, 68, 69, 70 or clause 71 is alleged or found to have been committed (hereafter in this clause referred to as the victim), with imprisonment of either description for a term which may extend to two years and shall also be liable to fine subject to certain conditions.

It further provides conditions under which sub-clause (*1*) shall not apply.

It also explains the term "recognised welfare institution or organisation" and the printing or publication of the judgment of any High Court or the Supreme Court does not amount to an offence within the meaning of this clause.

Clause 73 of the Bill seeks to provide that whoever prints or publishes any matter relating to any Court proceeding with respect to any offence referred to in section 72 without previous permission of such Court shall be punished with imprisonment up to two years and fine.

Clause 74 of the Bill seeks to provide that whoever assaults or uses criminal force to any woman, intending to outrage or knowing it to be likely that he will thereby outrage her modesty, shall be punished with imprisonment of either description for a term which shall not be less than one year but which may extend to five years, and shall also be liable to fine.

Clause 75 of the Bill seeks to provide punishment for sexual harassment, such as physical contact and advances involving unwelcome and explicit sexual overtures; or a demand or request for sexual favours; or showing pornography against the will of a woman; with rigorous imprisonment for a term which may extend to three years, or with fine, or with both and for making sexually coloured remarks, with imprisonment of either description for a term which may extend to one year, or with fine, or with both.

Clause 76 of the Bill seeks to provide that whoever assaults or uses criminal force to any woman or abets such act with the intention of disrobing or compelling her to be naked, shall be punished with imprisonment of either description for a term which shall not be less than three years but which may extend to seven years, and shall also be liable to fine.

Clause 77 of the Bill seeks to provide for punishment that whoever watches, or captures the image of a woman engaging in a private act in circumstances where she would usually have the expectation of not being observed either by the perpetrator or by any other person at the behest of the perpetrator or disseminates such image.

It further explains the term "private act" and where the victim consents to the capture of the images or any act, but not to their dissemination to third persons and where such image or act is disseminated, such dissemination shall be considered an offence under this clause.

Clause 78 of the Bill seeks to define the offence of staking and punishment thereof.

Clause 79 of the Bill seeks to provide for punishment for intending to insult the modesty of any woman, utters any words, makes any sound or gesture, or exhibits any object in any form, intending that such word or sound shall be heard, or that such gesture or object shall be seen, by such woman, or intrudes upon the privacy of such woman, with simple imprisonment for a term which may extend to three years, and also with fine.

Clause 80 of the Bill seeks to provide where the death of a woman is caused by any burns or bodily injury or occurs otherwise than under normal circumstances within seven years of her marriage and it is shown that soon before her death she was subjected to cruelty or harassment by her husband or any relative of her husband for, or in connection with, any demand for dowry, such death shall be called "dowry death", and such husband or relative shall be deemed to have caused her death.

It also provides punishment for dowry death with imprisonment for a term which shall not be less than seven years but which may extend to imprisonment for life and explains that "dowry" shall have the same meaning as in section 2 of the Dowry Prohibition Act, 1961.

Clause 81 of the Bill seeks to provide punishment for cohabitation or sexual intercourse by a man deceitfully inducing a woman to belief of lawful marriage, with imprisonment of either description for a term which may extend to ten years, and shall also be liable to fine.

Clause 82 of the Bill seeks to provide that whoever, having a husband or wife living, marries in any case in which such marriage is void by reason of its taking place during the life of such husband or wife, shall be punished with imprisonment of either description for a term which may extend to seven years, and shall also be liable to fine.

It further provides in *Exception* that when sub-clause (*1*) of this clause shall not apply.

Clause 83 of the Bill seeks to provide that whoever, dishonestly or with a fraudulent intention, goes through the ceremony of being married, knowing that he is not thereby lawfully married, shall be punished with imprisonment of either description for a term which may extend to seven years, and shall also be liable to fine.

Clause 84 of the Bill seeks to provide that whoever takes or entices away any woman who is and whom he knows or has reason to believe to be the wife of any other man, with intent that she may have illicit intercourse with any person, or conceals or detains with that intent any such woman, shall be punished with imprisonment of either description for a term which may extend to two years, or with fine, or with both.

Clause 85 of the Bill seeks to provide that whoever, being the husband or the relative of the husband of a woman, subjects such woman to cruelty shall be punished with imprisonment for a term which may extend to three years and shall also be liable to fine.

Clause 86 of the Bill defines the term "cruelty" for the purposes of clause 85.

Clause 87 of the Bill seeks to provide for punishment for kidnapping abducting or inducing woman to compel her marriage against her will for illicit intercourse, with an imprisonment for a term which may extend to ten years, and shall also be liable to fine.

Clause 88 of the Bill seeks to provide for punishment for causing voluntary miscarriage if not caused for good faith for the purpose of saving the life of the woman, with imprisonment for a term which may extend to three years, or with fine, or with both; and, if the woman be quick with child, shall be punished with imprisonment of either description for a term which may extend to seven years, and shall also be liable to fine.

It further explains that a woman who causes herself to miscarry, is within the meaning of this clause.

Clause 89 of the Bill seeks to provide punishment for miscarriage without consent of woman, for a term which may extend to ten years and also for fine.

Clause 90 of the Bill seeks to provide that punishment whoever, with intent to cause the miscarriage of a woman with child, does any act which causes the death of such woman, shall be punished with imprisonment of either description for a term which may extend to ten years, and shall also be liable to fine; and when done without the consent of woman with imprisonment for life or which may extend to ten years or with fine.

It further explains that it is not essential to this offence that the offender should know that the act is likely to cause death.

Clause 91 of the Bill seeks to provide that whoever before the birth of any child does any act with the intention of thereby preventing that child from being born alive or causing it to die after its birth, and does by such act prevent that child from being born alive, or causes it to die after its birth, shall, if such act be not caused in good faith for the purpose of saving the life of the mother, be punished with imprisonment of either description for a term which may extend to ten years, or with fine, or with both.

Clause 92 of the Bill seeks to provide that whoever does any act under such circumstances, that if he thereby caused death he would be guilty of culpable homicide, and does by such act cause the death of a quick unborn child, shall be punished with imprisonment of either description for a term which may extend to ten years, and shall also be liable to fine.

Clause 93 of the Bill seeks to provide that whoever being the father or mother of a child under the age of twelve years, or having the care of such child, shall expose or leave such child in any place with the intention of wholly abandoning such child, shall be punished with imprisonment of either description for a term which may extend to seven years, or with fine, or with both.

It further explains that this clause is not intended to prevent the trial of the offender for murder or culpable homicide, as the case may be, if the child die in consequence of the exposure.

Clause 94 of the Bill seeks to provide that whoever, by secretly burying or otherwise disposing of the dead body of a child whether such child die before or after or during its birth, intentionally conceals or endeavours to conceal the birth of such child, shall be punished with imprisonment of either description for a term which may extend to two years, or with fine, or with both.

Clause 95 of the Bill seeks to provide that whoever hires, employs or engages any child to commit an offence shall be punished with imprisonment of either description which shall not be less than three years but which may extend to ten years, and with fine; and if the offence be committed shall also be punished with the punishment provided for that offence or fine provided for that offence as if the offence has been committed by such person himself.

It further explains that hiring, employing, engaging or using a child for sexual exploitation or pornography is covered within the meaning of this clause.

Clause 96 of the Bill seeks to provide that whoever, by any means whatsoever, induces any child to go from any place or to do any act with intent that such child may be, or knowing that it is likely that such child will be, forced or seduced to illicit intercourse with another person shall be punishable with imprisonment which may extend to ten years, and shall also be liable to fine.

Clause 97 of the Bill seeks to provide that whoever kidnaps or abducts any child under the age of ten years with the intention of taking dishonestly any movable property from the person of such child, shall be punished with imprisonment of either description for a term which may extend to seven years, and shall also be liable to fine.

Clause 98 of the Bill seeks to provide that whoever sells, lets to hire, or otherwise disposes of child with intent that such child shall at any age be employed or used for the purpose of prostitution or illicit intercourse with any person or for any unlawful and immoral purpose, or knowing it to be likely that such child will at any age be employed or used for any such purpose, shall be punished with imprisonment of either description for a term which may extend to ten years, and shall also be liable to fine.

It further explains that when a female under the age of eighteen years is sold, let for hire, or otherwise disposed of to a prostitute or to any person who keeps or manages a brothel, the person so disposing of such female shall, until the contrary is proved, be presumed to have disposed of her with the intent that she shall be used for the purpose of prostitution and also to explain the term "illicit intercourse".

Clause 99 of the Bill seeks to provide that whoever buys, hires or otherwise obtains possession of any child with intent that such child shall at any age be employed or used for the purpose of prostitution or illicit intercourse with any person or for any unlawful and immoral purpose, or knowing it to be likely that such child will at any age be employed or used for any such purpose, shall be punished with imprisonment of either description for a term which shall not be less than seven years but which may extend to fourteen years, and shall also be liable to fine.

It further explains that any prostitute or any person keeping or managing a brothel, who buys, hires or otherwise obtains possession of a female under the age of eighteen years shall, until the contrary is proved, be presumed to have obtained possession of such female with the intent that she shall be used for the purpose of prostitution and also to explain the term "illicit intercourse".

Clause 100 of the Bill seeks to provide that whoever causes death by doing an act with the intention of causing death, or with the intention of causing such bodily injury as is likely to cause death, or with the knowledge that he is likely by such act to cause death, commits the offence of culpable homicide.

It further explains that when bodily injury shall be deemed to have caused the death and causing of the death of a child in the mother's womb is not homicide. But it may amount to culpable homicide to cause the death of a living child, if any part of that child has been brought forth, though the child may not have breathed or been completely born.

Clause 101 of the Bill seeks to provide that the culpable homicide is murder under the given circumstances.

It is proposed to insert *Exceptions* 1 to 5 to provide that when culpable homicide is not murder.

Clause 102 of the Bill seeks to provide that if a person, by doing anything which he intends or knows to be likely to cause death, commits culpable homicide by causing the death of any person, whose death he neither intends nor knows himself to be likely to cause, the culpable homicide committed by the offender is of the description of which it would have been if he had caused the death of the person whose death he intended or knew himself to be likely to cause.

Clause 103 of the Bill seeks to provide punishment for murder which shall be punished with death or imprisonment for life, and also fine. Sub-clause (*2*) further provides that when a murder is committed by a group of five or more persons acting in concert on the ground of race, caste or community, sex, place of birth, language, personal belief or any other similar ground each member of such group shall be punished with death or with imprisonment for life and shall also be liable to fine.

Clause 104 of the Bill seeks to provide that whoever, being under sentence of imprisonment for life, commits murder, shall be punished with death or with imprisonment for life, which shall mean the remainder of that person's natural life.

Clause 105 of the Bill seeks to provide the punishment for culpable homicide not amounting to murder.

Clause 106 of the Bill seeks to provide that whoever causes death of any person by doing any rash or negligent act not amounting to culpable homicide, shall be punished with imprisonment of either description for a term which may extend to five years and shall also be

liable to fine. It further provides that whoever causes death of any person by rash and negligent driving of vehicle not amounting to culpable homicide and escapes without reporting it to a police officer or a Magistrate soon after the incident, shall be punished with imprisonment of either description of a term which may extend to ten years and shall also be liable to fine.

Clause 107 of the Bill seeks to provide that if any child, any person with unsound mind, any delirious person or any person in a state of intoxication, commits suicide, whoever abets the commission of such suicide, shall be punished with death or imprisonment for life, or imprisonment for a term not exceeding ten years, and shall also be liable to fine.

Clause 108 of the Bill seeks to provide that if any person commits suicide, whoever abets the commission of such suicide, shall be punished with imprisonment of either description for a term which may extend to ten years, and shall also be liable to fine.

Clause 109 of the Bill seeks to provide punishment for attempt to murder and if by that death is caused, he would be guilty of murder and shall be punished with imprisonment which may extend to ten years and also for fine and further provides that if hurt is caused by such act the punishment shall be imprisonment for life, or with fine, or with both.

Clause 110 of the Bill seeks to define attempt to commit culpable homicide not amounting to murder and provides for punishment which may extend to three years, or with fine, or with both; and, if hurt is caused to any person by such act, shall be punished with imprisonment of either description for a term which may extend to seven years, or with fine, or with both.

Clause 111 of the Bill seeks to define organised crime to mean that any continuing unlawful activity including kidnapping, robbery, vehicle theft, extortion, land grabbing, contract killing, economic offence, cyber-crimes, trafficking of persons, drugs, weapons or illicit goods or services, human trafficking for prostitution or ransom, by any person or a group of persons acting in concert, singly or jointly, either as a member of an organised crime syndicate or on behalf of such syndicate, by use of violence, threat of violence, intimidation, coercion, or by any other unlawful means to obtain direct or indirect, material benefit including a financial benefit, shall constitute organised crime.

It further explains the terms "organised crime syndicate", "continuing unlawful activity" and "economic offence".

It further provides imprisonment and fine.

Clause 112 of the Bill seeks to define petty organised crime as whoever, being a member of a group or gang, either singly or jointly, commits any act of theft, snatching, cheating, unauthorised selling of tickets, unauthorised betting or gambling, selling of public examination question papers or any other similar criminal act, is said to commit petty organised crime.

It further explains the term "theft".

It also provides that whoever commits any petty organised crime shall be punished with imprisonment for a term which shall not be less than one year but which may extend to seven years, and shall also be liable to fine.

Clause 113 of the Bill seeks to provide that whoever does any act with the intent to threaten or likely to threaten the unity, integrity, sovereignty, security, or economic security of India or with the intent to strike terror or likely to strike terror in the people or any section of the people in India or in any foreign country in the given circumstances, committed terrorist act.

It further explains the terms "public functionary" and "counterfeit Indian currency". It also provides punishment of imprisonment, fine

It also explains that the officer not below the rank of Superintendent of Police shall decide whether to register the case under this clause or under the Unlawful Activities (Prevention) Act, 1967.

Clause 114 of the Bill seeks to provide whoever causes bodily pain, disease or infirmity to any person is said to cause hurt.

Clause 115 of the Bill seeks to define voluntarily causing hurt and punishment thereof.

Clause 116 of the Bill seeks to provide that hurt namely, emasculation, permanent privation of the sight of either eye, permanent privation of the hearing of either ear privation of any member or joint, destruction or permanent impairing of the powers of any member or joint, permanent disfiguration of the head or face, fracture or dislocation of a bone or tooth, and any hurt which endangers life or which causes the sufferer to be during the space of fifteen days in severe bodily pain, or unable to follow his ordinary pursuits are grievous hurt.

Clause 117 of the Bill seeks to define voluntarily causing grievous hurt and punishment thereof.

It further explains that a person is not said voluntarily to cause grievous hurt except when he both causes grievous hurt and intends or knows himself to be likely to cause grievous hurt, however, he is said voluntarily to cause grievous hurt, if intending or knowing himself to be likely to cause grievous hurt of one kind, he actually causes grievous hurt of another kind.

Clause 118 of the Bill seeks to define voluntarily causing hurt or grievous hurt by dangerous weapons or means and punishment thereof.

Clause 119 of the Bill seeks to define voluntarily causing hurt or grievous hurt to extort property, or to constrain to an illegal to an act and punishment thereof.

Clause 120 of the Bill seeks to define voluntarily causing hurt or grievous hurt to extort confession, or to compel restoration of property and punishment thereof.

Clause 121 of the Bill seeks to define voluntarily causing hurt or grievous hurt to deter public servant from his duty and punishment thereof.

Clause 122 of the Bill seeks to define voluntarily causing hurt or grievous hurt on provocation and punishment thereof.

It further explains that this clause is subject to the same proviso as *Exception* 1 of clause 101.

Clause 123 of the Bill seeks to define causing hurt by means of poison, etc., with intent to commit an offence and punishment thereof.

Clause 124 of the Bill seeks to define voluntarily causing grievous hurt by use of acid, etc., and punishment thereof.

It further explains the term "acid" and permanent or partial damage or deformity or permanent vegetative state shall not be required to be irreversible for the purpose of this clause.

Clause 125 of the Bill seeks to define act endangering life or personal safety of others and punishment for such act, hurt and grievous hurt.

Clause 126 of the Bill seeks to define wrongful restraint and punishment thereof.

It further provides that the obstruction of a private way over land or water which a person in good faith believes himself to have a lawful right to obstruct, is not an offence within the meaning of this clause.

Clause 127 of the Bill seeks to define wrongful confinement and punishment thereof.

Clause 128 of the Bill seeks to define force.

Clause 129 of the Bill seeks to define criminal force as whoever intentionally uses force to any person, without that person's consent, in order to the committing of any offence, or intending by the use of such force to cause, or knowing it to be likely that by the use of such force he will cause injury, fear or annoyance to the person to whom the force is used, is said to use criminal force to that other.

Clause 130 of the Bill seeks to define assault.

It further provides that mere words do not amount to an assault. But the words which a person uses may give to his gestures or preparation such a meaning as may make those gestures or preparations amount to an assault.

Clause 131 of the Bill seeks to provide punishment for assault or criminal force otherwise than on grave provocation.

It further provides that under given circumstances grave and sudden provocation will not mitigate the punishment for an offence under this clause and whether the provocation was grave and sudden enough to mitigate the offence, is a question of fact.

Clause 132 of the Bill seeks to provide punishment for assault or criminal force to deter public servant from discharge of his duty.

Clause 133 of the Bill seeks to provide punishment for assault or criminal force with intent to dishonour person, otherwise than on grave provocation.

Clause 134 of the Bill seeks to provide punishment assault or criminal force in attempt to commit theft of property carried by a person.

Clause 135 of the Bill seeks to provide punishment assault or criminal force in attempt wrongfully to confine a person.

Clause 136 of the Bill seeks to provide punishment assault or criminal force on grave provocation.

Clause 137 of the Bill seeks to define kidnapping from India and from Lawful

Guardianship and punishment thereof.

It further explains the term "lawful guardian" and this clause does not extend to the act of any person who in good faith believes himself to be the father of an illegitimate child or who in good faith believes himself to be entitled to the lawful custody of such child, unless such act is committed for an immoral or unlawful purpose.

Clause 138 of the Bill seeks to provide that whoever by force compels, or by any deceitful means induces, any person to go from any place, is said to abduct that person.

Clause 139 of the Bill seeks to define kidnapping or maiming a child for purposes of begging and punishment thereof and also define the begging for the purpose of this clause.

Clause 140 of the Bill seeks to provide for kidnapping or abducting in order to murder or for ransom, etc., and punishment thereof.

Clause 141 of the Bill seeks to provide for importation of girl or boy from foreign country and punishment thereof.

Clause 142 of the Bill seeks to provide for wrongfully concealing or keeping in confinement, kidnapped or abducted person punishment thereof.

Clause 143 of the Bill seeks to provide for means and purposes of trafficking of person and punishment thereof.

It further explains the term "trafficking" and "consent of the victim".

Clause 144 of the Bill seeks to provide for exploitation of a trafficked person and punishment thereof.

It *inter alia* provides that whoever, knowingly or having reason to believe that a child has been trafficked, engages such child for sexual exploitation in any manner, shall be punished with rigorous imprisonment for a term which shall not be less than five years, but which may extend to ten years, and shall also be liable to fine.

Clause 145 of the Bill seeks to provide for habitual dealing in slaves and punishment thereof.

Clause 146 of the Bill seeks to provide for unlawful compulsory labour and punishment thereof.

Clause 147 of the Bill seeks to provide that whoever wages war against the Government of India, or attempts to wage such war, or abets the waging of such war, shall be punished with death, or imprisonment for life and shall also be liable to fine.

Clause 148 of the Bill seeks to provide for conspiracy to commit offences punishable by clause 147 and punishment thereof.

It further provides that to constitute a conspiracy under this clause, it is not necessary that any act or illegal omission shall take place in pursuance thereof.

Clause 149 of the Bill seeks to provide for collecting arms, etc., with intention of waging war against the Government of India and punishment thereof.

Clause 150 of the Bill seeks to provide for concealing with intent to facilitate design to wage war and punishment thereof.

Clause 151 of the Bill seeks to provide for assaulting President, Governor, etc., with intent to compel or restrain the exercise of any lawful power and punishment thereof.

Clause 152 of the Bill seeks to provide for acts endangering sovereignty unity and integrity of India and punishment thereof.

It further provides that comments expressing disapprobation of the measures, or administrative or other action of the Government with a view to obtain their alteration by lawful means without exciting or attempting to excite the activities referred to in this Clause do not constitute an offence under this clause.

Clause 153 of the Bill seeks to provide for waging war against Government of any foreign State at peace with the Government of India and punishment thereof.

Clause 154 of the Bill seeks to provide for committing depredation on territories of foreign State at peace with the Government of India and punishment thereof.

Clause 155 of the Bill seeks to provide for receiving property taken by war or depredation mentioned in clauses 153 and 154 and punishment thereof.

Clause 156 of the Bill seeks to provide for public servant voluntarily allowing prisoner of state or war to escape and punishment thereof.

Clause 157 of the Bill seeks to provide for public servant negligently suffering such prisoner to escape and punishment thereof.

Clause 158 of the Bill seeks to provide for aiding escape of, rescuing or harbouring such prisoner and punishment thereof.

It further provides that State prisoner or prisoner of war, who is permitted to be at large on his parole within certain limits in India, is said to escape from lawful custody if he goes beyond the limits within which he is allowed to be at large.

Clause 159 of the Bill seeks to provide that whoever abets the committing of mutiny by an officer, soldier, sailor or airman, in theArmy, Navy orAir Force of the Government of India or attempts to seduce any such officer, soldier, sailor or airman from his allegiance or his duty, shall be punished with imprisonment for life, or with imprisonment of either description for a term which may extend to ten years, and shall also be liable to fine.

Clause 160 of the Bill seeks to provide for abetment of mutiny, if mutiny is committed in consequence and punishment thereof.

Clause 161 of the Bill seeks to provide for abetment of assault by soldier, sailor or airman on his superior officer, when in execution of his office and punishment thereof.

Clause 162 of the Bill seeks to provide that whoever abets an assault by an officer, soldier, sailor or airman, in the Army, Navy or Air Force of the Government of India, on any superior officer being in the execution of his office, shall, if such assault be committed in consequence of that abetment be punished with imprisonment of either description for a term which may extend to seven years, and shall also be liable to fine.

Clause 163 of the Bill seeks to provide that whoever abets the desertion of any officer, soldier, sailor or airman, in the Army, Navy orAir Force of the Government of India, shall be punished with imprisonment of either description for a term which may extend to two years, or with fine, or with both.

Clause 164 of the Bill seeks to provide for harbouring deserter and punishment thereof. It further provides in the *Exception* that this provision does not extend to the case in

which the harbour is given by the spouse of the deserter.

Clause 165 of the Bill seeks to provide for deserter concealed on board, merchant vessel through negligence of master and punishment thereof.

Clause 166 of the Bill seeks to provide for abetment of act of insubordination by soldier, sailor or airman and punishment thereof.

Clause 167 of the Bill seeks to provide that no person subject to the Air Force Act, 1950, the Army Act, 1950 and the Navy Act, 1957, or shall be subject to punishment under this Sanhita for any of the offences defined in this Chapter.

Clause 168 of the Bill seeks to provide for wearing garb or carrying token used by soldier, sailor or airman and punishment thereof.

Clause 169 of the Bill seeks to define "candidate" and "electoral right".

Clause 170 of the Bill seeks to provide provisions for bribery relating to electoral right. It *inter alia* provides that whoever gives a gratification to any person with the object

of inducing him or any other person to exercise any electoral right or of rewarding any person for having exercised any such right; or accepts either for himself or for any other person any gratification as a reward for exercising any such right or for inducing or attempting to induce any other person to exercise any such right, commits the offence of bribery.

Clause 171 of the Bill seeks to define undue influence at elections under given circumstances.

It also provides that a declaration of public policy or a promise of public action or the mere exercise or a legal right without intent to interfere with an electoral right, shall not be deemed to be interference within the meaning of this clause.

Clause 172 of the Bill seeks to define personation at elections.

Clause 173 of the Bill seeks to provide that whoever commits the offence of bribery shall be punished with imprisonment of either description for a term which may extend to one year, or with fine, or with both. However, bribery by treating shall be punished with fine only.

It further explains that "treating" means that form of bribery where the gratification consists in food, drink, entertainment, or provision.

Clause 174 of the Bill seeks to provide punishment for undue influence or personation at an election.

Clause 175 of the Bill seeks to provide for false statement in connection with an election and punishment of fine.

Clause 176 of the Bill seeks to provide for illegal payments in connection with an election and punishment thereof.

Clause 177 of the Bill seeks to provide for failure to keep election account and punishment thereof.

Clause 178 of the Bill seeks to provide for counterfeiting coin, Government stamps, currency-notes or bank-notes and punishment thereof.

It further explains the terms "bank-note", "coin", "counterfeiting Government stamp" and "counterfeiting coin".

Clause 179 of the Bill seeks to provide for using as genuine, forged or counterfeit coin, Government stamp, currency-notes or bank-notes and punishment thereof.

Clause 180 of the Bill seeks to provide for possession of forged or counterfeit coin, Government stamp, currency-notes or bank-notes and punishment thereof.

It further explains that if a person establishes the possession of the forged or counterfeit coin, stamp, currency-note or bank-note to be from a lawful source, it shall not constitute an offence under this clause.

Clause 181 of the Bill seeks to provide for making or possessing instruments or materials for forging or counterfeiting coin, Government stamp, currency notes or bank-notes and punishment thereof.

Clause 182 of the Bill seeks to provide for making or using documents resembling currency-notes or bank-notes and punishment thereof.

Clause 183 of the Bill seeks to provide for effacing writing from substance bearing Government stamp, or removing from document a stamp used for it, with intent to cause loss to Government and punishment thereof.

Clause 184 of the Bill seeks to provide for using Government stamp known to have been before used and punishment thereof.

Clause 185 of the Bill seeks to provide for fraudulently or with intent to cause loss to Government, erases or removes from a stamp issued by Government for the purpose of revenue, any mark, put or impressed upon such stamp for the purpose of denoting that the same has been used, or knowingly has in his possession or sells or disposes of any such stamp from which such mark has been erased or removed, or sells or disposes of any such stamp which he knows to have been used, and punishment thereof.

Clause 186 of the Bill seeks to provide for prohibition of fictitious stamps and punishment thereof.

Clause 187 of the Bill seeks to provide for, being employed in any mint lawfully established in India, does any act, or omits what he is legally bound to do, with the intention of causing any coin issued from that mint to be of a different weight or composition from the weight or composition fixed by law, and punishment thereof.

Clause 188 of the Bill seeks to provide for unlawfully taking coining instrument from mint and punishment thereof.

Clause 189 of the Bill seeks to provide that under given common objects an assembly of five or more persons is designated an "unlawful assembly".

It further provides the punishment for unlawful assembly.

It also explains that an assembly which was not unlawful when it assembled, may subsequently become an unlawful assembly.

Clause 190 of the Bill seeks to provide that if an offence is committed by any member of an unlawful assembly in prosecution of the common object of that assembly, or such as the members of that assembly knew to be likely to be committed in prosecution of that object, every person who, at the time of the committing of that offence, is a member of the same assembly, is guilty of that offence.

Clause 191 of the Bill seeks to provide for rioting and punishment thereof.

Clause 192 of the Bill seeks to provide for want only giving provocation with intent to cause riot- if rioting be committed; if not committed and punishment thereof.

Clause 193 of the Bill seeks to provide for liability of owner, occupier, etc., of land on which an unlawful assembly or riot takes place and punishment thereof.

Clause 194 of the Bill seeks to provide for affray and punishment thereof.

Clause 195 of the Bill seeks to provide for assaulting or obstructing public servant when suppressing riot, etc., and punishment thereof.

Clause 196 of the Bill seeks to provide for promoting enmity between different groups on ground of religion, race, place of birth, residence, language, etc., and doing acts prejudicial to maintenance of harmony and punishment thereof.

Clause 197 of the Bill seeks to provide for imputations, assertions prejudicial to national integration and punishment thereof.

Clause 198 of the Bill seeks to provide for public servant disobeying law, with intent to cause injury to any person and punishment thereof.

Clause 199 of the Bill seeks to provide for public servant disobeying direction under law and punishment thereof.

Clause 200 of the Bill seeks to provide that whoever, being in charge of a hospital, public or private, whether run by the Central Government, the State Government, local bodies or any other person, contravenes the provisions of section 397 of the Bharatiya Nagarik Suraksha Sanhita, 2023, shall be punished with imprisonment for a term which may extend to one year, or with fine, or with both.

Clause 201 of the Bill seeks to provide for public servant framing an incorrect document with intent to cause injury and punishment thereof.

Clause 202 of the Bill seeks to provide for public servant unlawfully engaging in trade and punishment thereof.

Clause 203 of the Bill seeks to provide for public servant unlawfully buying or bidding for property and punishment thereof.

Clause 204 of the Bill seeks to provide for personating a public servant and punishment thereof.

Clause 205 of the Bill seeks to provide for wearing garb or carrying token used by public servant with fraudulent intent and punishment thereof.

Clause 206 of the Bill seeks to provide for absconding to avoid service of summons or other proceeding and punishment thereof.

Clause 207 of the Bill seeks to provide for preventing service of summons or other proceeding, or preventing publication and punishment thereof.

Clause 208 of the Bill seeks to provide for non-attendance in obedience to an order from public servant and punishment thereof.

Clause 209 of the Bill seeks to provide for non-appearance in response to a proclamation under clause 84 of the Bharatiya Nagarik Suraksha Sanhita, 2023 and punishment thereof.

Clause 210 of the Bill seeks to provide for omission to produce document or electronic record to public servant by person legally bound to produce it and punishment thereof.

Clause 211 of the Bill seeks to provide for omission to give notice or information to public servant by person legally bound to give it and punishment thereof.

Clause 212 of the Bill seeks to provide for furnishing false information and punishment thereof.

It further explains the terms "offence" and "offender".

Clause 213 of the Bill seeks to provide for refusing oath or affirmation when duly required by public servant to make it and punishment thereof.

Clause 214 of the Bill seeks to provide for refusing to answer public servant authorised to question and punishment thereof.

Clause 215 of the Bill seeks to provide that whoever refuses to sign any statement made by him, when required to sign that statement by a public servant legally competent to require that he shall sign that statement, shall be punished with simple imprisonment for a term which may extend to three months, or with fine which may extend to three thousand rupees, or with both.

Clause 216 of the Bill seeks to provide for false statement on oath or affirmation to public servant or person authorised to administer an oath or affirmation and punishment thereof.

Clause 217 of the Bill seeks to provide for false information, with intent to cause public servant to use his lawful power to injury of another person and punishment thereof.

Clause 218 of the Bill seeks to provide for resistance to taking of property by lawful authority of a public servant and punishment thereof.

Clause 219 of the Bill seeks to provide for obstructing sale of property offered for sale by authority of public servant and punishment thereof.

Clause 220 of the Bill seeks to provide for illegal purchase or bid for property offered for sale by authority of public servant and punishment thereof.

Clause 221 of the Bill seeks to provide for obstructing public servant in discharge of public functions and punishment thereof.

Clause 222 of the Bill seeks to provide for omission to assist public servant when bound by law to give assistance and punishment thereof.

Clause 223 of the Bill seeks to provide for disobedience to order duly promulgated by public servant and punishment thereof.

It further provides that it is not necessary that the offender should intend to produce harm, or contemplate his disobedience as likely to produce harm. It is sufficient that he knows of the order which he disobeys, and that his disobedience produces, or is likely to produce, harm.

Clause 224 of the Bill seeks to provide for threat of injury to public servant and punishment thereof.

Clause 225 of the Bill seeks to provide for threat of injury to induce person to refrain from applying for protection to public servant and punishment thereof.

Clause 226 of the Bill seeks to provide for attempt to commit suicide to compel or restrain exercise of lawful power and punishment thereof.

Clause 227 of the Bill seeks to provide for giving false evidence. It further explains the "statement" and "false statement".

Clause 228 of the Bill seeks to provide for fabricating false evidence. *Clause* 229 of the Bill seeks to provide for punishment for false evidence. It further explains the "judicial proceeding" and "investigation".

Clause 230 of the Bill seeks to provide for giving or fabricating false evidence with intent to procure conviction of capital offence and punishment thereof.

Clause 231 of the Bill seeks to provide for giving or fabricating false evidence with intent to procure conviction of offence punishable with imprisonment for life or imprisonment and punishment thereof.

Clause 232 of the Bill seeks to provide for threatening any person to give false evidence and punishment thereof.

Clause 233 of the Bill seeks to provide for using evidence known to be false and punishment thereof.

Clause 234 of the Bill seeks to provide for issuing or signing false certificate and punishment thereof.

Clause 235 of the Bill seeks to provide for using as true a certificate known to be false and punishment thereof.

Clause 236 of the Bill seeks to provide for false statement made in declaration which is by law receivable as evidence and punishment thereof.

Clause 237 of the Bill seeks to provide for using as true such declaration knowing it to be false and punishment thereof.

It further explains the term "declaration".

Clause 238 of the Bill seeks to provide for causing disappearance of evidence of offence, or giving false information to screen offender and punishment thereof.

Clause 239 of the Bill seeks to provide for intentional omission to give information of offence by person bound to inform and punishment thereof.

Clause 240 of the Bill seeks to provide for giving false information respecting an offence committed and punishment thereof.

Clause 241 of the Bill seeks to provide for destruction of document or electronic record to prevent its production as evidence and punishment thereof.

Clause 242 of the Bill seeks to provide for false personation for purpose of act or proceeding in suit or prosecution and punishment thereof.

Clause 243 of the Bill seeks to provide for fraudulent removal or concealment of property to prevent its seizure as forfeited or in execution and punishment thereof.

Clause 244 of the Bill seeks to provide for fraudulent claim to property to prevent its seizure as forfeited or in execution and punishment thereof.

Clause 245 of the Bill seeks to provide for fraudulently suffering decree for sum not due and punishment thereof.

Clause 246 of the Bill seeks to provide that whoever fraudulently or dishonestly, or with intent to injure or annoy any person, makes in a Court any claim which he knows to be false, shall be punished with imprisonment of either description for a term which may extend to two years, and shall also be liable to fine.

Clause 247 of the Bill seeks to provide for fraudulently obtaining decree or order for sum not due and punishment thereof.

Clause 248 of the Bill seeks to provide for false charge of offence made with intent to injure and punishment thereof.

Clause 249 of the Bill seeks to provide for harbouring offender and punishment thereof. It further explains the term "Offence".

It also provides in *Exception* that this clause shall not extend to any case in which the harbour or concealment is by the spouse of the offender.

Clause 250 of the Bill seeks to provide for taking gratification, etc., to screen an offender from punishment and punishment thereof.

Clause 251 of the Bill seeks to provide for offering gratification or restoration of property in consideration of screening offender and punishment thereof.

It further provides in *Exception* that the provisions of this clause and clause 250 do not extend to any case in which the offence may lawfully be compounded.

Clause 252 of the Bill seeks to provide for taking gratification to help any person to recover stolen property, etc., and punishment thereof.

Clause 253 of the Bill seeks to provide for harbouring offender who has escaped from custody or whose apprehension has been ordered and punishment thereof.

It further explains the term "Offence" for this clause.

It is also provides in *Exception* that the provisions of this clause do not extend to the case in which the harbour or concealment is by the spouse of the person to be apprehended.

Clause 254 of the Bill seeks to provide for penalty for harbouring robbers or dacoits and punishment thereof.

It further provides that for the purposes of this clause it is immaterial whether the robbery or dacoity is intended to be committed, or has been committed, within or without India.

It is also provides in *Exception* that the provisions of this clause do not extend to the case in which the harbour is by the spouse of the offender.

Clause 255 of the Bill seeks to provide for public servant disobeying direction of law with intent to save person from punishment or property from forfeiture and punishment thereof.

Clause 256 of the Bill seeks to provide for public servant framing incorrect record or writing with intent to save person from punishment or property from forfeiture and punishment thereof.

Clause 257 of the Bill seeks to provide for public servant in judicial proceeding corruptly making report, etc., contrary to law and punishment thereof.

Clause 258 of the Bill seeks to provide for commitment for trial or confinement by person having authority who knows that he is acting contrary to law and punishment thereof.

Clause 259 of the Bill seeks to provide for intentional omission to apprehend on part of public servant bound to apprehend and punishment thereof.

Clause 260 of the Bill seeks to provide for intentional omission to apprehend on part of public servant bound to apprehend person under sentence or lawfully committed to custody and punishment thereof.

Clause 261 of the Bill seeks to provide for escape from confinement or custody negligently suffered by public servant and punishment thereof.

Clause 262 of the Bill seeks to provide for resistance or obstruction by a person to his lawful apprehension and punishment thereof.

It further explains that the punishment in this clause is in addition to the punishment for which the person to be apprehended or detained in custody was liable for the offence with which he was charged, or of which he was convicted.

Clause 263 of the Bill seeks to provide *inter alia* for resistance or obstruction to lawful apprehension of another person and punishment thereof.

Clause 264 of the Bill seeks to provide for omission to apprehend, or sufferance of escape, on part of public servant, in cases not otherwise, provided for and punishment thereof.

Clause 265 of the Bill seeks to provide for resistance or obstruction to lawful apprehension or escape or rescue in cases not otherwise provided for and punishment thereof.

Clause 266 of the Bill seeks to provide for violation of condition of remission of punishment and punishment thereof.

Clause 267 of the Bill seeks to provide for intentional insult or interruption to public servant sitting in judicial proceeding and punishment thereof.

Clause 268 of the Bill seeks to provide for personation of assessor and punishment thereof.

Clause 269 of the Bill seeks to provide for failure by person released on bail or bond to appear in court and punishment thereof.

It further provides that the punishment under this clause is in addition to and also without prejudice to the power of the Court to order forfeiture of the bond.

Clause 270 of the Bill seeks to provide for public nuisance.

Clause 271 of the Bill seeks to provide for negligent act likely to spread infection of disease dangerous to life and punishment thereof.

Clause 272 of the Bill seeks to provide for malignant act likely to spread infection of disease dangerous to life and punishment thereof.

Clause 273 of the Bill seeks to provide for disobedience to quarantine rule and punishment thereof.

Clause 274 of the Bill seeks to provide for adulteration of food or drink intended for sale and punishment thereof.

Clause 275 of the Bill seeks to provide for sale of noxious food or drink and punishment thereof.

Clause 276 of the Bill seeks to provide for adulteration of drugs and punishment thereof.

Clause 277 of the Bill seeks to provide for sale of adulterated drugs and punishment thereof.

Clause 278 of the Bill seeks to provide for sale of drug as a different drug or preparation and punishment thereof.

Clause 279 of the Bill seeks to provide for fouling water of public spring or reservoir and punishment thereof.

Clause 280 of the Bill seeks to provide for making atmosphere noxious to health and punishment thereof.

Clause 281 of the Bill seeks to provide for rash driving or riding on a public way and punishment thereof.

Clause 282 of the Bill seeks to provide for rash navigation of vessel and punishment thereof.

Clause 283 of the Bill seeks to provide for exhibition of false light, mark or buoy and punishment thereof.

Clause 284 of the Bill seeks to provide for conveying person by water for hire in unsafe or overloaded vessel and punishment thereof.

Clause 285 of the Bill seeks to provide for danger or obstruction in public way or line of navigation and punishment thereof.

Clause 286 of the Bill seeks to provide for negligent conduct with respect to poisonous substance and punishment thereof.

Clause 287 of the Bill seeks to provide for negligent conduct with respect to fire or combustible matter and punishment thereof.

Clause 288 of the Bill seeks to provide for negligent conduct with respect to explosive substance and punishment thereof.

Clause 289 of the Bill seeks to provide for negligent conduct with respect to machinery and punishment thereof.

Clause 290 of the Bill seeks to provide for negligent conduct with respect to pulling down, repairing or constructing buildings, etc., and punishment thereof.

Clause 291 of the Bill seeks to provide for negligent conduct with respect to animal and punishment thereof.

Clause 292 of the Bill seeks to provide punishment for public nuisance in cases not otherwise provided for.

Clause 293 of the Bill seeks to provide for continuance of nuisance after injunction not to repeat or continue and punishment thereof.

Clause 294 of the Bill seeks to provide for sale, etc., of obscene books, etc., and punishment thereof.

It further provides in *Exception* that in the interest of science, literature, art or learning or other objects of general concern or which is kept or used *bona fide* for religious purposes, this clause shall not apply.

Clause 295 of the Bill seeks to provide for sale, etc., of obscene objects to child and punishment thereof.

Clause 296 of the Bill seeks to provide for obscene acts and songs and punishment thereof.

Clause 297 of the Bill seeks to provide for keeping lottery office and punishment thereof.

Clause 298 of the Bill seeks to provide for injuring or defiling place of worship, with intent to insult the religion of any class and punishment thereof.

Clause 299 of the Bill seeks to provide for deliberate and malicious acts, intended to outrage religious feelings of any class by insulting its religion or religious beliefs and punishment thereof.

Clause 300 of the Bill seeks to provide for disturbing religious assembly and punishment thereof.

Clause 301 of the Bill seeks to provide for trespassing on burial places, etc., and punishment thereof.

Clause 302 of the Bill seeks to provide for uttering words, etc., with deliberate intent to wound religious feelings and punishment thereof.

Clause 303 of the Bill seeks to provide that whoever, intending to take dishonestly any movable property out of the possession of any person without that person's consent, moves that property in order to such taking, is said to commit theft.

It further explains the subject, severance, removing, moving and consent in respect of commission of theft.

Clause 304 of the Bill seeks to define the offence snatching and provide that when theft is snatching and punishment thereof.

Clause 305 of the Bill seeks to provide for theft in a dwelling house, or means of transportation or place of worship, etc., and punishment thereof.

Clause 306 of the Bill seeks to provide for theft by clerk or servant of property in possession of master and punishment thereof.

Clause 307 of the Bill seeks to provide for theft after preparation made for causing death, hurt or restraint in order to committing of theft and punishment thereof.

Clause 308 of the Bill seeks to define the offence extortion and punishment thereof.

Clause 309 of the Bill seeks to define the offence robbery and punishment thereof.

It further provides that the offender is said to be present if he is sufficiently near to put the other person in fear of instant death, of instant hurt, or of instant wrongful restraint.

Clause 310 of the Bill seeks to define the offence dacoity, its preparation and commission of various perspective and punishment thereof.

Clause 311 of the Bill seeks to provide for robbery, or dacoity, with attempt to cause death or grievous hurt and punishment thereof.

Clause 312 of the Bill seeks to provide for attempt to commit robbery or dacoity when armed with deadly weapon and punishment thereof.

Clause 313 of the Bill seeks to provide for punishment for belonging to gang of robbers, etc.

Clause 314 of the Bill seeks to provide for dishonest misappropriation of property and punishment thereof.

It further provides in *Explanations* 1 and 2 that a dishonest misappropriation for a time only is a misappropriation within the meaning of this clause and *inter alia* a person who finds property not in the possession of any other person, and takes such property for the purpose of protecting it for, or of restoring it to, the owner, does not take or misappropriate it dishonestly, and is not guilty of an offence; but he is guilty of the offence above defined, if he appropriates it to his own use, when he knows or has the means of discovering the owner, or before he has used reasonable means to discover and give notice to the owner and has kept the property a reasonable time to enable the owner to claim it.

Clause 315 of the Bill seeks to provide for dishonest misappropriation of property possessed by deceased person at the time of his death and punishment thereof.

Clause 316 of the Bill seeks to provide for criminal breach of trust under given circumstances and punishment thereof.

It further explains the dishonestly used the amount of the employee's contribution in violation of a direction of law.

Clause 317 of the Bill seeks to define stolen property and punishment thereof if received, retained, dealt with, assisted, concealed, disposed or made away under given circumstances.

Clause 318 of the Bill seeks to define cheating and punishment thereof.

It further explains that a dishonest concealment of facts is a deception within the meaning of this clause.

Clause 319 of the Bill seeks to define cheating by personation and punishment thereof. It further explains that the offence is committed whether the individual personated is a

real or imaginary person.

Clause 320 of the Bill seeks to provide for dishonest or fraudulent removal or concealment of property to prevent distribution among creditors and punishment thereof.

Clause 321 of the Bill seeks to provide whoever dishonestly or fraudulently prevents any debt or demand due to himself or to any other person from being made available according to law for payment of his debts or the debts of such other person, shall be punished with imprisonment of either description for a term which may extend to two years, or with fine, or with both.

Clause 322 of the Bill seeks to provide for dishonest or fraudulent execution of deed of transfer containing false statement of consideration and punishment thereof.

Clause 323 of the Bill seeks to provide for dishonest or fraudulent removal or concealment of property and punishment thereof.

Clause 324 of the Bill seeks to define mischief and punishment thereof.

It further provides in *Explanations* 1 and 2 that it is not essential to the offence of mischief that the offender should intend to cause loss or damage to the owner of the property injured or destroyed. It is sufficient if he intends to cause, or knows that he is likely to cause, wrongful loss or damage to any person by injuring any property, whether it belongs to that person or not and mischief may be committed by an act affecting property belonging to the person who commits the act, or to that person and others jointly.

Clause 325 of the Bill seeks to provide for mischief by killing or maiming animal and punishment thereof.

Clause 326 of the Bill seeks to provide for mischief by injury, inundation, fire or explosive substance, etc., and punishment thereof.

Clause 327 of the Bill seeks to provide *inter alia* whoever commits mischief to any rail, aircraft, or a decked vessel or any vessel of a burden of twenty tons or upwards, intending to destroy or render unsafe, or knowing it to be likely that he will thereby destroy or render unsafe, that rail, aircraft or vessel, shall be punished with imprisonment of either description for a term which may extend to ten years, and shall also be liable to fine.

Clause 328 of the Bill seeks to provide for punishment for intentionally running vessel aground or ashore with intent to commit theft, etc., and punishment thereof.

Clause 329 of the Bill seeks to provide for criminal trespass and house-trespass and punishment thereof.

It further explains that the introduction of any part of the criminal trespasser's body is entering sufficient to constitute house-trespass.

Clause 330 of the Bill seeks to provide for house-trespass and house-breaking.

It further explains that any out-house or building occupied with a house, and between which and such house there is an immediate internal communication, is part of the house within the meaning of this clause.

Clause 331 of the Bill seeks to provide for punishment for house-trespass or house breaking.

Clause 332 of the Bill seeks to provide for house-trespass in order to commit offence and punishment thereof.

Clause 333 of the Bill seeks to provide for house-trespass after preparation for hurt, assault or wrongful restraint and punishment thereof.

Clause 334 of the Bill seeks to define dishonestly breaking open receptacle containing property.

Clause 335 of the Bill seeks to define making a false document.

Clause 336 of the Bill seeks to provide for forgery and forgery for the purpose of cheating and punishment thereof.

Clause 337 of the Bill seeks to provide for forgery of record of Court or of public register, etc., and punishment thereof.

It further explains the term "register".

Clause 338 of the Bill seeks to provide for forgery of valuable security, will, etc., and punishment thereof.

Clause 339 of the Bill seeks to provide for having possession of document specified in clause 337 or 338, knowing it to be forged and intending to use it as genuine and punishment thereof.

Clause 340 of the Bill seeks to provide for forged document or electronic record and using it as genuine and punishment thereof.

Clause 341 of the Bill seeks to provide for making or possessing counterfeit seal, etc., with intent to commit forgery punishable under clause 338 and punishment thereof.

Clause 342 of the Bill seeks to provide for counterfeiting device or mark used for authenticating documents described in clause 338, or possessing counterfeit marked material and punishment thereof.

Clause 343 of the Bill seeks to provide for fraudulent cancellation, destruction, etc., of will, authority to adopt, or valuable security and punishment thereof.

Clause 344 of the Bill seeks to provide for falsification of accounts and punishment thereof.

It further provides that it shall be sufficient in any charge under this clause to allege a general intent to defraud without naming any particular person intended to be defrauded or specifying any particular sum of money intended to be the subject of the fraud, or any particular day on which the offence was committed.

Clause 345 of the Bill seeks to provide for property mark and punishment thereof.

Clause 346 of the Bill seeks to provide for tampering with property mark with intent to cause injury and punishment thereof.

Clause 347 of the Bill seeks to provide for counterfeiting a property mark and punishment thereof.

Clause 348 of the Bill seeks to provide for making or possession of any instrument for counterfeiting a property mark and punishment thereof.

Clause 349 of the Bill seeks to provide for selling goods marked with a counterfeit property mark and punishment thereof.

Clause 350 of the Bill seeks to provide for making a false mark upon any receptacle containing goods and punishment thereof.

Clause 351 of the Bill seeks to provide for criminal intimidation and punishment thereof. It further explains that a threat to injure the reputation of any deceased person in whom

the person threatened is interested, is within this clause.

Clause 352 of the Bill seeks to provide for intentional insult with intent to provoke breach of peace and punishment thereof.

Clause 353 of the Bill seeks to provide for statements conducing to public mischief and punishment thereof.

It further provides in *Exception* that it does not amount to an offence, within the meaning of this clause, when the person making, publishing or circulating any such statement, false information, rumour or report, has reasonable grounds for believing that such statement, false information, rumour or report is true and makes, publishes or circulates it in good faith and without any such intent as aforesaid.

Clause 354 of the Bill seeks to provide for act caused by inducing person to believe that he will be rendered an object of Divine displeasure and punishment thereof.

Clause 355 of the Bill seeks to provide for misconduct in public by a drunken person and punishment thereof.

Clause 356 of the Bill seeks to define defamation and punishment thereof.

It further provides in *Explanations* 1 to 4 that when any words, signs or visible representation is amount to defamation and when no imputation is said to harm a person's reputation.

It also provides in *Exceptions* 1 to 10 that there is no any defamation under given circumstances.

Clause 357 of the Bill seeks to provide that whoever, being bound by a lawful contract to attend on or to supply the wants of any person who, by reason of youth, or of unsoundness of mind mental illness, or of a disease or bodily weakness, is helpless or incapable of providing for his own safety or of supplying his own wants, voluntarily omits so to do, shall be punished with imprisonment of either description for a term which may extend to three months, or with fine which may extend to five thousand rupees, or with both.

Clause 358 of the Bill seeks to provide for repeal and savings of the Indian Penal Code.

FINANCIAL MEMORANDUM

The proposed legislation if enacted, is not likely to involve any expenditure, either recurring or non-recurring, from and out of the Consolidated Fund of India.

131

LOK SABHA

A

BILL

(*Shri Amit Shah, Minister of Home Affairs and Cooperation*)

MGIPMRND—460LS(S3)—09.12.2023.

to consolidate and amend the provisions relating to offences and for matters connected therewith or incidental thereto.